Commemorating Conflict

Greek Monuments of the Persian Wars

Xavier Duffy

Archaeopress Archaeology

Archaeopress Publishing Ltd
Summertown Pavilion
18-24 Middle Way
Summertown
Oxford OX2 7LG
www.archaeopress.com

ISBN 978 1 78491 839 2
ISBN 978 1 78491 840 8 (e-Pdf)

© Archaeopress and X Duffy 2018

All rights reserved. No part of this book may be reproduced, stored in retrieval system, or transmitted, in any form or by any means, electronic, mechanical, photocopying or otherwise, without the prior written permission of the copyright owners.

This book is available direct from Archaeopress or from our website www.archaeopress.com

Contents

Preface v

Acknowledgements vi

Abbreviations vii

Chapter 1 Introduction 1
1.1 Aim 1
1.2 What were the Persian Wars? 1

Chapter 2 Contextualising the Commemorations of the Persian Wars 5
2.1 Reliability of the Evidence 5
2.2 Commemoration in Ancient Greece 10
    2.2.1 Athenian Dominance 10
    2.2.2 Looking beyond Athens 12
    2.2.3 Commemorative Monumentalisation 14
2.3 Commemoration of the Persian Wars 15

Chapter 3 Commemorative Groups and Commemorative Places 17
3.1 Commemorative Groups 17
    3.1.1 The *Polis* 17
    3.1.2 The Delphic Amphictyony 18
    3.1.3 Pan-Hellenic / Pan-Hellenism 20
3.2 Commemorative Places 21
    3.2.1 Battlefield 21
    3.2.2 Urban centre 22
    3.2.3 Pan-Hellenic Sanctuary 24
    3.2.4 Other 25

Chapter 4 Monuments by Type 27
4.1 What is a Monument? 29
4.2 Monument Types 29
    4.2.1 Cenotaphs 29
    4.2.2 Trophies 30
        4.2.2.1 Perishable 31
        4.2.2.2 Permanent 32
    4.2.3 Inscriptions 34
        4.2.3.1 Epigrams 34

  4.2.3.2 Epitaphs 35
  4.2.3.3 Casualty Lists 36
 4.2.4 Burials 36
  4.2.4.1 Collective 36
  4.2.4.2 Commander 38
 4.2.5 Dedications 39
  4.2.5.1 Dedications of Spoils of War 40
  4.2.5.2 Statues 41
  4.2.5.3 Votive offerings 43
 4.2.6 Structures 45
  4.2.6.1 Altars 45
  4.2.6.2 Sacred Precincts, Temples and Stoas 46
  4.2.6.3 Non-Religious Structures 47
 4.2.7 Non-Physical Monuments 48
  4.2.7.1 Military Vow 48
  4.2.7.2 Oaths 49
  4.2.7.3 Behavioural Commemoration 50
 4.2.8 Other 51

Chapter 5 The Monuments and the Evidence 53
5.1 Assessing the Evidence 53
5.2 The Monuments 56
 Marathon: **Nos. 1-20** 56
 Artemisium: **Nos. 21 and 22** 97
 Thermopylae: **Nos. 23-33** 99
 Salamis: **Nos. 34-48** 110
 Plataea: **Nos. 49-79** 126
 General: **Nos. 80-105** 158

Bibliography 193

List of Figures

Figure 1. Establishing boundaries to the battlefield space............................ 22

Figure 2. Athenian burial mound at Marathon 57

Figure 3. Plataean burial mound 61

Figure 4. Athenian trophy at Marathon 64

Figure 5. Inscribed stele mentioning the Herakleia 67

Figure 6. Herakleia inscription 68

Figure 7. Athenian treasury at Delphi 73

Figure 8. Stone A I (I 303 a, Agora Excavations, The American School of Classical Studies at Athens)... 78

Figure 9. Stone A II (I 303 b, Agora Excavations, The American School of Classical Studies at Athens)... 79

Figure 10. Stone B 79

Figure 11. Squared block on Salamis.. 113

Figure 12. Corinthian epitaph from Salamis... 115

Figure 13. Burial Mound on Salamis 116

Figure 14. Drawing of boundary stone 141

Figure 15. Section of Acropolis wall displaying Temple of Athena Polias' entablature 169

Figure 16. Section of Acropolis Wall displaying column drums of the Older Parthenon 169

List of Tables

Table 1. Full monument list 27
Table 2. Full monument list cont. 28
Table 3. Cenotaphs 30
Table 4. Trophies 34
Table 5. Epigrams and epitaphs 35
Table 6. Casualty lists 36
Table 7. Collective burials 37
Table 8. Commander burials 39
Table 9. Spoils of war 41
Table 10. Statues 43
Table 11. Votive offerings 45
Table 12. Altars 45
Table 13. Sacred precincts, temples and stoas 47
Table 14. Non-religious structures 48
Table 15. Military vow 49
Table 16. Oaths 50
Table 17. Behavioural commemoration 51
Table 18. Other 51
Table 19. Confidence attributed to the acceptance of each monument 54
Table 20. Confidence attributed to the acceptance of each monument cont. .. 55
Table 21. Provisions of the Oath of Plataea 136

Preface

This work originated from my PhD thesis 'Monuments, Memory and Place: Commemorations of the Persian Wars'. While researching the commemorative practices employed by the ancient Greeks, I found myself looking through numerous sources to gather information about the particular monuments. As I progressed through the process of postgraduate research, I amassed a good deal of material on the individual Greek monuments commemorating the Persian Wars and the confidence I attributed to the evidence. This material was eventually included as my thesis' Appendix. By compiling the information I discovered while researching, and publishing that data here, I hope for this work to serve as a point of reference for those interested in these particular monuments.

Acknowledgements

This work has been made possible by the support and assistance of many. Firstly, I would like to thank my PhD supervisor, John Carman. From the outset of my postgraduate research, from which this study originated, John has provided scholarly guidance but encouraged independence which allowed me to make this project my own. Thank you also to Caspar Meyer, whose encouragement during the completion of my Masters enabled me to believe postgraduate research was possible and whose door has proven to always be open. My fieldwork in Greece was enabled by generous funding from the College of Arts and Law, University of Birmingham, which gave me the opportunity to explore the places and examine the (existing) monuments which fill the pages to come.

My mum is singlehandedly responsible for my interest in the ancient world and without her support this project simply would not have been possible. Lastly, I thank Alex for her unwavering belief which I relied upon more than she knows, and for taking this journey with me.

Abbreviations

Aen. Tact.	-	Aeneas Tacticus
Aesch.	-	Aeschines
Agora	-	*The Athenian Agora*
Arist.	-	Aristotle
Aristides	-	Aristides, Aelius
Aristoph.	-	Aristophanes
Ath.	-	Athenaeus
CEG	-	*Carmina Epigraphica Graeca*
CIG	-	*Corpus Inscriptionum Graecarum*
Cic.	-	Cicero
CVA	-	*Corpus Vasorum Antiquorum*
Dem.	-	Demosthenes
[Dem.]	-	Pseudo Demosthenes
Dio Chr.	-	Dio Chrysostom
Diod.	-	Diodorus Siculus
Eurip.	-	Euripides
FD	-	*Fouilles de Delphes*
FGrH	-	*Die Fragmente der Griechischen Historiker* (Jacoby, F., 1923-1958)
GHI	-	*A Selection of Greek Historical Inscriptions* (Tod, M. N., 1946)
Harp.	-	Harpocration
Hdts.	-	Herodotus
IG	-	*Inscriptiones Graecae*
IvO	-	*Die Inschriften von Olympia* (Dittenberger, W. and Purgold K., 1986)
Isoc.	-	Isocrates
LSAG	-	*Local Scripts of Archaic Greece* (Jeffery, L.H., 1990)
Lyc.	-	Lycurgus
MGHI	-	*A Manual of Greek Historical Inscriptions* (Hicks, E.L., 1882)
ML	-	*A Selection of Greek Historical Inscriptions* (Meiggs, R. and Lewis D, 1969)
Nep.	-	Cornelius Nepos
OCD	-	*Oxford Classical Dictionary*
Od.	-	Homer's *The Odyssey*
Pal. Anth.	-	*Palatine Anthology*
Paus.	-	Pausanias
Phil.	-	Philostratus the Athenian
Pind.	-	Pindar
Plut.	-	Plutarch

RO	-	*Greek Historical Inscriptions 404-323 BC* (Rhodes P.J and Osborne R. 2003)
SEG	-	*Supplementum Epigraphicum Graecum*
Steph. Byz.	-	Stephanus of Byzantium
Syll.	-	*Sylloge Inscriptionum Graecarum*
Theo.	-	Theopompus
Thuc.	-	Thucydides
Vitr.	-	Vitruvius
Xen.	-	Xenophon

Chapter 1
Introduction

1.1 Aim

This study is concerned with how ancient Greek people, of primarily the classical period (480-323 BC), collectively commemorated the Persian Wars.[1] The aim of this work is to reveal the methods, in their known entirety, by which Greeks of this period commemorated the Persian Wars.

1.2 What were the Persian Wars?

In attempting to define which particular battles the Persian Wars comprised of, and indeed whether they were a collection of conflicts or a single conflict, it will be necessary to address the periodisation of the Persian invasion(s). A brief overview of the variations in the ancient Greek perceptions of the periodisation of the conflict(s) will reveal the multiplicity of both points of view concerning the Persian War(s) and, as a result, the multiplicity of narratives which necessarily emerged.

Herodotus, in justifying the writing of his history, tells us that the cause of the fighting between the Greeks and the Persians can be traced back to Croesus, the King of Lydia; Croesus was the first of the barbarians to force some of the Greek communities to pay tribute.[2] The Greco-Persian War, according to Herodotus, is not restricted to one or two invasions but is presented as a much wider conceptual event spanning about eighty years from c. 560 BC.[3] Herodotus later states that the Athenian ships sent to aid the Ionian revolt (in 499 BC) were the beginning of evils for the Greeks and barbarians.[4] As Cawkwell notes, Herodotus is here presenting the point of view of mainland Greeks as the troubles between Ionians and the Persians had begun much earlier when Cyrus had initially incorporated them into

---

[1] All translations have been obtained from the Perseus Digital Library unless otherwise stated.
[2] Hdts. 1.6.2; see also 1.92.1.
[3] See Yates 2011: 45 for further references.
[4] Hdts. 5.97.3.

the Persian Empire (c. 547 BC).[5] Despite Herodotus framing the conflict as beginning with the Ionian revolt by using individuals from various *poleis* to state as much in speeches, it has been suggested that Herodotus' notion of a larger Greco-barbarian conflict (within which the Persian invasions took place) was heavily influenced by his own cultural background in Asia Minor 'where his earliest conception of the war likely developed'.[6] Although Herodotus does not state that the end of his history was to be understood as the end of the conflict, Diodorus understood Herodotus to have implied the culmination of the conflict took place at the battle of Mycale and the siege of Sestos in 479 BC.[7] Herodotus' depiction of the larger conflict began with Ionian Greeks being forced to pay tribute to Persia and after the victories of 479 BC the Greek world was returned to its prior state of freedom.[8]

Thucydides, in his presentation of the Persian Wars, in general tends to limit the temporal scope of the conflict. This may be because he is comparing the war against Persia with the Peloponnesian War and while attempting to accentuate the latter it would suit his purpose to present the Persian Wars in the narrowest sense possible.[9] In Thucydides' work, the beginning of the Persian Wars is not clearly defined. For example, the beginning of the conflict is mentioned in relation to Darius' death (in 485 BC) in a brief description on the political landscape of Greece before the Peloponnesian War and to contrast the sizes of the Persian and Peloponnesian Wars.[10] The relation with Darius' death implies the exclusion of the Ionian revolt as part of the conflict. Secondly, Marathon appears to be treated as a separate conflict when describing the general happenings in Greece and, furthermore, Thucydides explains how the conflict was resolved quickly over four battles, two on land and two on sea.[11] The battles which are meant are not stated but it is possible that Thucydides intended

---

[5] Cawkwell 2005: 66.
[6] Yates 2011: 52; for an Athenian point of view see Hdts. 8.22.2; for a Spartan point of view see Hdts. 8.142.2.
[7] Diod. 11.37.6; Mycale: Hdts 9.98-107; Sestos: Hdts. 9.114 ff.
[8] Yates 2011: 51; for the prior state of freedom see Hdts. 1.6.3.
[9] Yates 2011: 60.
[10] Darius' death: Thuc. 1.14.2; political landscape in Greece: Thuc. 1.18.1-2; comparing conflict size: Thuc. 1.23.1.
[11] See Yates 2011: 55 for discussion and further references.

the Persian Wars to only include Xerxes' invasion and possibly subsequent immediate battles.

Thucydides is apparently in agreement with Herodotus in his dating for the culmination of the Persian Wars which he places around 478 BC.[12] Within Thucydides' narrative however, Athenians, Mytilenians and Corinthians all express their views on the scope of the Persian Wars. The Athenians and the Mytilenians both express similar views of an extended period of conflict which ranged beyond 478 BC.[13] In contrast, the Corinthians clearly state that they believe the conflict to have ended in 479/8 BC, when blaming Sparta for allowing the Athenians to fortify their city.[14] It has been suggested that the Athenians and Mytilenians may have been expressing views that were popular among Athens and her allies and subject states while the Corinthians were expressing views more prevalent in the Peloponnese which had limited involvement in the Persian conflict before and after Xerxes' invasion.[15]

Plato clearly presents a periodisation of the Persian Wars which ranges from Marathon to Plataea.[16] Similarly, Aristotle presents a periodisation ranging from Marathon to 479/8 BC, which could, it may be argued, include the battle of Mycale.[17] Further agreement on the Marathon – Plataea periodisation can be found in Aeschines, Demosthenes and Apollodorus.[18] In addition to the 4th century BC examples there are other concurrent Athenian variations. Isocrates initially frames the conflict as the repulsion of both Darius and Xerxes, which would include the battles between Marathon and Plataea.[19] However, it is later clarified in Isocrates' *Panegyricus* that Salamis is presented as the final battle of the conflict and is related as the final threat faced by the Greeks.[20] This particular deviation

---

[12] Thuc. 1.97.
[13] Athenian view: Thuc. 1.75.2; Mytilenian view: Thuc. 3.10.2.
[14] Thuc. 1.69.1.
[15] Yates 2011: 59-60.
[16] Plato *Laws* 707c 1-5; see Jung 2006: 13.
[17] Beginning at Marathon: Arist. *Posterior Analytics* 94a; conclusion: Arist. *Athenian Constitution* 25.1.
[18] Aesch. *On the Embassy* 74-75; Dem. *On the Crown* 208; for Apollodorus see [Dem.] *Against Neaera* 94 and 96.
[19] Isoc. *Panegyricus* 71.
[20] Isoc. *Panegyricus* 92.

is unique amongst known periodisations of the Persian Wars. Furthermore, in another of Plato's works the culmination of the conflict is suggested to have been as late as 449 BC.[21]

This discussion illustrates that, even within Athens, a common narrative concerning the periodisation of the Persian Wars never existed. It is therefore necessary to outline at the outset which temporal framework will be adopted in this study. While Herodotus' cultural background may have influenced his temporal framework of the conflict and Thucydides, perhaps, aimed at diminishing the Persian Wars in scope in comparison to the Peloponnesian War, this study follows the majority of sources outlined above: Aeschines, Demosthenes, Apollodorus, and Plato. This work therefore follows the Marathon – Plataea periodisation and is concerned with the invasions of both Darius in 490 BC and Xerxes in 480-479 BC. The battles for which commemorative data is compiled include Marathon, Artemisium, Thermopylae, Salamis and Plataea. In addition monuments are included here that were raised in memory of the Persian Wars in general.

---

[21] Plato *Menexenus* 241e-242a; see Yates 2011: 43.

Chapter 2
Contextualising the Commemorations of the Persian Wars

2.1 Reliability of the Evidence

Many monuments commemorating the Persian Wars have been lost and so, in these instances, it is necessary to rely fully on literary sources to verify their identification (or, indeed, existence). There is much deliberation over the identification of several of the monuments compiled here and so ancient, antiquarian and modern literary sources are addressed to support each monument's identification. Each monument is verified on a case by case basis, and the confidence with which the monuments are accepted are discussed individually in chapter 5. Considering the basis for many of the monuments' identification rests on ancient testimony, it is necessary to initially discuss the reliability of this evidence. When particular monuments are mentioned in the text, for ease of reference, they are hereafter referred to by their corresponding number; e.g. **no. 1**.

Herodotus is our primary source for the Persian Wars; however Herodotus' scope in mentioning monuments specifically is somewhat limited. This is because Herodotus' narrative stops at 479 BC and although the History is relating the events of the Persian Wars, it is not his specific purpose to relate the monuments which commemorated the conflicts. Herodotus does mention multiple monuments which are included here and, for the monuments he does mention, is to be considered a trustworthy source.[22] For example Herodotus, as a 5th century BC writer, provides the earliest literary attestations of the epigrams which stood on the battlefield at Thermopylae.[23] These quotations of the epigrams cannot be verified as the monument is no longer extant (see **no. 23** for discussion of Herodotus and the Thermopylae epigrams); however we do have evidence of Herodotus' reliability elsewhere. Herodotus quotes the inscription on a monument which commemorated the Athenian victory over the Boeotians and Chalcidians in 506 BC.[24] Fragments of the 6th century BC inscription

---
[22] West (1965: xx) also agrees on this point.
[23] Hdts. 7.228.
[24] Hdts. 5.77.

have survived and so Herodotus' quote may be verified and as a result a certain level of confidence may be attributed to Herodotus' reporting of epigrams.[25] In addition, two other of Herodotus' reported monuments included in this study have been attested by archaeology such as the serpent column (see discussion in **no. 80**) and, with less certainty, the Athenian portico at Delphi (see discussion in **no. 84**).

Thucydides' history, in relation to the identification of monuments of the Persian Wars, is peripheral. Thucydides mentions only four objects which are included in this study. However Thucydides as a 5th century BC writer and a near contemporary source has, in a similar way to Herodotus, had his epigraphic reference reliability confirmed. Thucydides reports an inscription on an altar dedicated by Pisistratus to Apollo and it has been preserved which confirms the quotation.[26] On the strength of this verification, some trust may be afforded to Thucydides' quotation of the initial epigram inscribed on the pan-Hellenic dedication of the serpent column at Delphi, which was erased in antiquity.[27] It is worthy of note, however, that Thucydides' reliability should not be taken for granted. For example, a fragment of the inscribed Athenian version of the alliance between Athens, the Argives, Mantineians, and Eleians in 420 BC was discovered in 1876.[28] This alliance is also related by Thucydides,[29] and clear discrepancies are evident concerning dialect, insertions, omissions, and transposed passages.[30] However, it has been suggested that Thucydides may have been drawing upon a version of the alliance set up at Argos, Mantinea, or Olympia which deviated from the Athenian version.[31]

It was in the 4th century BC that monuments would have been used as examples by Athenian authors in order to set up the victories in the Persian Wars as ideals for Athenians of the period to emulate.[32] Such authors from this century include Aeschines, Demosthenes, Lycurgus and Isocrates. The

---

[25] Fragment: *IG* I³ 501a/501b; see also *GHI* 12, and for commentary see no. 43; see also West 1965: xiv.
[26] Quote: Thuc. 6.54; inscription fragment: *IG* I³ 948.
[27] Thuc. 1.132.2; West 1965: xv.
[28] *IG* I³ 83; see Liddel and Low 2013: 15.
[29] Thuc. 5.47.
[30] The discrepancies are presented in *GHI* 72.
[31] Liddel and Low 2013: 15; for differing versions of the alliance see *GHI* 72.
[32] West 1965: xxii.

primary use for these literary references, in this study, is to provide the context against which the material evidence is assessed and evaluated.

Plutarch, who was writing in the 1st and 2nd centuries AD, provides many of the references to epigrams addressed in this work. It has been argued that Plutarch was not interested in discussing inscriptions for their own sake, but values epigraphy as a source material for the historian when reconstructing the lives of great individuals or the great deeds of ancient Greek peoples.[33] Furthermore, inscriptions have been said to have held little interest for him, with literary sources proving the backbone of his research.[34] Despite these criticisms Plutarch utilises this form of evidence for a number of purposes: they act as proofs in arguments;[35] they provide insights into the characters who read them, write them, and react to them;[36] or they act as a starting point for philosophical enquiry.[37]

Plutarch as a source must be treated with some care because, for example, the inscription quoted as being from the Corinthian epitaph is of four lines while the original inscription is preserved and contains only two lines (see discussion and image in **no. 36**). Utilising this inscription, Plutarch demonstrates how he uses epigraphical evidence in scholarly polemic by criticising Herodotus' description of Corinthian forces fleeing at the battle of Salamis.[38] In addition, with regard to inscriptions on the victory Herms in the Athenian agora, Plutarch's quotation differs to that given by Aeschines, although the opening lines correspond.[39] Despite these slight variations, it is possible to gain an impression of Plutarch's efforts in gathering information. It is revealed in Plutarch's work on Nicias that he would deliberately consult multiple forms of evidence to enhance his understanding of a particular character.[40] Furthermore, Plutarch provides an example of original research when he notes that he

---

[33] Liddel 2008: 126 and 136.
[34] Buckler 1992: 4799.
[35] Plut. *Lycurgus* 1-2.
[36] Plut. *On the Fortune of Alexander* 1.9; Plut. *Pompey* 27.3; Plut. *Demosthenes* 20.2; Plut. *Alexander* 69.2.
[37] Plut. *The E at Delphi* 1 ff.; for more examples see Liddel 2008: 126.
[38] Hdts. 8.94.1; Liddel 2008: 130-131.
[39] Plut. *Kimon* 7.4-6; Aesch. *Against Ctesiphon* 3.184-185.
[40] In *Nicias* 1.5 Plutarch describes how, in addition to consulting literary sources such as Thucydides and Philistus, he gathers inscriptions from votive offerings and public decrees.

had read an inscription bearing the name of Aristides as *choregos* and used this information to prove that Aristides was born into nobility.[41] Despite Plutarch applying his greatest efforts to literary sources, and having not expressed a true appreciation of epigraphic evidence,[42] it may be argued that the diligence of his information gathering is evident in his writings. Therefore West's judgement, that a certain level of confidence may be attributed to Plutarch as a reliable source, is followed here.[43]

Alongside Plutarch, the Palatine Anthology also provides many of the references to epigrams relating to the Persian Wars. It has been suggested that the dating of epigrams, whether mentioned by multiple authors or not, should be judged by its style: whether they are ornate or simple and whether it adorned a monument that was likely to have been erected.[44] As a result each reference is judged independently.

Pausanias, who was writing in the 2nd century AD, provides references for the majority of the monuments addressed in this study, either verifying other authors or as a sole reference. Although Pausanias' purpose was to create a description of Greece, he described many of the monuments of the Persian Wars and so this study necessarily relies heavily on his writings. Furthermore, Pausanias does not state he intends to catalogue all monuments and the choices made as to which monuments to include were his.[45] The choices Pausanias made on which monuments to describe have been said to rest on two principles: his antiquarian taste, and his religious curiosity.[46] His preference for, and therefore descriptions of, works of the 5th and 4th centuries BC over those of later periods greatly benefits the current study.

It has been argued that when quoting or citing inscriptions Pausanias, in a good many cases (if not all), is doing so from autopsy.[47] For example,

---

[41] Plut. Aristides 1.3; see Buckler 1992: 4795.
[42] Buckler 1992: 4799.
[43] West 1965: xvii.
[44] West 1965: xvii.
[45] Frazer 1965: 1.xxxiii.
[46] Frazer 1965: 1.xxxiii.
[47] Whittaker 1991: 171-172; in addition Whittaker notes that 'tourism was a growth industry in second-century Greece, and inscriptions would have played an important role in documenting the historical importance of places which by Pausanias' time had sunk into obscurity' (1991: 172-173).

on a number of occasions Pausanias refers to the actual appearance of inscriptions.[48] On the contrary, it has been suggested that Pausanias had seen little of what he was describing and was relying on second hand information from earlier writers such as Polemo of Ilium (of the 2nd century BC).[49] However, when Pausanias describes statues at Olympia which depict victors, the inscriptions are used to provide further information on the individual,[50] and if any information is deemed missing by Pausanias he explains that it was not provided by the inscription.[51] This suggests the information about Olympic victors was obtained from the specific statue's inscription opposed to a list of Olympic victors, for example.[52] Furthermore, many statue bases described by Pausanias have been discovered during excavations at Olympia which attest to the accuracy of his descriptions.[53] In relation to the treatment of inscriptions, Pausanias' accuracy has been described as 'as remarkable as is his economical style of reporting'.[54] Pausanias quotes 39 inscriptions and cites more than 200,[55] and the quantity of these references has been interpreted as Pausanias' understanding of how trustworthy epigraphical evidence was in comparison to some of the literary and oral information available to him.[56] Therefore, while not infallible (e.g. see **no. 70**), Pausanias is accepted here as a generally reliable source.

Thucydides notes the difficulty in verifying the truth of eyewitness accounts due to 'the want of coincidence between accounts of the same

---

[48] Pausanias notes that Attic letters were used when describing inscriptions (1.2.4, 6.19.6), that an inscription is written in a circle (5.20.1), and that letters are worn or the inscription has disappeared over time (6.15.8, 8.40.1). Pausanias does mention a number of inscriptions from places which he does not describe (e.g. 1.13.2, 5.10.3, 10.12.6) and therefore it is quite possible that he hadn't examined them in person and copied them from a literary source (Whittaker 1991: 180-182).
[49] Habicht 1985: 165; a review of the criticisms of Pausanias work by 19th and 20th century scholars is presented in Habicht (1985: 165-175) with further bibliography on criticisms and defence; see Frazer 1965 1.xcvi for examples of Pausanias' fallibility.
[50] Such as their father's name and where they came from, e.g. Paus. 6.3.4.
[51] E.g. Paus. 6.2.9.
[52] Whittaker 1991: 174.
[53] Whittaker 1991: 174; Habicht 1984: 55; Frazer 1965: 1.xcv-xcvi.
[54] Habicht 1984: 55.
[55] Whittaker 1991: 171.
[56] Habicht 1984: 56.

occurrences by different eye-witnesses, arising sometimes from imperfect memory, sometimes from undue partiality for one side or the other'.[57] A writer, at any time, may choose to misrepresent a situation for various purposes; alternatively, the misrepresentation may not be intentional. It is understood here, therefore, that there is no direct correlation between the temporal proximity of a source with a particular event and that source's reliability.[58]

2.2 Commemoration in Ancient Greece

2.2.1 Athenian Dominance

Much of the existing scholarly work on ancient Greek commemoration has focussed on Athens, mainly due to the predominance of Athenian evidence.[59] In addition, much of the work concerning Athenian commemoration relates to how the surviving population remembered the war dead and understands the collective burial in the context of the emerging Athenian democracy.[60] It has been noted that 'an overly narrow focus on the democratic implications of Athenian commemorative practice has led to a sometimes oversimplified reading of both its intended purpose and its actual reception'.[61] The Athenians would commemorate their war dead through a complex set of rituals and monuments including burial (on the battlefield or in the *demosion sema*), casualty lists, epigrams, sculpture, dedications, speeches, processions, and graves. The temptation is there, but must be avoided, to focus on the evidence which is well preserved and extrapolate the findings to the whole.[62] The available material can often lead to an interpretation of a narrow and singular state-dominated intention of the commemorative narrative.

The burial and commemoration of the Athenian war dead in the classical period represented the honour which is bestowed upon the war

---

[57] Thuc. 1.22.3.
[58] As also noted in Hall 2007: 19.
[59] Low 2003: 99.
[60] See Clairmont 1983: 15.
[61] Low 2010: 341; for relationship between Athenian collective burial and Athenian democracy see Loraux 2006.
[62] Noted in Low 2010: 342.

dead by the city; the city takes over the formalities of burial from the family in the case of those who died in war but also the state removes the possibility for families to create their own sites and symbols of memory and mourning.[63] Commemoration has been described as a 'weapon of social control'[64] with centralising authorities often exercising control over commemorative cultures,[65] and in this way Athenian families were denied the chance to construct their own forms of commemoration.[66] Although this interpretation of the Athenian war dead commemoration has become conventional, Low argues that in fact the true essence of Athenian commemoration is more inclusive or at least more complex than a strictly patriotic (and democratic) expression.[67] Families are permitted to take part in the burial ceremony, albeit by invitation, for example, and foreigners and women were also permitted to observe the funeral.[68] Non Athenians have also been commemorated on steles, although they are identified as such by the terms '*xenoi*' or '*barbaroi toxsotai*'.[69]

Much of our knowledge of the Athenian treatment of their war dead is flawed and much information is yet unclear and possibly irretrievable with the surviving evidence. Many details concerning public burial are unknown such as the date at which it was instituted, the timing and frequency of the commemorative festivals and the precise locations of almost all the monuments. In addition it is very difficult to gain a sense of the role these monuments would have played in the social life of the Athenian citizens throughout the classical period. The evidence, particularly the material evidence, goes some way to reflect the complex social system which existed in Athens when the monuments were erected. The traditional view of Athenian commemoration as monologic can be revisited as a more diverse picture of a society with blurred divisions in practice emerges.[70]

---

[63] Low 2012: 14-15.
[64] Samuel 1994: 17.
[65] Low and Oliver 2012: 3.
[66] Low 2012: 15.
[67] Low 2012: 15-23.
[68] See Thuc. 2.34.4.
[69] *IG* 1³ 1172, (mid-5th century BC), 1180 (430's BC), 1184 (423 BC), 1190 (c. 411 BC), 1192 (second half of the 5th century BC).
[70] Low 2012: 36.

The focus in studies on commemoration is often on remembrance within and around the bounded confines of the city. For example, studies on commemoration which are reliant on Athenian evidence often focus on the *demosion sema*.[71] This particular place has been identified as an area shaped by the nascent democracy of the 5th century BC for a more communal self-representation.[72] Despite the Greek casualties of the Persian Wars having been buried on the battlefields, Arrington argues that a cenotaph for the Marathon dead was raised in the *demosion sema*. With these visual links to their heroic past, it is argued that the Athenians utilised this space to forge a new collective identity and celebrate a new communal outlook.[73]

In contrast to focussing on a single site within a single city (such as the *demosion sema*), this study compiles commemorative material from a range of site types including urban centres, battlefields and pan-Hellenic sanctuaries. The aim of including a wider range of commemorative places is to provide a more complete impression of the distribution of commemorative monuments, particularly relating to the Persian Wars. By highlighting the diverse range of commemorative places, this study contributes to a fuller understanding of ancient Greek commemoration.

2.2.2 Looking beyond Athens

Recent studies in the commemoration of ancient Greek warfare have looked at case studies beyond Athens. For example, commemorative activity at Sparta has been the focus of study.[74]

Focussing on Spartan commemoration, Pausanias mentions a stele with names and fathers' names of the warriors who fought at Thermopylae which was erected in Sparta.[75] While there is no guarantee this was erected in the classical period, the existence of this monument is evidence that the 300 warriors, marked individually, were commemorated as a distinct and somehow special group.[76] Where the Spartans provided

---

[71] Clairmont 1983: 29-45; Arrington 2010; Low 2012: 23-32.
[72] Arrington 2010: 499.
[73] Arrington 2010: Marathon cenotaph: 504-506; collective identity: 533.
[74] See Low 2011; furthermore, studies of military commemoration have been undertaken which focus on the Hellenistic period (Chaniotis 2005, especially ch.11, Chaniotis 2012) and the Roman period (Hölscher 2006: 27-48, Cooley 2012).
[75] Paus. 3.14.1; discussed in Low 2011.
[76] Low 2011: 6.

civic commemoration, the memorials seem to focus on the collective (for example the Battle of the Champions),[77] but the list of individual names suggests other trends. Only the names are recalled in the monument mentioned by Pausanias and the bodies do not play a physical part in the memorial landscape. Absence of the body should not be dismissed as trivial, however, as the body was central to private mourning.[78] Without the focus for individual mourning, perhaps, it becomes easier to treat the dead as abstract, heroic figures which exemplify the glory of the *polis*.[79]

The commemorative material which dominates the acropolis area in Sparta (and starts to do so before the Persian Wars) celebrates a different sort of achievement; inscriptions set up here focus primarily on athletic victories, such as the stele of Damonon.[80] The practice of individual commemorations of athletic victories is a peculiarly Spartan phenomenon. The connection between athletic prowess and military strength is well attested, in activities at festivals such as the *Gymnopaedia* or by placing Olympic victors at prestigious places in the battle line.[81] The question has been posed as to whether the placing of monuments commemorating the Persian Wars near these individualistic displays of prowess encouraged a reading of the monument that promoted individual glory rather than promoting the message of the collective and self-sacrifice for the good of the *polis*.[82] Olick emphasises the way in which current memory is constrained by earlier commemorations of historical events.[83] Olick asserts that there is a dialogue between current and earlier memorialisations which produce 'genre memories'; the present is immersed in these preordained pasts. Multiple readings of commemorative structures may have been possible as the burials and the stele would not, necessarily, be viewed in isolation.[84]

In contrast to focussing on commemorations by larger *poleis*, which are sometimes better represented in the archaeological record or literary sources, this study compiles monuments from a range of commemorative

---

[77] Pettersson 1992: 51.
[78] Chaniotis 2006: 219-226.
[79] Low 2011: 8.
[80] See Low 2011: 14 for further examples and image.
[81] *Gymnopaedia*: Pettersson 1992: 50; athletic victors in the battle line: Plut. *Lycurgus* 22.4.
[82] Low 2011: 15.
[83] Olick 1999.
[84] Low 2011: 15.

groups; these groups include *poleis* (regardless of size or renown), the Delphic Amphictyonic League and the pan-Hellenic. The aim of presenting commemorative material from a wider range of commemorative groups is to provide a more complete impression of the commemorative tradition, particularly relating to the Persian Wars.

2.2.3 Commemorative Monumentalisation

The over representation of research undertaken on the remembrance of the war dead in Athens has been mentioned above. However, in relation to the types of commemoration, the remembrance of the Greek war dead specifically is also a popular topic. The individual soldiers are remembered in a variety of ways and these commemorative styles are often studied individually, for example casualty lists, burial customs, and funeral orations.[85]

In addition, a range of monument types have also been studied individually; for example, votive offerings, spoils of war, and trophies.[86] The trend of dealing with particular monument types individually is probably best represented in Pritchett's five volume study on the Greek state at war.[87] These volumes deal with ancient Greek warfare comprehensively. Within these volumes Pritchett allocates individual chapters to specific aspects of warfare. Within Pritchett's body of work, particular commemorative monument types are allocated individual chapters; for example military vows, cenotaphs, casualty lists and many others.[88]

In contrast to providing an in depth study on one particular form of commemorative monument, this study compiles a set of commemorative monuments ranging broadly in type. By presenting the full range of monument types, relating particularly to the Persian Wars, this study demonstrates the possible diversity in ancient Greek commemorative practices.

---

[85] Casualty lists: Bradeen 1969; burial customs: Clairmont 1983, Kurtz and Boardman 1971; funeral orations: Loraux 2006.
[86] Votive offerings: Rouse 1902; spoils: Thompson 1956; trophies: Vanderpool 1966, West 1969.
[87] Pritchett 1971-1991: volumes 1-5.
[88] Vows: Pritchett 1979: 3.230-239; cenotaphs: Pritchett 1985: 4.257-259; casualty lists: Pritchett 1985: 4.139-144.

2.3 Commemoration of the Persian Wars

In addition to the general scholarly trends in commemoration outlined above, two trends in the study of remembering the Persian Wars particularly have drawn attention away from a more holistic presentation of the commemorations: the categorisation of commemorations by battle,[89] and, again, an overemphasis on Athenian commemorations.[90]

In the early 20th century Macan published a study on a selection of Herodotus' chapters. Several monuments of the Persian Wars are discussed in Macan's work but with particular reference to how these monuments shed light on Herodotus' narrative.[91] However, this is primarily a literary exercise with little focus on the archaeological material. The 5th century BC public monuments of the Persian Wars were catalogued for the first time in 1965 and the volume was intended, as far as possible, to gather together in one place evidence of all known monuments utilising inscriptions, literary references, and archaeological research.[92] The catalogue divides the monuments by city and, unsurprisingly, Athens is best represented due to either lack of wealth of other cities or the general pro-Athenian nature of the literary tradition.[93]

More recently Jung has conducted an expansive treatment of two battles; Marathon and Plataea.[94] Jung's work includes an assessment of the material evidence and memorialisation of the two battles from immediately after the conflict to the Roman period. Yates takes a more temporally restricted approach, dealing with the classical period ending with the death of Alexander.[95] With the rise of Macedon, Yates presents competition between the free Greek states undergoing a significant transformation.

In contrast to focussing on singular monument types, individual commemorative places, a particular commemorating group or specific battle, this study provides a more holistic impression of the

---

[89] Marathon: Flashar 1995, Hölkeskamp 2001, Gehrke 2003 and 2007; Thermopylae: Albertz 2006; Marathon and Plataea: Jung 2006.
[90] Harrison 2000, Jung 2006, Loraux 2006, see Yates 2011: 4 for further references.
[91] Macan 1908: 6-7, n. 1; see also West 1965: v.
[92] West 1965: v.
[93] West 1965: lxviii.
[94] Jung 2006.
[95] Yates 2011.

commemorations of the Persian Wars. In doing so, this study presents a comprehensive compilation of all known Greek commemorations of the Persian Wars, at all known sites, from all commemorative groups and assesses the reliability of the available evidence.

Chapter 3
Commemorative Groups and Commemorative Places

3.1 Commemorative Groups

The Persian Wars were commemorated collectively and the ancient Greek commemorative community may be divided into three distinct commemorative collectives who are represented in the compiled body of monuments: the *polis*, the Amphictyonic League, and the pan-Hellenic. These groups varied in size and structure, the *polis* was the smallest collective and represents a single city-state, the Amphictyonic League represents a select collection of city-states, and the pan-Hellenic represents the ancient Greek community at large. Definitions of each of these groups will be offered in turn below.

3.1.1 *The* Polis

In order to define a group who collectively commemorated the Persian Wars, the *polis* is regarded here as a state. It is necessary to follow the definition of the *polis* as a state because this study analyses commemorations from individual *poleis* that clearly differentiate themselves from each other. The inhabitants of Greek *poleis* would have shared their ethnic identity (language, culture, history and religion) with neighbouring Greek *poleis*.[96] However, the sense of political identity was focussed on the individual *polis*, and therefore differentiated any *polis* from its neighbours.[97]

The basic definition which is followed here in regarding the *polis* as a state is the city-state as 'a centralized authority with administrative and judicial institutions, along with cleavages of wealth, privilege, and status, which correspond to the distribution of power and authority'.[98] In following this definition the 'centralised authority', in using the 'cleavages of wealth', would be able to construct monuments in representation of the collective. In modern day terminology we refer to states in the singular

---

[96] As defined by Hansen 2006: 64; *contra.* Berent (1996) who argues that the Greek *polis* was not a state; See also Hall 2013: 10-11 for further references on this debate.
[97] Hansen 2006: 64; see also Hansen and Nielsen 2004: 128-129.
[98] Hall 2013: 11.

e.g. France, America, China, while ancient Greeks referred to the *polis* in the plural e.g. the Athenians, or the Corinthians.⁹⁹ The focus was therefore primarily on the collective. Due to the fact that this study is concerned with public monuments, suggestions will not be made as to who, out of those living in the city, is considered 'of the collective'; the *polis* is the smallest denominator of commemorator to be analysed. Private commemorations, for example the epitaph raised at Thermopylae by Simonides for the seer Magistias, will not be included in this study.¹⁰⁰

3.1.2 The Delphic Amphictyony

The word 'amphictyon' is derived from the Greek *amphi*: 'around' and *ktizein*: 'dwell' and is therefore generally understood to refer to those people who dwell around.¹⁰¹ The term 'amphictyony' was initially intended to refer to the Anthela and Delphic League. Only later was this terminology applied to other leagues of city-states. The term, however, was used quite rarely and no specific typology of an amphictyony can be derived from the ancient sources.¹⁰² By the 4th century BC the views of Amphictyonic leagues was that they were based heavily on spatial organisation.¹⁰³ This prerequisite of residing in a similar geographical area took precedence over other forms of bonds, for example ethnic bonds. A league's sanctuaries, as cultic centres, acted as predetermined and accepted sites to come together and interact. An Amphictyonic League, from its beginning 'was not only a cultic league; at the same time it was an early interstate league.'¹⁰⁴ An Amphictyonic League, therefore, was a creation of an area which enabled the interaction of a number of city-states and without the necessity of tribal or ethnic links; the included members were politically independent.¹⁰⁵

---

⁹⁹ Strauss 2013: 23.
¹⁰⁰ See Hdts. 7.228.4.
¹⁰¹ *OCD*: 73 'amphictiony'; see also Funke 2013: 452.
¹⁰² Funke 2013: 454.
¹⁰³ Anaximenes of Lampsakus: *FGrH* no. 72, F.2; Androtion of Athens: *FGrH* no. 324, F.58 which cites Paus. 10.8.1.
¹⁰⁴ Funke 2013: 454.
¹⁰⁵ Funke 2013: 462-463.

> Amphictyonic leagues were a particular phenomenon of early Greek history. They were an attempt to overcome the fragmentation of the Greek system of developing city-states as early as the Dark Ages and the Archaic period.[106]

This study is concerned solely with the Delphic Amphictyony because this group of communities were the only league to commemorate the Persian Wars as a distinct amphictyony. The Delphic Amphictyony can probably be dated back to the 8th century BC when a group of independent, neighbouring tribes formed a league who based their cultic centre initially at the sanctuary of Demeter at Anthela in the region of Malis, near Thermopylae.[107] Over an undetermined period of time Delphi (as a *polis*) became encompassed within this league and the Delphic sanctuary rose to greater fame than the sanctuary at Anthela and as a result also became one of the league's cultic centres.[108]

The aims of the Delphic Amphictyony may be understood as both religious and political; '[w]e find it true here, as always in Greece, that to make an absolute separation between the spheres of religion and politics does violence to the facts.'[109] We learn from Strabo, who is albeit a late source (writing in the early 1st century AD), that the Amphictyony was responsible for both the control of the temple and to deliberate over common affairs.[110] In fact, the earliest evidence available for the Amphictyonic League's responsibility for repairs at the Delphi sanctuary was Herodotus' account of the rebuilding of the temple of Apollo after the fire of 548 BC.[111] With regard to the Persian Wars, the 'common affairs' closely link with the spatial organisation of its members. For example, the Amphictyons were particularly active in both commemorating the battle of Thermopylae, which was within their territory, and commemorating at Delphi. The 'current affairs' would also relate to upholding rules of behaviour between city-states.[112] Incidentally, again with relevance to the

---

[106] Funke 2013: 463.
[107] Funke 2013: 453; for the sanctuary of Demeter at Anthela as the original assembly place see Hdts. 7.200.2 and Soph. *Trachiniae* 638-639.
[108] Funke 2013: 453.
[109] Ehrenberg 1969: 109.
[110] Strabo 9.3.7.
[111] Hdts. 2.180.
[112] Ehrenberg 1969: 109.

Persian Wars, the League announced a bounty for the capture of Ephialtes (a Malian, of whom were members of the Amphictyony), who guided the Persians around to the Spartan rear at Thermopylae. Again, this interest in Thermopylae and the regional focus of the league's actions reaffirms the idea that the Amphictyonic League was particularly focussed on the immediate area of their members' territories.[113]

3.1.3 Pan-Hellenic / Pan-Hellenism

Pan-Hellenism is the idea that what the ancient Greeks had in common was more important than what divided them. This idea distinguished Greeks from others, such as 'barbarians'.[114] It has been stated that the idea of pan-Hellenism was fostered when Greeks began to increasingly interact with non-Greeks, particularly in the early 5th century BC during the combined Greek resistance during the Persian Wars.[115] The term itself is an invention by modern scholars to describe the 'various appeals made by the late fifth and early fourth-century BC intellectuals to foster Hellenic unity and to submerge interstate differences in a common crusade against the "eternal enemy", Persia.'[116] Pan-Hellenism as a concept is difficult both to define and even detect. This is due to the wide range of ways it manifests itself throughout Greek history.[117] There is a general consensus among modern scholars, however, that the idea of pan-Hellenism is closely associated with both Greek identity and notions of barbarism.[118] As Flower states:

> *In modern usage 'pan-Hellenism' has two distinct, but related meanings. In one sense it refers to the notion of Hellenic identity and the concomitant polarization of Greek and barbarian as generic opposites... In its other sense, panhellenism is the idea that the various Greek city-states could solve their political disputes and simultaneously enrich themselves by uniting in common cause and conquering all or part of the Persian Empire.*[119]

---

[113] Funke 2013: 457; for the bounty on Ephialtes see Hdts. 7.213.
[114] *OCD*: 1075 'panhellenism'.
[115] *OCD*: 1075 'panhellenism'.
[116] Hall 2002: 205.
[117] Mitchell 2007: xviii.
[118] Mitchell 2007: xviii, see also xv-xvii for further references.
[119] Flower 2000: 65-66.

A true and equitable pan-Hellenism, it has been argued, was not in the interests of the states that were in the best position to foster it.[120] However, for the purpose of this study the term 'pan-Hellenic', with regard to the monuments attributed to it, represents a group of Greek communities (although not wholly inclusive), bound by a common sense of 'Greekness' who work together (however temporarily) to celebrate a victory over an enemy (consisting of both non-Greek and Greek Persian sympathisers) after the repulsion of the Persian invasions.

3.2 Commemorative Places

The Persian Wars were commemorated throughout the Greek world. The original locations of these monuments may be divided into four general site types which are represented in the compiled body of monuments: the battlefield, the urban centre, the pan-Hellenic sanctuary and other. Definitions of each of these site types will be offered in turn below.

3.2.1 *Battlefield*

The purpose of defining what a battlefield consists of is to identify the boundaries of the site of conflict and therefore delineate a commemorative place. The conflict sites of the Persian Wars provide a varied collection of battlefield types: Marathon was fought on a coastal plain; Thermopylae was fought in a pass, restricted on both lateral sides by physical boundaries; Artemisium and Salamis were naval battles, one fought in more open water and the other in the restricted strait between Athens and the island of Salamis; and Plataea was fought on an undulating inland plain. It will be necessary to apply a broad definition of what a battlefield is and the space it occupies within the broader landscape to encompass the varied collection of battlefield types represented in the Persian Wars. Therefore, Carman and Carman are followed here in their definition of the term 'battlefield':

> *so far as can be identified, those places where troops concentrated with the intention of fighting are considered by us to be inside the battlefield space, and locations where no fighting either took place or was intended (as far as we can ascertain) lie outside.*[121]

---
[120] Hall 2002: 228.
[121] Carman and Carman 2006: 134.

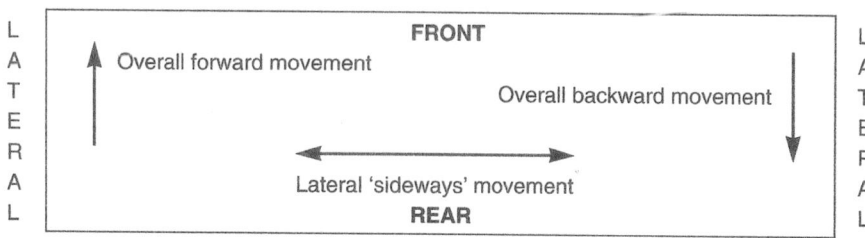

Figure 1. *Establishing boundaries to the battlefield space (after Carman and Carman 2006: 135. Reproduced by kind permission of Dr John Carman).*

As Carman and Carman explain, to simplify the battlefield space is to acknowledge that it has 'four edges'.[122]

As Figure 1 illustrates, the battlefield is understood to have a 'front' which marks the edge of any forward movement; a 'rear' which marks the extent of any movement in the opposite direction and 'sides' which mark the extent of movement to either side. The range of battlefield types mentioned above illustrate how some boundaries are physical, for example the pass at Thermopylae and the Attic and Salamis coast lines at Salamis, and some were less physical (as far as it is possible to ascertain) such as the lateral boundaries at Plataea. Broadly defining the edges to the battlefield makes it possible to attribute the construction of certain monuments to particular site types. Presenting battlefields as places with edges enables the differentiation of the space outside of these boundaries. The boundaries are necessarily loose due to the varied collection of battlefield types, and it is understood here that commemorative monuments were built upon the battlefield if they were constructed where, or nearby where, fighting took place.

3.2.2 Urban centre

The 'urban centre' site type is understood here as the ancient Greek city: the *polis*. The *polis* may be thought of as both a city and as a state.[123] However, for the purpose of presenting the *polis* as a place of commemoration, it is understood here as a city (for the *polis* as a state and as a commemorative group, see chapter section 3.1.1). The urban centre is understood here as a

---

[122] Carman and Carman 2006: 134.
[123] Hansen 1997: 10; Hansen 2006: 62-65.

dense collection of individuals with a higher population density than the area surrounding it. Density of population as representative of a city is outlined by Aristotle:

> A city is an aggregate made up of houses and land and property, self-sufficient with regard to a good life.[124]

The *polis* has always been linked to the surrounding countryside (*chora*).[125] When the *polis* is understood as a state, the term *chora* is used to denote the territory of which the urban centre was a part. However when the term *polis* is used to denote an urban centre, as it is here when denoting a commemorative place, *chora* usually refers to the countryside and is often opposed to the *polis*.[126]

The defining line between urban and non-urban in this study is understood, for the vast majority of *poleis*, to be the city walls.[127] For example, in the classical period it was regarded as exceptional and old fashioned for a *polis* to not be protected by walls.[128] However, it should be noted that the ancient intention of constructing a wall was for defensive purposes only and not to create a barrier between those individuals living within the urban centre and those individuals living in the surrounding countryside. During peace times people could enter or exit the city gates at will, while they were guarded during times of war.[129] Therefore urban centres, when considered as commemorative places, are differentiated from the space around it by the walls which demarcate it in the landscape. Therefore, everything inside the walls falls under the title 'urban centre'; urban sanctuaries are therefore necessarily included. In short, for the purpose of defining a place of commemoration, the urban centre is presented as a physical thing with clearly defined boundaries.

---

[124] Arist. *Economics* 1343a10; trans. Hansen.
[125] Hansen 1997: 17, see n. 73 for further references.
[126] Hansen 1997: 17; see Arist. *Politics* 5.1303b7-10 for an example of differentiating *polis* and *chora*.
[127] For city walls see Hansen and Nielsen 2004: 135-137.
[128] Hansen 1997: 52; Sparta: Xen. *Hellenica* 6.5.28; Elis: Xen. *Hellenica* 3.2.27.
[129] See Thuc. 7.29.3 for an account of a surprise attack finding the city gates open and unguarded; see Aen. Tact. 28.1-4 for guarding the gates during times of war; see also Hansen 1997: 52.

3.2.3 Pan-Hellenic Sanctuary

At the most basic level a sanctuary would have consisted of an altar and a boundary. The animal sacrifice, which was the primary act of worship, would have been performed at the altar and the boundary would have separated the sacred area from the secular.[130] These two aspects would be among the defining features of sanctuaries. In addition, the altar and boundary could be accompanied by temples, groves, statues, and other offerings; all these aspects taken together, or various combinations, would have comprised a sanctuary.[131] Sanctuaries varied greatly in size. The smaller sanctuaries may not have had many or any structures apart from a hearth, or altar, to perform the sacrifice and perhaps even an imaginary boundary. The larger sanctuaries, however, had many buildings which would have been constructed to accommodate the ritual behaviour. For example, at Delphi the paved sacred way is clearly defined and lined with structures and would have served as the route for processions towards the altar. Many of the treasuries which lined the sacred way at Delphi were not orientated towards the temple or the altar but were situated to be visible to visitors.[132]

Sanctuaries were either local or pan-Hellenic. Local sanctuaries were maintained by a particular *polis* and were intended for the use of citizens from that city-state, while pan-Hellenic sanctuaries were intended for use by all Greeks.[133] The main four pan-Hellenic sanctuaries were Olympia, Delphi, Isthmia and Nemea. According to the data compiled in this study, no monuments commemorating the Persian Wars were erected at Nemea and so only Olympia, Delphi and Isthmia are represented. Pan-Hellenic sanctuaries were likely to be politically neutral and were often situated away from the more powerful *poleis*. These sanctuaries were run by either local administrations or federations representing local interests and so provided an equitable place at which Greek city-states could come to meet and interact.[134] Sanctuaries of this scale would have provided a neutral place to argue, compete in athletic and musical contests or display

---

[130] Emerson 2007: 4.
[131] Pedley 2005: 6.
[132] Pedley 2005: 6-8.
[133] Emerson 2007: 5-6.
[134] Pedley 2005: 40;

social prowess. By winning victories in competition or dedicating lavish gifts to the gods (either individually or as a collective city-state), both the individual and their *polis* would be glorified. Dedications on an individual and collective scale could have taken the form of, for example, weapons and art and these sites have been described as 'museums'.[135] On a purely collective scale treasuries were constructed at pan-Hellenic sanctuaries in order to display the wealth and construction skills of the dedicating *polis*. Some city-states used materials from their home territory so the treasury became a home territory in a distant sanctuary.[136] As neutral sites, these sanctuaries became focal points for the exchange of both political and artistic ideas.[137]

The unified idea of a pan-Hellenic sanctuary has recently been challenged, and it has been argued that these pan-Hellenic sites were sites of disunity, were not active at all times, and would have experienced an irregular flow of visitors.[138] Furthermore, it is suggested that the term 'pan-Hellenic' is vague and ill-fitting when considering the variety of activities that took place at these sanctuaries over time by various groups. While the vagueness of the 'pan-Hellenic' label is acknowledged here, it is utilised to set apart four specific sanctuaries: Delphi, Olympia, Isthmia, and Nemea.[139]

3.2.4 Other

Monuments are attributed to this category when they cannot be attributed to the three main general categories. This category includes monuments erected at non-urban, non-pan-Hellenic sanctuaries and when a monument cannot be allocated a specific physical commemorative place, for example in the case of vows and oaths. Non-urban, non-pan-Hellenic sanctuaries would have functioned in the same manner as other sanctuaries but they were usually not as large as pan-Hellenic sanctuaries and they were situated outside the walls of the *polis*. Vows and oaths were non-physical monuments and would have, initially, consisted of a verbal agreement with

---

[135] Pedley 2005: 41.
[136] Pedley 2005: 40.
[137] Pedley 2005: 41.
[138] Scott 2010: esp. 256-264, with further bibliography.
[139] For similarities between these four sanctuaries particularly, see Roux 1980; Scott (2010: 257-258) also accepts these sanctuaries are set apart.

the divine. This verbal component of commemoration will therefore not be assigned a specific site type or specific place of commemoration. However, in cases in which a vow is repaid with behavioural commemoration, such as sacrifice, the commemorative act is associated with a specific place.

Chapter 4
Monuments by Type

Table 1. Full monument list

Battle	No.	Monument	Commemorating Group	Location
Marathon	1	Burial Mound	Athens	Battlefield
	2	Burial Mound	Plataea	Battlefield
	3	Trophy	Athens	Battlefield
	4	Grave of Miltiades	Athens	Battlefield
	5	*Herakleia*	Athens	Battlefield
	6	Epigram for the Athenians	Athens	Battlefield
	7	Casualty List	Athens	Battlefield
	8	Treasury	Athens	Delphi
	9	Thank-Offering (Statue Group?)	Athens	Delphi
	10	Callimachus Monument	Athens	Athens (Acropolis)
	11	Engraved Marble Base (Cenotaph?)	Athens	Athens
	12	Stoa *Poikile*	Athens	Athens (Agora)
	13	Temple of Eukleia	Athens	Athens (Agora)
	14	Sanctuary of Pan	Athens	Athens (Acropolis)
	15	Statue Group	Athens	Delphi
	16	Bronze Statue of Athena	Athens	Athens (Acropolis)
	17	'Old' Parthenon	Athens	Athens (Acropolis)
	18	Annual Sacrifice of 500 Kids	Athens	Athens (Agrai)
	19	Temple of Nemesis with Statue of Nemesis	Athens	Rhamnus
	20	Statue of Arimnestos	Plataea	Plataea
Artemisium	21	Circle of Marble Steles with an Epigram	Athens	Battlefield
	22	Shrine to Boreas	Athens	Athens
Thermopylae	23	Epigram for the Spartiates	Amphictyons	Battlefield
	24	Epigram for Peloponnesians	Amphictyons	Battlefield
	25	Epigram for the Opuntian Locrians	Opus	Battlefield
	26	Epigram for the Thespians	Thespiae	Battlefield
	27	Stone Lion over Leonidas' grave	Spartans or Amphictyons	Battlefield
	28	Burial mound	Sparta & Thespiae	Battlefield
	29	Tomb of Leonidas	Sparta	Sparta
	30	List of Spartans Who Fought at Thermopylae	Sparta	Sparta
	31	Shrine of Maron and Alpheius	Sparta	Sparta (Agora)
	32	Hero-Cult practices for the fallen	Sparta	Sparta
	33	Epigram for Leonidas	Sparta	Sparta
Salamis	34	Trophy on the Island of Psyttaleia	Athens	Battlefield
	35	Trophy on the Island of Salamis (Cynosoura)	Athens	Battlefield
	36	Gravestone with Epitaph for the Corinthians	Corinth	Battlefield
	37	Burial Mound		Battlefield
	38	Tomb of Themistocles	Athens	Battlefield
	39	Thank-Offering of Three Triremes (1)	Panhellenic	Isthmus
	40	Thank-Offering of Three Triremes (2)	Panhellenic	Sunium
	41	Thank-Offering of Three Triremes (3)	Panhellenic	Salamis
	42	Statue of Apollo Holding the Beak of a Ship	Panhellenic	Delphi
	43	Tomb of Eurybiades	Sparta	Sparta
	44	Painting of Salamis Holding the Beak of a Ship	Athens	Olympia
	45	Sanctuary of the Hero Cychreus	Athens	Salamis
	46	Epigram Engraved on a Cenotaph	Corinth	Isthmus
	47	Bronze Mast with Three Gold Stars	Aegina	Delphi
	48	Pedimental Sculptures of the Temple of Aphaea	Aegina	Aphaea sanctuary, Aegina

Table 2. Full monument list cont.

Battle	No.	Monument	Commemorating Group	Location
Plataea	49	Trophy	Panhellenic	Battlefield
	50	Trophy	Sparta	Battlefield
	51	Trophy	Athens	Battlefield
	52	Epigram for Athenians	Athens	Battlefield
	53	Epigram for Spartans	Sparta	Battlefield
	54	Epigram for Corinthians	Corinth	Battlefield
	55	Epigram for Tegeans	Tegea	Battlefield
	56	Burial Mound	Sparta	Battlefield
	57	Burial Mound	Athens	Battlefield
	58	Burial Mound	Tegea	Battlefield
	59	Burial Mound	Megara	Battlefield
	60	Burial Mound	Phlius	Battlefield
	61	Burial Mound (Empty?)	Aegina	Battlefield
	62	Empty Burial Mounds	Others	Battlefield
	63	Ruins of Sanctuaries as Memorial of Persian Impiety	Panhellenic	
	64	Tithing of Medising Greeks	Panhellenic	
	65	*Eleutheria*	Panhellenic	Battlefield
	66	Inviolability of Plataea	Panhellenic	
	67	Altar of Zeus *Eleutherios*	Panhellenic	Battlefield
	68	Annual Rites Performed at the Greek Tombs	Plataea	Battlefield
	69	Tomb of Mardonius	Plataea	Battlefield
	70	Temple and Statue of Athena *Areia*	Plataea	Plataea
	71	Tomb of Pausanias	Sparta	Sparta
	72	Spoils Displayed in the Parthenon	Athens	Athens (Acropolis)
	73	Odeum at Athens	Athens	Athens
	74	Shields Hung on Temple Architraves	Athens	Delphi
	75	Bronze Statue of Artemis the Saviour	Megara	Megara
	76	Bronze Statue of Artemis the Saviour	Pagae (in Megarid)	Pagae
	77	Grave of Euchidas with Engraved Stele	Plataea	Plataea
	78	Statue of an Ox	Plataea	Delphi
	79	Manger of Mardonius Dedicated to Athena *Alea*	Tegea	Tegea
General	80	Serpent Column	Panhellenic	Delphi
	81	Bronze Statue of Zeus	Panhellenic	Olympia
	82	Bronze Statue of Poseidon	Panhellenic	Isthmus
	83	Persian Stoa	Sparta	Sparta (Agora)
	84	Athenian Portico Displaying Spoils	Athens	Delphi
	85	North Wall of the Acropolis	Athens	Athens (Acropolis)
	86	'New' Parthenon	Athens	Athens (Acropolis)
	87	Statue of Zeus *Eleutherios*	Athens	Athens (Agora)
	88	Statue of Miltiades	Athens	Athens (Agora)
	89	Statue of Themistocles	Athens	Athens (Agora)
	90	Tomb of Aristides	Athens	Athens (Phalerum)
	91	Epigram in Thanks to Aphrodite	Corinth	Corinth
	92	Epigram Engraved on a Cenotaph	Megara	Megara (Agora)
	93	Statues of Skyllis and His Daughter Hydna	Amphictyons	Delphi
	94	Altar Dedicated to Helios *Eleutherios*	Troezen	Troezen
	95	Statues of Women and Children	Troezen	Troezen (Agora)
	96	Trophy with Epigram	Delphi	Delphi
	97	Altar of the Winds	Delphi	Thyia
	98	Statue of Apollo	Epidaurus	Delphi
	99	Bronze Statue of an Ox	Carystus	Delphi
	100	Statue Group	Hermionae	Delphi
	101	Gilded statue of Alexander I	Macedon	Delphi
	102	Bronze Apollo	Peparethos	Delphi
	103	Bronze Apollo	Samos	Delphi
	104	Bronze Bull	Eretria	Olympia
	105	Inscribed Persian Helmet	Athens	Olympia

4.1 What is a Monument?

Alcock has defined monuments as 'places, structures, or objects deliberately designed, or later agreed, to provoke memories'.[140] However, this study modifies Alcock's definition slightly on two separate points. Firstly, within this definition behavioural commemoration is included as a 'monument'. Behavioural commemoration is considered here to be the repetitive behaviour with a communally accepted relevance to a particular place and/or event. By considering behavioural commemoration as a monument, this study aims to highlight the importance of non-material experiences which are less easily detected by the archaeologist.

Secondly, while Alcock's 'types of data' include monuments and places such as urban centres and sanctuaries,[141] this study separates the 'types of data' into separate categories. The monuments, which include behavioural commemoration, form the compilation of commemorations discussed here in chapter 4 and in chapter 5, while the places such as specific urban centres, sanctuaries and battlefields provide the setting within which the monument is (or at least was originally) situated. Therefore, the monuments which are collated within this study are either physical commemorative objects located, or behavioural commemorative activities enacted, at particular places.

4.2 Monument Types

The commemorations of the Persian Wars encompass a range of monument types which illustrate the variety of methods used by Greek communities to commemorate the Persian Wars. The range of monument types may be broadly categorised as: cenotaphs, trophies, inscriptions, burials, dedications, structures, non-physical monuments and other.

4.2.1 Cenotaphs

Page suggests the term 'cenotaph' 'should be reserved for memorials for the bodies not recovered for burial'.[142] Pritchett notes that throughout Page's study 'he recognizes only a war-memorial at home and a cenotaph

---

[140] Alcock 2002: 28.
[141] Alcock 2002: 31.
[142] Page 1981: 220; see also Xen. *Anabasis* 6.4.9.

Table 3. Cenotaphs

Battle	No.	Monument	Dedicator	Location
Marathon	11	Engraved Marble Base (Cenotaph?)	Athens	Athens
Salamis	46	Epigram Engraved on a Cenotaph	Corinth	Isthmus
General	92	Epigram Engraved on a Cenotaph	Megara	Megara (Agora)

on the field of battle' when honouring the war dead in the absence of their bodies.[143] However, as Pritchett argues, this 'is counter to Greek usage'.[144] For example Plutarch clearly states the monument at the Isthmus of Corinth was a *cenotaphion* (**no. 46**) and it was not erected on the battlefield.[145] Also, the monument raised in the *demosion sema* in Athens to commemorate the Athenian war dead, in absence of the bodies themselves, has been suggested to have been a 'cenotaph' (see **no. 11** for discussion). In the case of the Marathon war dead the bodies were recovered for burial but were buried on the battlefield (see **no. 1**). Therefore, the only consistent aspect of a cenotaph is the physical lack of a body, or bodies (even if their location is known to be elsewhere): they may be considered as empty graves.[146]

The practice of erecting cenotaphs can be traced back to the Homeric period and the forms which cenotaphs could take varied widely.[147] Cenotaphs may range from pits containing dedicated objects made specifically for dedication to the enormous tumulus cenotaph at Salamis, Cyprus, covering a mud-brick platform and ramp.[148]

4.2.2 Trophies

A clear physical divide can be made between the two forms of trophy: those which were destined to decay relatively rapidly, and those which

---

[143] Pritchett 1985: 4.258-259.
[144] Pritchett 1985: 4.259.
[145] Plut. *On the Malice of Herodotus* 39; Pritchett (1985: 4.259) puts the confusion over classifying ancient Greek commemorative monuments down to there being 'no separate word to designate what we call a war-memorial'.
[146] Kurtz and Boardman 1971: 99.
[147] In *Od.* 1.291 Telemachus is advised to raise a cenotaph to Odysseus in Ithaca if it is discovered that Odysseus is dead; also in *Od.* 4.584 Menelaus raises a cenotaph for Agamemnon in Egypt.
[148] Pits containing objects: Kurtz and Boardman 1971: 99; tumulus cenotaph: Kurtz and Boardman 1971: 258, image on 252.

were meant to be more permanent markers of a historical event. The two forms will be described below in turn under the titles of 'perishable' and 'permanent'.

4.2.2.1 Perishable

The perishable monument would have been constructed at the culmination of battle. This monument would have consisted of a panoply of enemy armour placed on a stake, or a collection of pieces of enemy armour piled together.[149] The battlefield trophy, according to the ancient literature, would have marked the spot at which the enemy were routed.[150] These trophies were often erected in remote spots in enemy territory and therefore would have been difficult to interact with as objects of cult and thus access as focal points for repetitive behavioural commemoration.[151] Furthermore, it has been suggested that the perishable battlefield trophy was a symbol of prestige.[152] For example, Thucydides informs us that the Spartans returned to the site of conflict to erect a trophy after their naval victory over an Athenian squadron in 412/411 BC.[153] The return journey, which took place in winter, would have totalled fifty miles or more and Thucydides provides no other reason for this other than to erect a trophy.[154] The trophy was raised in territory occupied by the enemy and most probably would not have been intended as an object to return to; the trophy was to become an instrument 'of publicity for advertising the prowess of the victor'.[155]

The perishable form of trophy would slowly degrade over time and the renewal or repair of these monuments was forbidden. The purpose of this prohibition was to avoid prolonging hatreds caused in warfare by ensuring

---

[149] *OCD*: 1512 'trophies'; see West 1969: 10, n. 17 for visual representations of trophies.
[150] Thucydides refers to trophies of the turning point (*trope*) of battles on two occasions: 2.92.5 and 7.54; this is also attested in later literature: Diod. 13.51.7; Cassius Dio 42.40.5; see Pritchett 1974: 2.253 for further references; West 1965: xxxix-xl; see also *OCD*: 1512 'trophies'.
[151] Pritchett 1974: 2.272-273.
[152] Pritchett 1974: 2.273.
[153] See Thuc. 8.42.4.
[154] The distance between Knidos (where the Spartans were anchored after the conflict) and Syme (where they returned to in order to erect a trophy) has been estimated by Pritchett (1974: 2.273) to be approximately 40 km as the crow flies.
[155] Pritchett 1974: 2.273.

monuments on the battlefield had a finite lifespan.[156] The testimonies which explicitly support this point were writing in the 1st century BC, or the 1st century AD and are therefore considered late. However, it has been argued that their judgement is supported by the fact that Thucydides and Xenophon (authors of the 5th and 4th centuries BC) do not mention the use of either stone or bronze for the trophies of any battle that they describe.[157]

In order to erect a trophy, the victor must have control of the battlefield. Thucydides provides us with just one example of the destruction of a trophy, and the justification for violating the monument was that the victor was not in possession of the battlefield when the trophy was erected.[158] The Athenians sailed to Panormos in Milesian territory and defeated the Spartan rescue force, only to wait two days to erect a trophy which was subsequently pulled down by the Milesians. For one force to demonstrate control of the battlefield in a naval clash is more difficult than on land. As a result, opposing navies could both erect trophies to claim the victory and these monuments would be constructed at the nearest shore to where the clash took place.[159]

With the focus on a finite existence for this form of monument and the prohibition of permanent monuments it has been suggested that the perishable trophy may be considered a sign of the defeat of the enemy rather than a monument to victory.[160]

4.2.2.2 Permanent

The trophies of the Persian Wars were the first to be given permanent form; in the transformation process the meaning attributed to these monuments (still referred to as *tropaia*) altered from the traditional meaning (as a sign of the defeat of the enemy) to a victory monument.[161] It has been argued,

---

[156] Plut. *The Roman Questions* 273c-d; Cic. *On inventions* 2.23 (69-70); Diod. 13.24.5-6.
[157] West 1969: 9; furthermore, although it is not in reference to a 'trophy', Aeschines (*Against Ctesiphon* 116) describes how the Thebans requested the Athenians be fined for renewing hanging shields affixed to the temple of Apollo at Delphi after it was destroyed by fire early in the 4th century BC. For more detail on the monument see **no. 74**.
[158] Thuc. 8.24.1.
[159] Pritchett 1974: 2.260.
[160] West 1969: 13; for trophies as causes of shame for the defeated see Thuc. 1.105.6; Xen. *Hellenica* 6.4.14.
[161] West 1969: 18.

convincingly, that Aristophanes introduces us to a new usage of the term *tropaion*, when he references the trophy on the Marathon battlefield.[162] The *tropaion* on the battlefield of Marathon is put on par with the city of Athens itself,[163] and the regal treatment the Athenians enjoyed from cities paying them tribute is deemed worthy of both the land and the trophy.[164] West believes that Aristophanes is describing a permanent trophy, as a temporary trophy which had been decaying for two generations would hardly have been 'worthy of the city'.[165] Moreover, Aristophanes' reference in the *Knights* is the first reference in extant 5th century BC sources to the trophy as an object of emulation (see also **no. 3**).[166]

Chaniotis states that trophies were an important aspect of the cultural memory of 'Greeks'.[167] These structures were religiously protected and, although the form changed from perishable to permanent, it remained sacrilegious to destroy trophies. However, the permanent trophies would not degrade as quickly as their perishable predecessors and the prohibition of renewing or repairing trophies must only be understood as relevant to the perishable examples discussed above.[168] As a result measures could be taken by the defeated to remove the permanent trophy from sight; for example, the Rhodians constructed a building around a trophy to prevent it being seen so as to avoid destroying the structure itself.[169] Herodotus never mentions trophies in his histories of the Persian Wars. It has been argued that by the time of Herodotus' writing many imposing monuments stood on the battlefields and in sanctuaries referencing Greek victory and so 'Herodotus felt that his audience did not need to be told who won the great battles of the Persian wars'.[170] However, it should be noted that terminology may vary among authors as Plutarch refers to numerous monuments as *tropaia* which were not described as such by Herodotus. For

---

[162] West 1969: 12; see Aristoph. *Knights* 1333-1334 and Aristoph. *Wasps* 707-711.
[163] Aristoph. *Knights* 1333-1334.
[164] Aristoph. *Wasps* 707-711.
[165] West 1969: 12; Aristophanes' Knights and Wasps are dated to 424 and 422 BC respectively.
[166] West 1969: 12.
[167] Chaniotis 2005: 234.
[168] Pritchett 1985: 2.257.
[169] Vitr. 2.8.15.
[170] Pritchett 1985: 2.270.

Table 4. Trophies

Battle	No.	Monument	Dedicator	Location
Marathon	3	Trophy	Athens	Battlefield
Salamis	34	Trophy on the island of Psyttaleia	Athens	Battlefield
	35	Trophy on the island on Salamis (Cynosoura)	Athens	Battlefield
Plataea	49	Trophy	Panhellenic	Battlefield
	50	Trophy	Sparta	Battlefield
	51	Trophy	Athens	Battlefield
General	96	Trophy with epigram	Delphi	Delphi

example, the serpent column at Delphi described by Herodotus is referred to as a trophy by Plutarch.[171]

With regard to the data collated in this study, the only trophy of whose style we may be sure of is the Athenian trophy at Marathon. The permanent monument of Marathon, of which archaeological remains have been identified, was a 9 m column monument topped with an ionic capital, which was cut to receive a statue (see **no. 3**).[172] At Salamis and Plataea trophies are also said to have been constructed but no sources refer to the style.[173]

4.2.3 Inscriptions

Inscriptions regarded here as 'monuments' are divided into three parts: epigrams, epitaphs and casualty lists.

4.2.3.1 *Epigrams*

In the archaic period the epigram was a short inscription on an object or monument intended to inform the onlooker who it belonged to, who made it, who dedicated it and to which god, or who is buried beneath it.[174] During the classical period epigrams inscribed on monuments were normally anonymous. The earliest signed by the author can be dated to the mid-4th century BC.[175] Many epigrams are attributed to earlier poets, the earliest being Simonides. Multiple epigrams and epitaphs included in this

---

[171] Hdts. 9.81.1; Plut. *On the Malice of Herodotus* 837d and e.
[172] See Vanderpool 1966.
[173] Salamis: Paus. 1.36.1.; Psyttaleia: Plut. *Aristides* 9.2., Paus. 1.36.2.; Plataea: Plut. *Aristides* 20.3., Paus. 9.2.6.
[174] *OCD*: 515 'Epigram, Greek'.
[175] See *CEG* 2.819 and 888, ii; *OCD*: 515 'Epigram, Greek'.

study have been attributed to Simonides by different authors. However, it has been argued that only one (which incidentally is not included here as it is erected by, and commemorates, an individual) may be confidently attributed to Simonides; this is the epitaph for Magistias constructed at the Thermopylae field of conflict.[176]

4.2.3.2 Epitaphs

An epitaph is particular form of epigram in that it has direct relevance to the deceased. 'Epitaph' may be translated as 'over', or 'at a tomb' (made up from *epi*: 'at, or over' and *taphos*: 'tomb'). Epitaphs could be erected at the site of an individual tomb or a communal grave. At the site of an individual grave the epitaph would at the least give the name of the dead, and at the most give an account of the dead person's virtues, how he died, and bid for sympathy from the viewer who was often directly addressed.[177] At the beginning of the 5th century BC epitaphs were usually quite crude in design (e.g. **no. 36**) with just the text inscribed. However, by the late 5th century BC epitaphs had become more complex and figurative imagery was added to the stone.[178]

Table 5. Epigrams and epitaphs

Battle	No.	Monument	Dedicator	Location
Marathon	6	Epigram for fallen Athenians	Athens	Battlefield
	11	Marble base upon which 2 epigrams are engraved	Athens	Athens
Artemisium	21	Circle of marble stelae with epigram	Athens	Battlefield
Thermopylae	23	Epigram for Spartiates	Amphictyons	Battlefield
	24	Epigram for Peloponnesians	Amphictyons	Battlefield
	25	Epigram for the Opuntian Locrians	Opus	Battlefield
	26	Epigram for the Thespians	Thespiae	Battlefield
	33	Epigram for Leonidas	Sparta	Sparta
Salamis	36	Epitaph for Corinthians buried on Salamis	Corinth	Battlefield
	46	Epigram Engraved on a Cenotaph	Corinth	Isthmus
Plataea	52	Epigram for Athenians	Athens	Battlefield
	53	Epigram for Spartans	Sparta	Battlefield
	54	Epigram for Corinthians	Corinth	Battlefield
	55	Epigram for Tegeans	Tegea	Battlefield
	77	Grave of Euchidas with engraved stele	Plataea	Plataea
General	91	Epigram in thanks to Aphrodite	Corinth	Corinth
	92	Epigram engraved on a cenotaph	Megara	Megara (Agora)

---

[176] Hdts. 7.228; Page 1981: VI.
[177] Kurtz and Boardman 1971: 260.
[178] See Peek 1955: no. 1600.

4.2.3.3 Casualty Lists

The Athenian casualty lists of the 5th century BC found in the *Kerameikos* are by far the most numerous example of this type of monument, represented by over thirty examples.[179] In Athens, each year casualty lists would be set up denoting who had died in war. If there were no wars, no casualty lists were erected. Casualty lists could be inscribed and raised at a distance from the buried dead, or even if the dead were not recovered. In cases such as these the casualty list may form a part of a monument which, in turn, may be considered a cenotaph. This, arguably, occurs at the 'cenotaph' raised for the Marathon dead at Athens (see **no. 11**).[180] In contrast to the Athenian examples, only sixteen examples of casualty lists have been discovered outside of Athens.[181]

Casualty lists consisted of an upstanding stele inscribed with the names of the war dead. In the case of the recently discovered Marathon casualty list (**no. 7**) the list of names are preceded by a short inscription denoting who the named dead are and how they died. The form of the Marathon casualty lists suggests that, on this monument specifically, each Athenian tribe would have been designated their own stele and these would be lined up on a communal base.[182]

Table 6. Casualty lists

Battle	No.	Monument	Dedicator	Location
Marathon	7	Marathon casualty list	Athens	Battlefield
Thermopylae	30	List of those who fought at Thermopylae	Sparta	Sparta

4.2.4 Burials

4.2.4.1 Collective

A collective burial or *polyandrion* is the covering of multiple bodies with earth, an object (such as a monumental structure), or both. Funerary architecture above the ground would usually adhere to two basic types: the

---

[179] Bradeen 1969: 146; Kurtz and Boardman 1971: 112; Pritchett 1985: 4.139.
[180] See Matthaiou 2003: 197-200.
[181] Pritchett 1985: 4.140 ff.
[182] In the same way as casualty lists *IG* 1^3 1147 and *IG* 1^3 1147bis. A one-slab-per-tribe arrangement is only one possible form for casualty lists; for example, for multiple tribes-per-slab see Bradeen 1964: 43-55.

Table 7. Collective burials

Battle	No.	Monument	Dedicator	Location
Marathon	1	Burial mound	Athens	Battlefield
	2	Burial mound	Plataea	Battlefield
Thermopylae	28	Burial mound	Sparta/Thespiae	Battlefield
Salamis	37	Burial mound		Battlefield
Plataea	56	Burial mound	Sparta	Battlefield
	57	Burial mound	Athens	Battlefield
	58	Burial mound	Tegea	Battlefield
	59	Burial mound	Megara	Battlefield
	60	Burial mound	Phlius	Battlefield
	61	Burial mound (empty?)	Aegina	Battlefield
	62	Empty burial mounds	Others	Battlefield

round and rectangular mounds. The examples represented in this study which have survived and are viewable today, the Athenian and Plataean burial mounds at Marathon (**nos. 1** and **2**) and perhaps the burial mound on Salamis (**no. 37**), represent the round type. The rectangular mounds and built tombs were popular in the archaic period but continued into the classical period.[183] The bodies contained within these monuments can be cremated, partly cremated, or buried. In the classical period in Athens both cremation and inhumation were practised. The collective burials addressed in this study represent cremations and inhumations. For example, at Marathon the bodies of the dead Athenians 'were cremated and a tumulus was raised over a brick platform which some have seen as the cremation area, together with some vase offerings'.[184] Again at Marathon a contrasting method of communal burial can be seen; the Plataeans and slaves together were buried as opposed to having been cremated.[185] Inhumation was the less expensive and less time consuming form of burial. However, a pyre of offerings was found beside the inhumations in the grave of the Plataeans and slaves (**no. 2**).[186]

---

[183] Kurtz and Boardman 1971: 106, 111.
[184] Kurtz and Boardman 1971: 247.
[185] Paus. 1.32.3.
[186] Kurtz and Boardman 1971: 247.

4.2.4.2 Commander

All burials of military leaders in Table 8 are reliant on literary evidence as none have been identified with confidence. In addition all military leader burials represented in this study were buried, or at least reburied, alone.

With regard to the examples of the burial of Greek military leaders from the Persian Wars we only have evidence from two city states: Athens and Sparta. The form and location of Miltiades' grave has been the subject of some debate (see **no. 4**) but may have consisted of a base with an inscribed stele identifying who was buried beneath.[187] The tombs of Leonidas and Pausanias at Sparta are referred to only by Pausanias.[188] Pausanias makes no reference to the form of the tombs but states that the bones of Leonidas were removed from the battlefield of Thermopylae about forty years after the battle (see **no. 29**). This suggests that Leonidas' body was still identifiable at the battlefield and the bones were interred at Sparta. We learn from literary sources that the bodies of the dead Spartan leaders were carefully preserved for transport from the site of conflict; therefore, the general practice may have been inhumation.[189] The return of Themistocles' bones to Attica is mentioned by Thucydides.[190] However, the earliest information which has survived regarding the form of Themistocles' tomb is from Plutarch who states that 'there is a basement of goodly size, and that the altar-like structure upon this is the tomb of Themistocles.'[191] The literary evidence does not offer any information about the forms of Aristides' and Eurybiades' tombs.

I also include the tomb of Mardonius, the Persian General, who was killed at the battle of Plataea and supposedly buried on the battlefield.[192] Pausanias is the only literary source for this grave and does not give any information about its form.

It should be noted that only Leonidas, from the collection of commemorated Greek commanders represented in this study, died in battle. The remaining individuals died after the Persian Wars (as defined

---

[187] Paus. 1.32.4; West 1965: 13.
[188] Paus. 3.14.1.
[189] Pritchett 1985: 4.255; see Xen. *Hellenica* 5.3.19.; Plut. *Agesilaus* 40.3.
[190] Thuc. 1.138.5-6.
[191] Plut. *Them.* 32.4.
[192] Paus. 9.2.2.

Table 8. Commander burials

Battle	No.	Monument	Dedicator	Location
Marathon	4	Grave of Miltiades	Athens	Battlefield
Thermopylae	29	Tomb of Leonidas	Sparta	Sparta
Salamis	38	Tomb of Themistocles	Athens	Battlefield
Salamis	43	Tomb of Eurybiades	Sparta	Sparta
Plataea	69	Tomb of Mardonius	Plataea	Battlefield
Plataea	71	Tomb of Pausanias	Sparta	Sparta
General	90	Tomb of Aristides	Athens	Athens (Phalerum)

within this study). With regards to Spartan practice, despite Eurybiades and Pausanias dying at later dates,[193] the three Spartan commanders are all afforded tombs within the urban centre. Furthermore, no Athenian commander represented in Table 8 died during the Persian Wars.[194] However, Miltiades and Themistocles are given tombs on, or near, particular sites of conflict (Marathon and Salamis respectively) while Aristides is given a tomb at Phalerum (which is considered under the 'urban' site type). According to the examples presented in Table 8, Sparta is consistent with the treatment of their commanders despite the circumstances of the individual's death. On the other hand, variation can be seen in the site types selected for the Athenian commanders' tombs, with a preference being shown for battlefield burial.

4.2.5 Dedications

Dedications have been defined as the '[t]ransfer of a thing from the human into the divine sphere...indicating surrender of an object into divine ownership'.[195] The dedications addressed in this study include: the spoils of war (**nos. 9, 39, 40, 41, 72, 74, 79, 84** and **105**); statues of deities (**nos. 15,**

---

[193] Eurybiades survived the battle of Salamis, at which he commanded the Spartan navy, as according to Herodotus (8.124) he received an award for his valour and argued against destroying the Persian bridge over the Hellespont (8.108.2-4); Pausanias, according to Thucydides (1.134), was starved to death in Sparta.

[194] Miltiades is said to have died from a gangrenous leg wound after an unsuccessful assault on Paros (Hdts. 6.132-136); Themistocles is said to have died of 'disease', or perhaps poison while exiled (Thuc. 1.138.4); according to Plutarch (*Aristides* 26.1-2) numerous stories existed about the time and whereabouts of Aristides' death, none of which tell of him dying in battle.

[195] *OCD*: 422 '*dedicatio*'.

16, 19, 42, 70, 75, 76, 81, 82, 87, 98, 100, 102 and 103), heroes (**no. 15**), mortals (**nos. 15, 93** and **101**) and animals (**nos. 78, 99** and **104**); and votive offerings (**nos. 8, 10, 44, 47, 48** and **80**). Each sub category of dedication will be discussed in turn below.

4.2.5.1 Dedications of Spoils of War

The dedication of the spoils of war is represented in the three major Greek victories: Marathon (**no. 9**), Salamis (**nos. 39, 40** and **41**) and Plataea (**nos. 72, 74** and **79**). Also, spoils of war were dedicated to represent the Persian Wars generally (**nos. 84** and **105**). These offerings were voluntary, but it would have been considered impious not to dedicate a portion of the spoils of war.[196] In addition to offering a portion of won goods to a particular deity, it has been suggested that the dedication of captured arms and armour is intended to show the mastery over the enemy.[197]

The arms and armour of the defeated would be collected and a portion would be set apart for the gods. The dedication of spoils can take either one of two forms. The first would be to dedicate a token immediately. Alternatively, the portion set aside could be sold in order to construct monuments in another form, for example a statue. These two forms of dedication are, however, not exclusive and may have at any time been carried out simultaneously. Table 9 contains examples of these two forms of dedications of spoils. For example, the shields hung on the temple architraves at Delphi (**no. 74**) were spoils reworked and dedicated; these shields were gilded and constructed from the spoils taken from the booty at Plataea.[198] Also the thank-offering positioned in front of the Athenian treasury at Delphi may have taken the form of a statue group (see **no. 9**). In contrast, the inscribed Persian helmet (**no. 105**) was dedicated at Olympia in its original form.

The only naval battle represented in this study which offers dedications of spoils is Salamis. We learn from Herodotus that three whole triremes were dedicated at three different commemorative sites.[199] There was no accepted mode of commemorative behaviour concerning captured naval spoils. For example, the three triremes in Table 9 were dedicated in their

[196] Rouse 1902: 99.
[197] West 1965: xliv.
[198] See Aesch. *Against Ctesiphon* 116.
[199] Hdts. 8.121.

Table 9. Spoils of war

Battle	No.	Monument	Dedicator	Location
Marathon	9	Thank-Offering (Statue Group?)	Athens	Delphi
Salamis	39	Thank-offering of three triremes (1)	Panhellenic	Isthmus
	40	Thank-offering of three triremes (2)	Panhellenic	Sunium
	41	Thank-offering of three triremes (3)	Panhellenic	Salamis
Plataea	72	Spoils dedicated in the Parthenon	Athens	Athens (Acropolis)
	74	Shields hung on the temple architraves	Athens	Delphi
	79	Manger of Mardonius dedicated to Athena Alea	Tegea	Tegea
General	84	Athenian portico displaying spoils	Athens	Delphi
	105	Inscribed Persian helmet	Athens	Olympia

entirety whereas captured ships in subsequent conflicts were commissioned and reused by the victor.[200] Alternatively to the dedication of entire ships, parts of ships taken in war were often dedicated to particular deities; the beak or the ram became the regular token of captured ships.[201] There was therefore a range of options of how to use captured naval spoils and there were no conventions, religious or otherwise, dictating how naval spoils should be used or dedicated.[202]

4.2.5.2 Statues

Statues can be divided into four categories which are represented in Table 10: deities, heroes, mortals, and animals. Statues were dedicated to specific deities and could be paid for by money made from the sale of booty. For example, the statue of Athena set up on the Acropolis **(no. 16)** was apparently paid for by the sale of booty from the battle of Marathon.[203]

The dedication of a statue of a god was a popular mode of showing thanks to the protecting deity and Table 10 shows that there are many examples included in commemorations of the Persian Wars.[204] In addition, it has been suggested that the dedication of a statue would demonstrate the acknowledgement of the deity's power.[205] Another form which falls within this category of monument type is the statues of heroes. Only one monument **(no. 15)** attests to this style of statue and the heroes from

---

[200] See Pritchett 1979: 3.279 for numerous examples.
[201] Pritchett 1979: 3.281.
[202] Pritchett 1979: 3.285.
[203] Paus. 9.4.1.
[204] See Rouse 1902: 126-127 for other collected examples.
[205] Rouse 1902: 129.

which the Athenian tribes' names were derived were depicted.²⁰⁶ Among this group was a statue of Miltiades and it has been suggested that the statue group honours the gods and heroes who aided Miltiades in defeating the Persians.²⁰⁷ Statues of animals are also represented in Table 10. It has been suggested that the oxen dedicated at Delphi by Plataea (**no. 78**) and Carystus (**no. 99**) may be intended to represent an agricultural state or possibly the strength of the dedicator.²⁰⁸ Pausanias believes that the oxen represent the victory over the barbarian and therefore the securing of the land which would now be free to plough.²⁰⁹ Alternatively, as Rouse suggests, the dedication of an animal statue may be representative of the entire act of sacrifice, including the procession.²¹⁰

In order to present all examples of statues together, those set up in a non-religious context are included in Table 10; these statues, for the most part, took the form of mortals. For example, a statue group of mortals set up by Troezen was to commemorate the assistance they offered Athens when Athens was evacuated in the months before the battle of Salamis (**no. 95**). In addition, statues of famous men such as Themistocles and Miltiades set up in the Athenian agora have been included in this study, despite Demosthenes' assertions that Conon was the first to receive such honours since Harmodius and Aristogeiton.²¹¹ The erection of a statue of a victorious commander in the 5th century BC is peculiar to the examples listed in Table 10 and Rouse states that he couldn't find evidence of victorious generals, other than these examples, receiving stand-alone statues in the 5th century BC (for further discussion see **nos. 88** and **89**).²¹² One mortal is dedicated as a stand-alone monument in a religious context; that is the Macedonian monument of the gilded statue of Alexander I (**no. 101**). This monument was not a typical Greek

---

[206] See West 1965: 53-54.
[207] West 1965: 53-54.
[208] West 1965: xlviii.
[209] Paus. 10.16.6.
[210] Rouse 1902: 145.
[211] Dem. *Against Leptines* 70; as noted in **nos. 88** and **89**, Demosthenes may be understood to be describing the lack of Themistocles' and Miltiades' statues in the 5th century BC specifically. Demosthenes (in his *Against Aristocrates* 196) states that *his ancestors* didn't raise statues to these men, not that the statues did not exist (author's emphasis). Therefore, statues of Themistocles and Miltiades could have been constructed in the Athenian agora after that of Conon but still within the classical period.
[212] Rouse 1902: 137.

Table 10. Statues

Battle	No.	Monument	Dedicator	Location
Marathon	15	Statue Group	Athens	Delphi
	16	Bronze Statue of Athena	Athens	Athens (Acropolis)
	19	Temple of Nemesis with Statue of Nemesis	Athens	Rhamnus
	20	Statue of Arimnestos	Plataea	Plataea
Salamis	42	Statue of Apollo Holding the Beak of a Ship	Panhellenic	Delphi
Plataea	70	Temple and Statue of Athena *Areia*	Plataea	Plataea
	75	Bronze Statue of Artemis the Saviour	Megara	Megara
	76	Bronze Statue of Artemis the Saviour	Pagae (in Megarid)	Pagae
	78	Statue of an Ox	Plataea	Delphi
General	81	Bronze Statue of Zeus	Panhellenic	Olympia
	82	Bronze Statue of Poseidon	Panhellenic	Isthmus
	87	Statue of Zeus *Eleutherios*	Athens	Athens (Agora)
	88	Statue of Miltiades	Athens	Athens (Agora)
	89	Statue of Themistocles	Athens	Athens (Agora)
	93	Statues of Skyllis and His Daughter Hydna	Amphictyons	Delphi
	95	Statues of Women and Children	Troezen	Troezen (Agora)
	98	Statue of Apollo	Epidaurus	Delphi
	99	Bronze Statue of an Ox	Carystus	Delphi
	100	Statue Group	Hermionae	Delphi
	101	Gilded statue of Alexander I	Macedon	Delphi
	102	Bronze Apollo	Peparethos	Delphi
	103	Bronze Apollo	Samos	Delphi
	104	Bronze Bull	Eretria	Olympia

dedication as it was not the usual practice to depict a mortal in a dedication within a religious sanctuary and thus equate him with the gods.[213]

4.2.5.3 Votive offerings

Votive offerings are voluntary offerings to deities and are closely related to the vows made to deities, usually in periods of anxiety or achievement. Votive offerings illustrates the 'if-then' relationship both individuals and communities shared with deities.[214] This form of dedication is both equally an expression of thanks to the deity for favour and a reflection of the piety of the dedicator.[215] However, as represented by Table 11 there is little consistency in the style of votive monuments.

Tripods were a popular form of dedication. Initially this form of object was dedicated for its value; however, the tripod, over time, became a traditional object of dedication.[216] In the 8th and 7th centuries BC tripods

---

[213] West 1965: xlviii.
[214] *OCD*: 1564 'votive offerings'.
[215] West 1965: xlii.
[216] Rouse 1902: 146.

had mostly been dedicated by individuals at Olympia and Delphi as status symbols, cult objects or prizes. However, by the beginning of the 5th century BC these objects became more popular amongst city-states as dedicatory items and were utilised, particularly at Delphi, to commemorate victories in battle.[217] The tripod is represented in Table 11 (**no. 80**) and forms part of, arguably, the most famous commemorative monument of the Persian Wars: the serpent column. The tripod was placed on top of a pedestal of three intertwined snakes and a list of Greek city-states that fought against Persia was inscribed on the bodies of the snakes.

Although objects such as tripods had become traditional dedicatory objects, votive offerings could take multiple forms. For example in pan-Hellenic sanctuaries individual *poleis* may have dedicated a *'thesauros'*, a term commonly translated as 'treasury'. However to define the structure as a treasury, a structure built to merely store offerings, is misleading. The Athenian treasury (**no. 8**) is included in this section on votive offerings because treasury buildings may be considered as offerings in their own right.[218] Other forms of votive offering include a mast adorned with three gold stars dedicated by the Aeginetans (**no. 47**).[219] Herodotus is the only source for this monument and after mentioning the offering does not explain the choice in form. It has been suggested that the monument was influenced by natural phenomena understood to be a positive omen or the stars were intended to symbolise nautical skill.[220] Pausanias is the only source to refer to the painting of the personification of Salamis holding the beak of a ship dedicated by the Athenians at Olympia (**no. 44**).[221] The painting is accompanied by eight others containing mythological characters, apparently unrelated to the Persian Wars. This painting is the only attested votive offering of this type.

Taken together, the variety of these votive offerings has been suggested as evidence for the beginning of a change in attitude towards the style of commemorative monument; the idea that celebrating victory was becoming more important than traditional religious attitudes.[222]

---

[217] Scott 2010: 77.
[218] *OCD*: 1315 'sanctuaries, Greek'; see Scott 2010: 77-81.
[219] Hdts. 8.122.
[220] Natural phenomenon (St. Elmo's fire): Rouse 1902: 135; nautical skill: West 1965: 186.
[221] Paus. 5.11.5-6.
[222] West 1965: xlviii.

MONUMENTS BY TYPE

Table 11. Votive offerings

Battle	No.	Monument	Dedicator	Location
Marathon	8	Treasury	Athens	Delphi
	10	Callimachus Monument	Athens	Athens (Acropolis)
Salamis	44	Painting of Salamis Holding the Beak of a Ship	Athens	Olympia
	47	Bronze Mast with Three Gold Stars	Aegina	Delphi
	48	Pedimental Sculptures of the Temple of Aphaea	Aegina	Aphaea sanctuary, Aegina
General	80	Serpent Column	Panhellenic	Delphi

4.2.6 Structures

Altars, sanctuaries and temples were not considered dedications *per se*. According to West, although these monuments were religious monuments offered to a specific god, they did not have to be set up in a specific sanctuary in order to be consecrated; certain areas were considered sacred to a certain deity.[223] The structures set up in commemoration of the Persian Wars are divided here into two categories: religious structures and non-religious structures. The religious structures include altars (**nos. 67, 94 and 97**) sacred precincts (**nos. 14, 22, 31 and 45**) and temples (**nos. 17, 19, and 70**) and a stoa (**no. 84**). The non-religious category includes a varied range of structures (**nos. 73, 83 and 85**) which will be discussed collectively.

4.2.6.1 Altars

The construction of an altar, in contrast to dedications discussed above in *Dedications*, implies the worship of a particular deity at a specific place opposed to the recognition of favour.[224] Altars would have usually been raised structures upon which a fire would be lit for worshippers to witness the cremation of parts of the sacrificial animal. The structure would usually have been made of 'dressed stone', were typically rectangular and occasionally approached by a flight of steps.[225]

Table 12. Altars

Battle	No.	Monument	Dedicator	Location
Plataea	67	Altar of Zeus *Eleutherios*	Panhellenic	Battlefield
General	94	Altar Dedicated to Helios *Eleutherios*	Troezen	Troezen
	97	Altar of the Winds	Delphi	Thyia

---

[223] West 1965: xliii.
[224] West 1965: xlix.
[225] *OCD*: 66 'altars'.

4.2.6.2 Sacred Precincts, Temples and Stoas

Within the broad spectrum of sacred precincts, both sanctuaries and shrines are included. Monuments of this scale would only be constructed when the spoils of war were considerable. Sanctuaries were 'areas set aside for religious purposes and separate from the normal secular world'.[226] Both sanctuaries and shrines were referred to in the ancient sources as *hieroi* which is defined here as sacred space, again demarcated from the secular world by either a wall or boundary markers.[227] Sufficient space was required to construct a sacred precinct as congregations would typically gather to participate in the ritual carried out on the behalf of the particular deity.[228] Within the sacred area, or *temenos*, other structures such as temples and altars could be constructed depending on the varying religious needs. Sanctuaries can be developed for specific communities and each *polis* would have one major site dedicated to its protecting deity. Other smaller sanctuaries may also be constructed which were designed to cater for smaller sections of one particular community. Alternatively, sanctuaries (such as pan-Hellenic sanctuaries) could grow to serve more than one community and attract worshippers from all of Greece.[229]

Within the sacred space a temple could be constructed. The temple, however, was not a prerequisite for a sanctuary. The Greek temple contained the image of the god and was considered the god's house. The statue was usually positioned inside the temple so it would be facing the open door and could 'see' the burning of the sacrificial animal on the altar which stood outside.[230] In addition to housing the cult statue, the temple would have served as a repository for the property of the god which would have included votive offerings. Stoas or porticoes within sanctuaries, such as the Athenian portico at Delphi (**no. 84**), would have been a structure of lesser importance in comparison to the main religious structures, such as the sanctuary temple.[231] The portico included in Table 13 can be broadly defined under the term stoa. This term encompasses various building types

---

[226] *OCD*: 1314 'sanctuaries, Greek'.
[227] Liddel *et al.* 1996: 'ἱερὸν'.
[228] *OCD*: 1314 'sanctuaries, Greek'.
[229] *OCD*: 1315 'sanctuaries, Greek'.
[230] *OCD*: 1438 'temple'.
[231] *OCD*: 1403 'stoa'.

Table 13. Sacred precincts, temples and stoas

Battle	No.	Monument	Dedicator	Location
	17	'Old' Parthenon	Athens	Athens (Acropolis)
Marathon	13	Temple of Eukleia	Athens	Athens (Agora)
	14	Sanctuary of Pan	Athens	Athens (Acropolis)
	19	Temple of Nemesis with Statue of Nemesis	Athens	Rhamnus
Artemisium	22	Shrine to Boreas	Athens	Athens
Thermopylae	31	Shrine of Maron and Alpheius	Sparta	Sparta (Agora)
Salamis	45	Sanctuary of the Hero Cychreus	Athens	Salamis
Plataea	70	Temple and Statue of Athena *Areia*	Plataea	Plataea
General	84	Athenian Portico Displaying Spoils	Athens	Delphi
	86	'New' Parthenon	Athens	Athens (Acropolis)

but can be characterised by an open colonnade with a roof over the top, adjoining to a rear wall.[232] Stoas are most commonly found in agoras where they would serve the purpose of defining a boundary, such as the stoa containing the painting of the battle of Marathon (**no. 12**).

4.2.6.3 Non-Religious Structures

Structures in commemoration of the Persian Wars could also be built with no overt reference to a particular deity. The forms of these structures vary widely and of the three examples discussed in this study, and presented in Table 14, no two are the same (**nos. 73, 83** and **85**).

The odeum of Pericles was, according to Pausanias, constructed in imitation of Xerxes' tent.[233] The tent of Xerxes, which was left behind for Mardonius, could have come into the hands of the Greeks after the battle of Plataea.[234] Odea were small theatres or roofed halls for musical competitions and other events. These structures would have usually taken the form of a miniature theatre and had the seats arranged in a semicircle.[235] However, the odeum of Pericles was a square hall with, according to Vitruvius, remnants of Persian ships used as roof beams.[236]

The stoa constructed at Sparta (**no. 83**) which, by the time of Pausanias, had statues of Persians acting as pillars to hold up the roof and is now known as the Persian Stoa was one of three presented in this study (the other two are

---

[232] *OCD*: 1402 'stoa'.
[233] Paus. 1.20.4.
[234] West 1965: 155.
[235] *OCD*: 1032 'odeum'.
[236] Square structure: Broneer 1944: 309; roof beams: Vitr. 5.9.1.

Table 14. Non-religious structures

Battle	No.	Monument	Dedicator	Location
Plataea	73	Odeum at Athens	Athens	Athens
General	83	Persian Stoa	Sparta	Sparta (Agora)
	85	North Wall of the Acropolis	Athens	Athens (Acropolis)

nos. 12 and 84). The usual form of the stoa has been explained above under the section title 'Sacred Precincts, Temples and Stoas', and the Persian Stoa fits in with the usual practice of erecting a building of this type in the agora.

The Athenians utilised fragments of destroyed temples, left by the Persian destruction of Athens, to build the north wall of the Acropolis (**no. 85**). It has been suggested that this was a practical solution to wall building at a period in which money was tight, however a counter argument has been put forward that suggests this was a purposeful method of commemoration.[237] They are viewable quite clearly from the lower city today, north of the Acropolis, and would have stood out far more in antiquity because they would have been brightly painted.[238] The varied designs of non-religious structures imply that there were no established conventions in the 5th century BC on how to commemorate in this way. In addition, the general lack of non-religious structures also implies that this was not a popular method of commemoration. For example, many more structures are erected in a religious context.

4.2.7 Non-Physical Monuments

4.2.7.1 Military Vow

The vow is a promise to a deity and would usually accompany a prayer which was the most common form of expression in ancient Greek religion.[239] It has been described as 'the proposal of a bargain that the recipient of the favour requested shall make suitable recompense.'[240] In making a vow to a deity for a particular purpose, the god would have to grant the favour first and only then would the deity receive the promised votive offering.[241] With regard to

---

[237] See Kousser 2009: 271.
[238] As stated by Kousser 2009: 271.
[239] *OCD*: 1205 'prayer'.
[240] Pritchett 1979: 3.230.
[241] Pritchett 1979: 3.236; see also Rouse 1902: 97.

Table 15. Military vow

Battle	No.	Monument	Dedicator	Location
Marathon	18	Annual Sacrifice of 500 Kids	Athens	Athens (Agrai)

warfare, rarely would a leader pay the vow before the battle was fought but if this was performed it could be interpreted as presumptuous by the deity and the army would be defeated.[242] Vows were malleable. For example, the vow the Athenian made to Artemis *Agrotera* that they would sacrifice one goat for every Persian killed was altered to an annual sacrifice of 500 goats as enough goats could not be found, the Persian dead amounting to 6400.[243]

4.2.7.2 Oaths

Oaths are promises undertaken by groups binding them to future behaviour. An oath has been described as 'a statement (assertory) or promise (promissory) strengthened by the invocation of a god as a witness and often with the addition of a curse in case of perjury'.[244] The maintenance of oaths was considered a central aspect of piety, both personal and public.[245] For example, the Spartans attribute their loss of the naval battle at Pylos in 425 BC and other losses to their disregard of an oath.[246]

Table 16 consists of two oaths: the Oath of Plataea and the Covenant of Plataea. Neither of these oaths are represented in this study as individual monuments; however, the clauses which (may have) made up each oath are represented in chapter 5. The Oath of Plataea was apparently sworn before the battle of Plataea which included three main clauses: to fight to one's utmost, obey orders, and bury the allied dead **(nos. 56-62)**; to punish the cities who had sided with the Persians **(no. 64)**; and to not rebuild sanctuaries destroyed by the Persians **(no. 63)**. What appears to be the inscribed text of the oath has been preserved on the stele of Acharnae.[247] This inscribed oath finishes by explaining how a curse was placed on those who did not abide by what

---

[242] For examples see Paus. 2.6.3; 4.25.1.
[243] Xen. *Anabasis* 3.2.12; Arist. *Knights* 658-662; Plut. *On the Malice of Herodotus* 26; casualty numbers: Hdts. 6.117.
[244] *OCD*: 1029 'oath'.
[245] *OCD*: 1029 'oath'.
[246] Thuc. 7.18.2.
[247] *RO* 88; see also **no. 63** for further discussion.

Table 16. Oaths

Battle	No.	Monument	Dedicator	Location
Plataea		Oath of Plataea		
		Covenant of Plataea		

was sworn. The oath is also mentioned by two literary sources and only these literary versions refer to the clause about leaving the ruined sanctuaries as a mark of Persian impiety.[248]

The second oath is known as the Covenant of Plataea and consists of four commemorative clauses: *theoroi* and *probouloi* were to assemble at Plataea every year (see discussion in **no. 68**); a victory festival, the *Eleutheria*, was to be celebrated at Plataea every four years (**no. 65**); a pan-Hellenic force was to be levied;[249] and Plataea was to be kept inviolate and sacrosanct, so that the Plataeans might offer sacrifices to Zeus on behalf of all the Greeks (**no. 66**, and also **no. 67**).

4.2.7.3 Behavioural Commemoration

The behavioural commemorations listed in Table 17 can be divided into three categories: commemorative festivals (**nos. 5** and **65**), annual ritual practice (**nos. 18** and **68**), and hero-cult practices (**no. 32**).

Festivals were at the centre of the social and political spheres of ancient Greek life.[250] According to Plato religious festivals are divinely ordained and athletic competition at games, both military and non-military, would have been similar in type.[251] For example, despite the evidence for the establishment of the *Eleutheria* (**no. 65**) in the 5th century BC being slim, once the games were fully established they consisted of running races including full armoured races, gymnastic contests, and horse racing.[252] The sacrificing of 500 Kids to Artemis was the result of a vow,[253] but the repetitious act warrants the monument's inclusion in the behavioural commemoration category (**no. 18**).

---

[248] Lyc. *Against Leocrates* 80-81; Diod. 11.29.2-3.
[249] This clause is not counted as a commemorative monument in this study as the levying of a force is interpreted here as a means to continue the conflict, see discussion in **no. 65**.
[250] Brandt and Iddeng 2012: 1.
[251] Plato *Laws* 2.653D; see also Pritchett 1979: 3.154.
[252] Running: Paus. 9.2.4; armoured races: Phil. *Gymnasticus* 8.24; gymnastics: *IG* 7 1666; horse races: *IG* 4 1136; see Pritchett 1979: 3.154.
[253] Xen. *Anabasis* 3.2.12; Plut. *On the Malice of Herodotus* 26.

Table 17. Behavioural commemoration

Battle	No.	Monument	Dedicator	Location
Marathon	5	Herakleia	Athens	Battlefield
	18	Annual Sacrifice of 500 Kids	Athens	Athens (Agrai)
Thermopylae	32	Hero-Cult practices for the fallen	Sparta	Sparta
Plataea	65	Eleutheria	Panhellenic	Battlefield
	68	Annual Rites Performed at the Greek Tombs	Plataea	Battlefield

Heroes were 'a class of beings worshipped by the Greeks, generally conceived as the powerful dead, and often as forming a class intermediate between gods and men.'[254] Hero-shrines were often constructed around tombs and the hero had a particular connection with a particular place. The *Herakleia* is included among religious festivals because Herakles was an exception to this rule and is considered 'as much god as hero' (**no. 5**).[255] We learn of the hero-cult carried out Sparta for the fallen of Thermopylae due to Diodorus, who relates a poem supposedly composed by Simonides (**no. 32**).[256] The poem makes it clear that the poem would be performed in a *sekos*, which is a sacred enclosure appropriate to a hero.[257]

4.2.8 Other

This category contains the sole monument which does not fit in to the broad monument types outlined above. The monument is the stone lion set up over Leonidas' grave at Thermopylae (see **no. 27**). No other grave or battlefield represented in this study was adorned with a monument similar to this. The monument is mentioned by Herodotus and this form of monument has been said to represent valour.[258]

Table 18. Other

Battle	No.	Monument	Dedicator	Location
Thermopylae	27	Stone Lion over Leonidas' grave	Spartans or Amphictyons	Battlefield

---

[254] *OCD*: 672 'hero-cult'.
[255] *OCD*: 672 'hero-cult'.
[256] Diod. 11.11.6.
[257] West 1965: 123.
[258] Monument: Hdts. 7.225; representing valour (Pausanias is here describing the lion at Chaeronea): Paus. 9.40.10; see West 1965: 185.

Chapter 5
The Monuments and the Evidence

5.1 Assessing the Evidence

There is deliberation over the identification of several of the monuments compiled here and so ancient, antiquarian and modern literary sources are addressed to support each monument's identification. Each monument is verified on a case by case basis, and the confidence with which the monuments are accepted are discussed individually. Tables 19 and 20 provide a quick reference for the level of confidence attributed to each monument, based on the available evidence. In these tables the levels of confidence are depicted in three colours: green indicates a confident acceptance, amber indicates a tentative acceptance, and red indicates a cautious acceptance.

For a monument to be accepted with confidence in this study, and therefore attributed to the green category, its existence, probable dating, and commemorative focus would have to be secure. This information may be gathered in a number of ways: near contemporary literary evidence may be supported by archaeological evidence, dateable archaeological evidence may be supported by literary evidence (varying in date), near contemporary literary sources may be supported by later literary sources, or later literary sources may be deemed reliable based on how the reported monument fits in to the general commemorative practices of the 5th century BC.

For a monument to be accepted tentatively, and therefore attributed to the amber category, uncertainties concerning the date, form, commemorative focus and even existence result from the more limited evidence. These uncertainties may be products of combinations of sources of evidence: multiple literary sources (of varying date) may conflict in their reports; near contemporary, or late, literary evidence may not explicitly associate a monument with the Persian Wars; fragmentary archaeological evidence may lead to multiple, yet credible, interpretations of the evidence; due to the reliance on late literary references for some monuments, reliable dating can often be difficult to achieve.

For a monument to be attributed to the red category, the evidence is accepted with caution. The uncertainties in this category are similar to those of the amber category but more acute, and concern unclear locations, uncertain dating, questionable connection to the Persian Wars, and even doubtful existence. These uncertainties are often the result of scant evidence: monuments may be mentioned in a single late literary source, with a lack of all other forms of evidence; multiple late literary sources

Table 19. Confidence attributed to the acceptance of each monument

Battle	No.	Monument	Commemorating Group	Location	Confidence
Marathon	1	Burial Mound	Athens	Battlefield	Green
	2	Burial Mound	Plataea	Battlefield	Green
	3	Trophy	Athens	Battlefield	Green
	4	Grave of Miltiades	Athens	Battlefield	Red
	5	*Herakleia*	Athens	Battlefield	Green
	6	Epigram for the Athenians	Athens	Battlefield	Red
	7	Casualty List	Athens	Battlefield	Green
	8	Treasury	Athens	Delphi	Green
	9	Thank-Offering (Statue Group?)	Athens	Delphi	Amber
	10	Callimachus Monument	Athens	Athens (Acropolis)	Green
	11	Engraved Marble Base (Cenotaph?)	Athens	Athens	Amber
	12	Stoa *Poikile*	Athens	Athens (Agora)	Green
	13	Temple of Eukleia	Athens	Athens (Agora)	Red
	14	Sanctuary of Pan	Athens	Athens (Acropolis)	Green
	15	Statue Group	Athens	Delphi	Green
	16	Bronze Statue of Athena	Athens	Athens (Acropolis)	Amber
	17	'Old' Parthenon	Athens	Athens (Acropolis)	Amber
	18	Annual Sacrifice of 500 Kids	Athens	Athens (Agrai)	Amber
	19	Temple of Nemesis with Statue of Nemesis	Athens	Rhamnus	Green
	20	Statue of Arimnestos	Plataea	Plataea	Red
Artemisium	21	Circle of Marble Steles with an Epigram	Athens	Battlefield	Amber
	22	Shrine to Boreas	Athens	Athens	Amber
Thermopylae	23	Epigram for the Spartiates	Amphictyons	Battlefield	Green
	24	Epigram for Peloponnesians	Amphictyons	Battlefield	Green
	25	Epigram for the Opuntian Locrians	Opus	Battlefield	Amber
	26	Epigram for the Thespians	Thespiae	Battlefield	Red
	27	Stone Lion over Leonidas' grave	Spartans or Amphictyons	Battlefield	Green
	28	Burial mound	Sparta & Thespiae	Battlefield	Green
	29	Tomb of Leonidas	Sparta	Sparta	Green
	30	List of Spartans Who Fought at Thermopylae	Sparta	Sparta	Amber
	31	Shrine of Maron and Alpheius	Sparta	Sparta (Agora)	Amber
	32	Hero-Cult practices for the fallen	Sparta	Sparta	Green
	33	Epigram for Leonidas	Sparta	Sparta	Amber
Salamis	34	Trophy on the Island of Psyttaleia	Athens	Battlefield	Amber
	35	Trophy on the Island of Salamis (Cynosoura)	Athens	Battlefield	Green
	36	Gravestone with Epitaph for the Corinthians	Corinth	Battlefield	Amber
	37	Burial Mound		Battlefield	Amber
	38	Tomb of Themistocles	Athens	Battlefield	Red
	39	Thank-Offering of Three Triremes (1)	Panhellenic	Isthmus	Green
	40	Thank-Offering of Three Triremes (2)	Panhellenic	Sunium	Green
	41	Thank-Offering of Three Triremes (3)	Panhellenic	Salamis	Green
	42	Statue of Apollo Holding the Beak of a Ship	Panhellenic	Delphi	Green
	43	Tomb of Eurybiades	Sparta	Sparta	Amber
	44	Painting of Salamis Holding the Beak of a Ship	Athens	Olympia	Amber
	45	Sanctuary of the Hero Cychreus	Athens	Salamis	Amber
	46	Epigram Engraved on a Cenotaph	Corinth	Isthmus	Green
	47	Bronze Mast with Three Gold Stars	Aegina	Delphi	Green
	48	Pedimental Sculptures of the Temple of Aphaea	Aegina	Aphaea sanctuary, Aegina	Red

Table 20. Confidence attributed to the acceptance of each monument cont.

Battle	No.	Monument	Commemorating Group	Location	Confidence
	49	Trophy	Panhellenic	Battlefield	
	50	Trophy	Sparta	Battlefield	
	51	Trophy	Athens	Battlefield	
	52	Epigram for Athenians	Athens	Battlefield	
	53	Epigram for Spartans	Sparta	Battlefield	
	54	Epigram for Corinthians	Corinth	Battlefield	
	55	Epigram for Tegeans	Tegea	Battlefield	
	56	Burial Mound	Sparta	Battlefield	
	57	Burial Mound	Athens	Battlefield	
	58	Burial Mound	Tegea	Battlefield	
	59	Burial Mound	Megara	Battlefield	
	60	Burial Mound	Phlius	Battlefield	
	61	Burial Mound (Empty?)	Aegina	Battlefield	
	62	Empty Burial Mounds	Others	Battlefield	
	63	Ruins of Sanctuaries as Memorial of Persian Impiety	Panhellenic		
Plataea	64	Tithing of Medising Greeks	Panhellenic		
	65	*Eleutheria*	Panhellenic	Battlefield	
	66	Inviolability of Plataea	Panhellenic		
	67	Altar of Zeus *Eleutherios*	Panhellenic	Battlefield	
	68	Annual Rites Performed at the Greek Tombs	Plataea	Battlefield	
	69	Tomb of Mardonius	Plataea	Battlefield	
	70	Temple and Statue of Athena *Areia*	Plataea	Plataea	
	71	Tomb of Pausanias	Sparta	Sparta	
	72	Spoils Displayed in the Parthenon	Athens	Athens (Acropolis)	
	73	Odeum at Athens	Athens	Athens	
	74	Shields Hung on Temple Architraves	Athens	Delphi	
	75	Bronze Statue of Artemis the Saviour	Megara	Megara	
	76	Bronze Statue of Artemis the Saviour	Pagae (in Megarid)	Pagae	
	77	Grave of Euchidas with Engraved Stele	Plataea	Plataea	
	78	Statue of an Ox	Plataea	Delphi	
	79	Manger of Mardonius Dedicated to Athena *Alea*	Tegea	Tegea	
	80	Serpent Column	Panhellenic	Delphi	
	81	Bronze Statue of Zeus	Panhellenic	Olympia	
	82	Bronze Statue of Poseidon	Panhellenic	Isthmus	
	83	Persian Stoa	Sparta	Sparta (Agora)	
	84	Athenian Portico Displaying Spoils	Athens	Delphi	
	85	North Wall of the Acropolis	Athens	Athens (Acropolis)	
	86	'New' Parthenon	Athens	Athens (Acropolis)	
	87	Statue of Zeus *Eleutherios*	Athens	Athens (Agora)	
	88	Statue of Miltiades	Athens	Athens (Agora)	
	89	Statue of Themistocles	Athens	Athens (Agora)	
	90	Tomb of Aristides	Athens	Athens (Phalerum)	
	91	Epigram in Thanks to Aphrodite	Corinth	Corinth	
General	92	Epigram Engraved on a Cenotaph	Megara	Megara (Agora)	
	93	Statues of Skyllis and His Daughter Hydna	Amphictyons	Delphi	
	94	Altar Dedicated to Helios *Eleutherios*	Troezen	Troezen	
	95	Statues of Women and Children	Troezen	Troezen (Agora)	
	96	Trophy with Epigram	Delphi	Delphi	
	97	Altar of the Winds	Delphi	Thyia	
	98	Statue of Apollo	Epidaurus	Delphi	
	99	Bronze Statue of an Ox	Carystus	Delphi	
	100	Statue Group	Hermionae	Delphi	
	101	Gilded statue of Alexander I	Macedon	Delphi	
	102	Bronze Apollo	Peparethos	Delphi	
	103	Bronze Apollo	Samos	Delphi	
	104	Bronze Bull	Eretria	Olympia	
	105	Inscribed Persian Helmet	Athens	Olympia	

may conflict in their reports; modern interpretations of archaeological material may be made which is unsupported by near contemporary, or other, literary evidence.

5.2 The Monuments

MARATHON

1. Athenian Burial Mound

The dead at Marathon were buried on the battlefield as is described by Thucydides:

> *The dead are laid in the public sepulchre in the most beautiful suburb of the city, in which those who fall in war are always buried; with the exception of those slain at Marathon, who for their singular and extraordinary valour were interred on the spot where they fell.*[259]

According to Thucydides, this was contrary to regular practice. Thucydides, in describing the usual practice of the burial of the Athenian war dead in the *demosion sema*, states that due to the soldiers' outstanding achievement at Marathon they were buried on the battlefield as an exceptional mark of honour.

Pausanias also mentions the Athenian grave:

> *It was at this point in Attica that the foreigners landed, were defeated in battle, and lost some of their vessels as they were putting off from the land. On the plain is the grave of the Athenians, and upon it are slabs giving the names of the killed according to their tribes;*[260]

The English antiquarian Richard Chandler visited Marathon in 1765 and identified the mound, otherwise described as the '*soros*', as the burial place of the 192 'gallant Athenians'.[261] What has been identified as the Marathon burial mound is still visible today on the plain of Marathon (see Figure 2). In October 1788, the French antiquarian Louis François Sébastian Fauvel excavated the *soros* in the hope of uncovering some material evidence to support the identification of the mound.[262] After eight days the excavation at the centre of the mound reached the level of the plain and, in addition,

---
[259] Thuc. 2.34.5.
[260] Paus. 1.32.3.
[261] Chandler 1776: 165-166.
[262] See Krentz 2010: 122-123.

Figure 2. Athenian burial mound at Marathon (author's own photograph).

two other smaller holes were begun on either side. We are informed by Philippe-Ernest Legrand, in his 1897 biography of Fauvel that 'nothing was found for his trouble, and Fauvel, mortified by his failure and harassed by the owner of the land, discontinues his research.'[263]

In the years following Fauvel's excavation, the numbers of travellers visiting the site increased in search of traces of the ancient battle. One such traveller, Edward Clarke, who visited Marathon in 1801, was critical of Fauvel's work on the mound, noting that 'it would be necessary to carry the excavation much lower' (i.e. below the current ground level).[264] However, on entering a passage that had been opened up into the *soros*, Clarke discovered and collected numerous arrow heads, made of common

---

[263] Legrand 1897: 56.
[264] Clarke 1818: 7.24.

flint.²⁶⁵ In 1802, another attempt to excavate the *soros* was made by Lord and Lady Elgin. In much the same vain as Fauvel's effort, the Elgins were largely unsuccessful in discovering finds that would put the identification of the *soros* beyond doubt.²⁶⁶ Thus, between 1800 and 1830, the Marathon *soros* had become a prime attraction to travellers in search of memorabilia relating to the famous battle, arrow heads in particular.²⁶⁷ Dodwell suggested that the mound was the burial mound for the Persian war dead, which was heavily based on the discovery of these arrow heads, and this theory gained some support in the early 19th century.²⁶⁸

By 1836, due to the regularity of visitors and the digging they undertook, the mound was considered to be in danger of destruction. On May 12, 1836, Iakovos Rizos Neroulos, the minister of education responsible for cultural affairs, sent a memorandum to the Provincial Directorate of Attica:

> *being informed that foreign travellers passing via Marathon are frequently excavating, with the help of the locals, in the very tumulus [mound] of those Athenians who fell in the battle (the so-called soros) in order to find arrow heads, and wishing this most ancient monument of Greek glory to remain untouched and untroubled, we ask you to issue as quickly as possible the necessary orders to the municipal authority of Marathon, so that it is not allowed for anyone on any pretext to excavate the afore-mentioned tumulus or the other monuments on the field of battle.*²⁶⁹

By the date of this quote, in 1836, scholarly opinion appears to identify the mound as the burial place of the Athenian warriors and does not reference Dodwell's theory that it may contain the remains of the Persian war dead.

In 1883, Heinrich Schliemann undertook excavations at the Marathon *soros*. Two holes were dug into the mound; the central trench reached a depth of 2 m below ground level, while the trench on the eastern side filled with water at half that depth below ground level. Schliemann, presented

---

²⁶⁵ Clarke 1818: 7.23; Leake 1829: 172.
²⁶⁶ See Nisbet Ferguson and Nisbet Hamilton Grant 1926: 204; also Krentz 2010: 123.
²⁶⁷ Dodwell 1819: 2.159-160; Gell 1827: 59; Leake 1835: 431-432; Gray 1840: 342; see also Forsdyke 1919-1920: 147.
²⁶⁸ Dodwell 1819: 2.159-160; see also Gell 1827: 59.
²⁶⁹ Translation by Petrakos 1996: 186, n. 43. See also Krentz 2010: 123.

with meagre finds, concluded that the mound could be dated to the 19th century BC.[270] Following Schliemann's efforts, in 1890 and 1891 the Greek archaeologist Valerios Staes conducted two seasons of excavations and managed to demonstrate that the mound was, indeed, the burial place of the Athenian dead from 490 BC. Following Clarke's observation, mentioned above, excavations would have to be carried out much lower than ground level. At 4 m below ground level, Staes found a funeral pyre on a brick lined tray with ashes and charred bones and black figured pottery dated no later than the early 5th century BC.[271]

Due to the 5th century BC literary reference to the communal grave, and the subsequent archaeological evidence, which supports a date from the early 5th century BC, this monument is accepted with confidence.

2. Plataean Burial Mound

Pausanias, after decribing the grave of the Athenians, mentions a separate grave for the Boeotian Plataeans and the slaves:

> and there is another grave for the Boeotian Plataeans and for the slaves, for slaves fought then for the first time by the side of their masters.[272]

Due to the vestiges of ancient monuments in the vicinity to the *soros*, Clarke identifies the Plataean sepulchre to be between the Marathon mound and the grave of Miltiades, as does Leake.[273] This is at odds with the modern and generally accepted identification of the Plataean tomb, which is situated to the west of the plain near Vrana. Gell, while writing on his travels from the 'plain of Marathon to Pentelicus', notices 'a very remarkable circular hillock, which seems too considerable to be artificial, but may be the common tumulus of the slain'.[274] The hillock is not investigated further on this occasion and we cannot be certain that the mound mentioned is indeed what we know today to be the Plataean burial mound. However, the mound is situated on Gell's path between the Marathon plain towards

---

[270] Schliemann 1884b: 139; also Schliemann 1884a.
[271] Staes 1890: 65-71; see also Krentz 2010: 124-125.
[272] Paus. 1.32.3.
[273] Clarke 1818: 28, also see map on 18; Leake 1829: 172.
[274] Gell 1827: 62.

Penteli. Leake locates the ancient site of Marathon at Vrana,[275] and so tentatively suggests that the main tumulus (that we may assume is that of the Plataeans) is the tomb of Xuthus who founded the 'Tetrapolis' of Attica, consisting of Oenoe, Marathon, Probalinthus, and Tricorynthus.[276]

In 1970 the Greek archaeologist Spyridon Marinatos excavated the tumuli in the area of Vrana, west of the plain of Marathon. It was during these investigations that material evidence was unearthed which allowed Marinatos to confidently identify the largest tumulus in the area as that of the Plataean dead from the battle of Marathon.[277] Interred skeletons were uncovered with the remnants of fires having been lit beside them and on the surface sacrificial meals and gifts had been offered.[278] The mound contained eleven males, consisting of ten adults and one child of about ten years. Two of the burials were cremations and steles marked several of the inhumations.[279] One skeleton who had his head protected by large stones, and had received gifts, was the only burial to have had his stele engraved and may have been a Plataean officer. The name 'Archias' can be read engraved on the stele and Marinatos asserts that although it is inscribed in the Ionic alphabet, Plataeans may still have engraved the name as they 'had put themselves under the protection of the Athenians'.[280] This, arguably weak, justification for the use of the Ionic alphabet has led to uncertainty among modern scholarshp about the identification of the tumulus.[281] Marinatos believes the child to have taken part in the battle as a messenger and states it would have been necessary with such an extended battle line.[282] The strongets link, however, between this mound and the Plataean dead is the material finds. The finds 'are absolutely identical to the finds of the Tumulus of the Athenians, both in date and in shapes of vases.'[283]

---

[275] Leake 1829: 165-167.
[276] Leake 1829: 171; see also Strabo 8.7.1.
[277] Marinatos 1970a: 164-166; Marinatos 1970b: 357-366.
[278] Marinatos 1970a: 165-166.
[279] Marinatos 1970b: 358.
[280] Hdts. 6.108.1, possibly as early as 519 BC, see Thuc. 3.68.
[281] Petrakos 1996: 65-67.
[282] Marinatos 1970b: 359-361.
[283] Marinatos 1970b: 361, see Figs. 20-30; see also Marinatos 1970a: Fig. 19. Compare with Marathon finds, *CVA* I pls. 10-14.

THE MONUMENTS AND THE EVIDENCE

Figure 3. Plataean burial mound (author's own photograph).

Based on the late literary reference to the separate grave of the Plataeans to that of the Athenians, and the questionable inscriptional evidence, this monument may only be accepted tentatively.

3. Trophy

The earliest literary mention of the Marathon trophy is by Aristophanes:

> Chorus: Hail! King of Greece, we congratulate you upon the happiness you enjoy; it is worthy of this city, worthy of the trophy of Marathon.[284]

Aristophanes also mentions the monument elsewhere:

> Bdelycleon: We have now a thousand towns that pay us tribute; let them command each of these to feed twenty Athenians; then twenty thousand of our citizens would be eating nothing but hare, would drink nothing but the purest of milk, and always crowned with garlands, would be enjoying the delights

---

[284] Aristoph. *Knights* 1333-1334; see West 1969: 12-13.

> to which the great name of their country and the trophy of Marathon give them the right.[285]

Plutarch describes how the Athenians, before the battle of Plataea, explain their past exploits to the Spartans:

> while we have not only like arms and bodies with our brethren of that day, but that greater courage which is born of our victories; and our contest is not alone for land and city, as theirs was, but also for the trophies which they set up at Marathon and Salamis, in order that the world may think that not even those were due to Miltiades only, or to fortune, but to the Athenians.[286]

Pausanias mentions the trophy in passing while relaying a story about divine intervention:

> They say too that there chanced to be present in the battle a man of rustic appearance and dress. Having slaughtered many of the foreigners with a plough he was seen no more after the engagement. When the Athenians made enquiries at the oracle the god merely ordered them to honour Echetlaeus (He of the Plough-tail) as a hero. A trophy too of white marble has been erected.[287]

Plato also mentions the Marathon trophy:

> but to the King she could not bring herself to lend official aid for fear of disgracing the trophies of Marathon, Salamis and Plataea[288]

Leake mentions the remains of a marble structure from the plain of Marathon, on the strength of an account from a fellow traveller, having not seen them himself:

---

[285] Aristoph. *Wasps* 707-711.
[286] Plut. *Aristides* 16.4.
[287] Paus. 1.32.5.
[288] Plato. *Menexenus* 245a.

> Mr. W. Bankes, who has more recently visited Marathon, and who examined the plain with his usual diligence, discovered near the south-western angle of the Great Marsh, and about a quarter of a mile from the sea, at the church of Misosporetissa, the remains of a single Ionic column, of two feet and a half in diameter, of the best period of the arts, and which had the appearance of not having belonged to any building. It may have been part of the trophy of white marble which was erected by the Athenians after the action, and which, from the remark of Pausanias on its material, seems to have still existed in his time; for this is precisely the spot where the chief slaughter of the barbarians took place, and where the victory of the Athenians was crowned by driving them to the shore, and into the marsh.[289]

Remnants of a marble structure, the very same as those identified by Bankes, which consisted of multiple column drums and fragments of sculpture found on the plain of Marathon were published by Vanderpool.[290] These pentelic marble fragments, Vanderpool argues, were part of the very white marble trophy Pausanias described in the 2nd century AD. This 'white marble' structure was subsequently destroyed and the remnants were in fact built in to a mediaeval tower. This tower too has also fallen and is nearly completely destroyed while its remains are to be found near the modern day chapel of the Panagia Mesosporitissa. Vanderpool, having examined the foundations of the mediaeval tower, ascertained that the structure sits on its own foundations, indicating the components from the classical era had been moved and brought to the site of the tower.[291] One may assume, judging by the size and weight of the pentelic marble fragments that they were scavenged from within the immediate vicinity. When examining the text surrounding Pausanias' reference to the marble monument quoted above, we see that the trophy, the burial place of the Persians, the Makaria spring, and the Great Marsh are all mentioned in swift succession. This may indicate that, although slightly dubious with a lack of exact topographical referencing, these monuments and natural landmarks were located in close proximity to one another: to the northeast of the plain. Vanderpool advocates the trophy would probably have

---

[289] Leake 1829: 173-174.
[290] Vanderpool 1966; see also West 1969: 7-15.
[291] Vanderpool 1966: 100.

been erected near the area where the heaviest losses were inflicted upon the Persians;[292] this would support the above interpretation of Pausanias' account, as the victorious Athenians would probably have covered the Persian dead in the close vicinity of where they fell.

The largest piece of the original structure, which was pulled from the remains of the mediaeval tower, is the Ionic capital which is now housed in the Marathon Museum. This piece has a cutting which, it is generally accepted, once held a statue, presumably also made of marble. According to Vanderpool, '[t]he existing cutting on the top of the capital is too large for just the trophy and we must suppose that there was something else besides, perhaps a Nike preparing or crowning the trophy such as is sometimes represented on vases, reliefs and coins'.[293] The monument has been dated to the second quarter of the 5th century BC (*c*. 460 BC) on stylistic grounds.[294] Thus the monument was a single column, 10 m high which supported a statue. If the dating is accurate one can assume, with some degree of confidence, that this is indeed a commemorative monument of the battle of Marathon.

Figure 4. Athenian trophy at Marathon (author's own photograph).

---

[292] Vanderpool 1966: 102; see also 105.
[293] Vanderpool 1966: 106.
[294] Vanderpool 1966: 100.

4. Grave of Miltiades

Pausanias, writing in the 2nd century AD is the earliest literary reference to the grave of Miltiades:

> In the plain...here is also a separate monument to one man, Miltiades, the son of Kimon, although his end came later, after he had failed to take Paros and for this reason had been brought to trial by the Athenians.[295]

Pausanias is the only ancient source to discuss this monument and clearly indicates it is on the plain of Marathon. Pausanias uses the word *mnēma* to describe the monument which would not necessarily indicate Miltiades' body was entombed at this site.

Clarke, in the 19th century, interpreted Pausanias' writing as describing a place of burial, and identified some squared blocks at Marathon as the tomb of Miltiades.[296] Clarke identifies the remains of this monument as 'standing in a line with [the *soros*], towards the south'.[297] Contrastingly, Leake identified the foundation of a square monument consisting of large marble blocks situated 500 yards 'northward' of the *soros* and suggests that it is the remains of the monument erected in honour of Miltiades; on the strength of the remains, it is suggested that the monument may have consisted of a 'cubical base supporting a short column.'[298] Frazer also situates a structural foundation north of the *soros*, but at 600 yards.[299] At this position, Frazer describes a 'tower' which is marked by some cypresses. Here are the foundations of a quadrangular building lying north-west to south-east measuring, roughly, 12 paces long by eight paces broad. Frazer believes this is a construction of Roman date as he thinks the foundation is constructed with bricks and mortar. In 1890 the blocks of 'well-hewn' pentelic marble which sat on top of these foundations were found by Greek archaeologists to have been removed, revealing the mortared foundations

---

[295] Paus. 1.32.4-5.
[296] Clarke 1818: 7.27-28.
[297] Clarke 1818: 7.27.
[298] Leake 1829: 172-3.
[299] Frazer 1965: 2.435.

below. Fraser, therefore, rejects that this particular site can be 'either the Greek trophy or the tomb of Miltiades.'[300]

This structure would have been a monument to an individual, as Pausanias notes. Due to the lack of archaeological evidence it is not certain whether this monument was, in fact, a tomb or a cenotaph. However if it was a burial, in justification of including a singular burial in a study of communal commemoration, the Athenians saw fit to honour Miltiades with an individual grave upon the field of conflict and thus would have established some form of public recognition of the monument.[301]

Miltiades was evidently held in high regard in Athens after his death, as he was portrayed fighting in the battle of Marathon in the painting in the Stoa *Poikile* (**no. 12**) and a statue of him was dedicated at Delphi (**no. 15**). However, given the late date of the sole literary reference to this monument, and the lack of consensus in later literature regarding any archaeological evidence, this monument may only be accepted with caution.

5. *Herakleia*

Pindar includes the games at Marathon when referring to victories in other games, firstly in his *Olympian Odes*:

> And then there were two other joyous victories at the gates of Corinth, and others won by Epharmostus in the vale of Nemea; and at Argos he won glory in a contest of men, and as a boy at Athens. And at Marathon, when he was barred from competing with the beardless youths, how he endured the contest for silver cups among the older men![302]

And secondly in his *Pythian Odes*:

> You have won a prize of honour at Megara, and in the valley of Marathon[303]

---

[300] Frazer 1965: 2.435.
[301] West 1965: 14.
[302] Pind. *Olympian Odes* 9.89. See also Pind. *Olympian Odes* 13.110.
[303] Pind. *Pythian Odes* 8.79.

A stele was discovered in the early 1930s in the southern part of the Marathon plain in the locality known as Valaria, just north of the small swamp of Vrexisa.[304] The stele contains parts of two inscriptions; one on the front and one on the back. The first is a legal document dating from the period of Kleisthenes' reforms in the last decade of the 6th century BC.[305] The second inscription, which interests us here, records some of the procedure concerning the selection of officials for the *Herekleia* (games held at Marathon) and dates from just after the battle of Marathon, between 490-480 BC.[306] The inscription relating to legal matters is read vertically and so, due to the damage inflicted on the stone, only a quarter of each line is legible. Thus, no complete reading can be made.[307] The inscription on the back regarding the *Herakleia*, given that the text is to be read horizontally, can be reconstructed with more success.

Figure 5. Inscribed stele mentioning the Herakleia *(author's own photograph).*

> *Herakleion games... The Athlothetai shall appoint thirty men for the contest. They shall select from the visitors three from each tribe, who have promised in the sanctuary to help in arranging the contest to the best of their ability, not less than thirty years of age. These men are to take the oath in the sanctuary over victims. A steward...*[308]

---

[304] Vanderpool 1942: 329, also see n. 1.
[305] *IG* I³ 2.
[306] *IG* I³ 3.
[307] See Vanderpool 1942: 332-333 for attempts and suggestions at restoration and interpretation.
[308] *IG* I³ 3; trans. Vanderpool 1942: 335.

Figure 6. Herakleia inscription (author's own photograph).

Vanderpool dates this inscription to the beginning of the 5th century BC on epigraphical and historical grounds.[309] Another inscription was found in close proximity to the inscription discussed above.[310] For the purpose of the current study this second inscription, arguably referring to the *Herakleia*, does little more than confirm the topography of the battle and reaffirm the likelihood of the *Herakleia* taking part in this area of the plain.[311]

The *Herakleia* festival is understood to have had a long history. The Marathonians, according to Pausanias, claimed they were the first to worship Herakles as a god.[312] When the Athenian forces rushed back in defence of Athens in 490 BC, after defeating the Persian forces having camped in 'the sacred precinct of Heracles in Marathon, they pitched camp in the sacred precinct of Heracles in Cynosarges'.[313] Therefore, it has been suggested that the sanctuaries of Herakles, particularly those at Marathon and Cynosarges (just outside the city walls) must have been held

---

[309] Vanderpool 1942: 333.
[310] *IG* I³ 1015bis.
[311] See Matthaiou 2003: 191-194 for a discussion on this inscription and further references.
[312] Paus. 1.15.2; 1.32.4.
[313] Hdts. 6.116.

in especially high regard by Athenians of the early 5th century BC.[314] After the Persian Wars, the festival, which was probably initially only of local importance, grew to pan-Attic importance and this idea is supported by the archaeological evidence (Figure 6) in that prominent men were selected, three from each of the ten tribes, to manage the games.[315]

The increasing importance of Herakles, post-Marathon, would make sense given that the Athenian soldiers camped in the sanctuary of Herakles before the battle and may have wanted to further honour their 'protector'.[316] It is possible the festival went on to pan-Hellenic renown, as we learn from Pindar that Epharmostos of Opus, Aristomenes of Aegina, and a certain relative of Xenophon of Corinth won victories there.[317]

Considering the 5th century BC literary evidence and the supporting archaeological evidence, athletic contests taking place at Marathon in this period is beyond doubt. However, while the memory of Marathon was constantly recalled by Athenians throughout the 5th century BC, the association between an already existing *Herakleia* festival and the battle is speculative. Therefore, this monument is accepted tentatively.

6. Epigram for the Athenians

The Athenian epigram is quoted by Lycurgus, writing in the 4th century BC:

Athenians, guarding Greece, subdued in fight
At Marathon the gilded Persians' might.[318]

Lycurgus includes this epigram in examples raised 'over graves',[319] which would make it an epitaph, but it does not reference the grave or the dead specifically, as epitaphs almost always do.[320] The epigram states that the Athenians were protecting Greece, which is an idea reminiscent of the epigram inscribed on a fragmented marble base (see **no. 11**).

---

[314] Woodford 1971: 217.
[315] Vanderpool 1942: 337.
[316] Hdts. 6.108, 116; Herakles was also portrayed in the painting in the Stoa *Poikile*, see Paus. 1.15.3.
[317] Pind. *Olympian* 9. 89-90; Pind. *Pythian* 8. 79; Pind. *Olympian* 8.110.
[318] Lyc. *Against Leocrates* 109.
[319] Prior to recounting the epigram in Lyc. *Against Leocrates* 109.
[320] Jacoby 1945: 160.

This phraseology therefore accords with the Athenian outlook after the repulsion of Xerxes' forces.[321]

This epigram is also mentioned in Suidas, in which it is implied the epigram was set up in the Stoa *Poikile* near to the famous painting of Marathon in the Athenian agora.[322] If this inscription stood in the Athenian urban centre, this placement would go some way to explaining the lack of reference to the war dead, or grave, specifically. However, this placement does conflict with Lycurgus' description of the inscription as 'funerary'.[323] Furthermore, the Stoa *Poikile* has been dated to between 470-450 BC (see **no. 12**),[324] which would in turn provide a tentative date for the epigram.[325]

This monument is counted here as having been raised on the battlefield on the strength of Lycurgus implying the epigram was raised over the communal grave at Marathon. However, considering the monument's placement in the reference from Suidas, this attribution is not beyond doubt. Due to the conflicting literary sources, and the lack of archaeological evidence, this monument may only be accepted with caution.

7. Casualty List at Marathon

Pausanias describes the casualty list as erected upon the burial mound:

> *On the plain is the grave of the Athenians, and upon it are slabs giving the names of the killed according to their tribes*[326]

A damaged stele was recently uncovered near Kunouria in the northern Peloponnese. The object was found in the villa of the 2nd century AD aristocrat Herodes Atticus at modern Loukou (ancient Eua). It has been suggested that Herodes Atticus, who had a lavish estate at Marathon, had the monument there renovated and removed the original inscriptions to his villa at Loukou; this suggestion does imply, however, that Pausanias would have seen and reported the replacement inscriptions.[327]

---

[321] West 1965: 12.
[322] Suidas s.v. *Poikile*.
[323] As noted by West 1965: 13.
[324] See Castriota 2005: 90-91.
[325] The epigram has been dated, by its style, to the early 5th century BC, see West 1965: 12.
[326] Paus. 1.32.3. See also *SEG* 49.370; 51.425; 53.354; 55.413; 56.430, 431, 432.
[327] Petrovic 2013; Keesling 2012; Proietti 2013.

Good report indeed, as it reaches always the furthest ends of well-lit earth, will report the arête of these men, how they died fighting against Medes and crowned Athens, a few having awaited the attack of many.[328]

The stele measures 68 cm high, 55.8 cm wide and 26.5 cm thick. The cuttings on the stele's sides indicate this object was slotted into a row beside others. One may assume that the names of the individuals from each tribe were inscribed on separate steles and were lined up next to one another in the same way as Matthaiou presents the 'cenotaph' erected for the *Marathonomachoi* in the *demosion sema* (see **no. 11**).[329] If each stone was inscribed with a four line epigram such as the stele above, at 40 lines the monument would boast the longest epigram until the 4th century BC. The inscription has been dated to the early 5th century BC on stylistic grounds but the strongest link to the Marathon plain and thus the battle is the circumstance of its survival; it was found in the villa of Herodes Atticus, the Marathon born aristocrat.

It has been questioned whether the Athenians would have put up a casualty list on the battlefield as early as 490 BC;[330] however the recent interpretations of the archaeological evidence would suggest that this practice was, in fact, carried out.[331] The names of the war dead appear to be divided by tribe which complements Herodotus' assertion that the Athenian army were positioned in the battle line in accordance to tribal affiliation.[332]

Considering the archaeological material, the stele's dating, and the circumstances of its discovery, the existence of a casualty list at Marathon in the early 5th century BC is accepted here with confidence.

---

[328] See Steinhauer 2004-2009: 679-692, with an image on 690.
[329] Matthaiou 2003: 197-200.
[330] West 1965: xxxii.
[331] See Keesling 2012 for further references on the early 5th century BC dating of the Marathon casualty list; Arrington (2014: 43) also accepts the stele was part of the set of casualty lists from 490 BC; *contra*. Proietti 2013, who argues the recovered casualty list may be a later reconstruction with archaising features.
[332] Hdts 6.111.

8.– 9. Athenian Treasury and Statue Group at Delphi

Pausanias identifies the Athenian Treasury at Delphi as having been constructed from the spoils taken at Marathon:

> *The Thebans have a treasury built from the spoils of war, and so have the Athenians. Whether the Cnidians built to commemorate a victory or to display their prosperity I do not know, but the Theban treasury was made from the spoils taken at the battle of Leuctra, and the Athenian treasury from those taken from the army that landed with Datis at Marathon.*[333]

In addition a base bearing an inscription abuts the treasury's south side:

> *The Athenians to Apollo as offerings from the Battle of Marathon, taken from the Mede*[334]

The Athenian Treasury was situated on the sacred way on a high podium with a triangular terrace directly in front of the entrance way (see Figure 7). Three retaining walls were placed around the treasury, which backed into the hillside. To the north of the treasury was the terrace of Apollo's Temple.[335] Furthermore, running along the south of the treasury was a triangular platform upon which the inscription noted above was engraved. According to the inscription, the Athenians dedicated a thank-offering at Delphi paid for from the spoils of Marathon. The form of the monument is not known but West offers either arms and armour taken from the enemy, or a statue group, as possible suggestions.[336] Cuttings on the top side of the base, which is in situ today, have more recently been interpreted as supporting ten statues, which may have been the Athenian Eponymous Heroes.[337]

---

[333] Paus. 10.11.5.
[334] *GHI*³ no. 19; trans. Neer 2004: 66.
[335] See Scott 2010: 76, Fig. 4.1 for the locations of the treasury (no. 96 in Scott's publication) and the statue group (no. 97 in Scott's publication).
[336] West 1965: 16.
[337] Neer (2004: 66) suggests a statue group of the eponymous heroes; Scott (2010: Appendix C, no. 97 and 81) agrees with this identification.

The Monuments and the Evidence

Figure 7. Athenian treasury at Delphi (author's own photograph).

The engraved monument base abutting the south side of the temple was originally discovered in eight fragments by French excavators in 1893 and was pieced together by the reconstruction of the dedicatory verse inscribed on the stone.[338] The inscription visible today is probably of the 3rd century BC, the original having been erased possibly for the refurbishment of the letters.[339] However, the text is inscribed in the archaic alphabet and the letter forms have been interpreted as evidence for dating the original inscription to shortly after Marathon.[340] Based

---

[338] See Homolle 1893: 612 and 1896: 608-617.

[339] West 1965: 19; see also Jacquemin 1999: 315, no. 77.

[340] For example a dotted theta and a three stroke sigma are used. West's conclusion (1965: 19) is based on the assumption that the inscription was copied faithfully; Scott 2010: Appendix C, no. 97 dates this monument to 490 BC; Jaquemin (1999: 315, no. 77) also agrees with this dating.

on the inscriptional evidence, the association of the statue group as commemorating Marathon is understood here as secure.

It has been argued that the base and the treasury are to be understood as distinct structures, both in date and meaning.[341] For example, West provides four reasons which indicate that the base is an insertion after the Treasury had been completed.[342] The third course of the south side of the Treasury is used as a support for the base of the dedication. The Treasury's third course is well finished like the courses above it. West follows Pomtow in concluding that when the third course was constructed, due to the differing appearances of both, it was not immediately planned for a base to abut against it.[343] 'Swallow Tail' clamps were used in the Treasury construction while the base is joined by 'T' and 'Z' clamps.[344] The sockets cut in the Treasury to receive the pedimental sculptures are rectangular, while those cut into the base are round.[345] Finally the Treasury is built entirely of Parian marble while the base is made from limestone. To follow West would be to disassociate the statue group's base and the treasury, therefore concluding that the treasury was built first and had nothing to do with commemorating Marathon.[346]

As an alternative to commemorating the battle of Marathon, the victory over Boeotians and Chalcidians in 507/6 BC has been suggested as prompting the construction of the treasury.[347] However, the proximity of

---

[341] E.g. Pomtow 1894: 43-45; Dinsmoor 1912: 456, 492.

[342] These reasons are set out in West 1965: 17.

[343] West 1965: 17; see also Pomtow 1894: 43-45.

[344] According to West (1965: 17) these differing clamps indicate a difference in periods of construction. 'Swallow Tail' clamps being indicative of the 6th century BC, while 'T' and 'Z' clamps being more popular in the 5th century BC; *contra.* Cooper (1990: 317) who argues that the Swallow Tail clamp is not a product of the 6th century BC but rather represents an 'extracted double-Γ or double-T clamp across joints of blocks reset into position after rebuilding or repair.'

[345] Again West (1965:17) interprets these differences as indicative of a difference in dating: rectangular sockets suggest a 6th century BC date, whereas round sockets suggest a 5th century BC date.

[346] West (1965) does not treat the Athenian treasury as a commemorative monument; in addition certain architectural features, presented by Partida (2000: 53-55) are interpreted as evidence for a late 6th century BC date for the construction of the temple, which would be too early to commemorate Marathon.

[347] West 1965: 18-19; Scott (2010: 78, n. 15), who dates the treasury to *c.* 490 BC, states that this date was the most likely alternative date; see also Partida 2000: 52.

the proposed dates (*c.* 507 BC or *c.* 490 BC) has been argued as too close to be able to choose on the basis of such architectural features mentioned above.[348]

Recent evidence has been produced which supports the connection between the Athenian treasury and the commemorations of Marathon. In 1989 excavations were undertaken at Delphi to further understand the relationship between the treasury and thank-offering base.[349] The treasury was discovered to have been architecturally linked to the triangular terrace which bore the dedicatory inscription. For example, it was discovered that a ledge of 0.3 m in width protruded from the treasury's stereobate along the south side only, which would have supported the base for the thank-offering. The planning of the treasury, then, appears to have taken the addition of the base into account from the earliest stages of construction.[350] The architectural linkage of the treasury with the securely dated statue group dedication has led to the treasury also being dated to about 490 BC.[351] Furthermore, this archaeological evidence supports the statement provided by Pausanias, in the excerpt above, which clearly attributes the funding of the treasury to the spoils of Marathon.

The statue group dedication has been interpreted as a near-simultaneous monument to the treasury.[352] However the statue group and treasury, while close in proximity and understood here as sharing a commemorative focus, are distinct and separate monuments.[353]

---

[348] *FD* III 2 1 286.

[349] The results are summarised in Amandry 1998.

[350] Neer 2004: 67; Partida (2000: 49), who argues for an earlier date for the treasury construction, nevertheless agrees that the treasury and terrace were contemporary;

[351] Scott 2010: 78; See Neer 2004:72-73, who suggests a more specific date of 488 BC; Jacquemin 1999: 315-316, no. 86, with further bibliography, dates the monument to the beginning of the 5th century BC.

[352] Scott 2010: 81, who further states that statues of the Eponymous Heroes would, in *c.* 490 BC, have been an unusual type of dedication at Delphi and therefore would have required an explanatory inscription to aid the viewer to engage with the monument. In contrast, such an explanatory inscription was absent from the more 'easily understood' treasury.

[353] This view is shared by Jacquemin (1999: nos. 86 and 77); Neer (2004: 67) and Scott (2010: Appendix C, nos. 96 and 97).

10. Callimachus Monument

> [Callimachus] of Aphidna dedicated me to Athena
> The mes[senger of the imm]ortals who dwell in their Olympian halls.
> [Callimachus the pole]march, the struggle of the Athenians
> at Mar[athon on behalf of the G]reeks [...]
> for the children of the Athenians a mem[orial?][354]

The reconstructed monument and fragmentary inscription survives and is on display in the Acropolis Museum today.[355] The inscription runs vertically downwards in two flutings apparently cut for the engraving. The form of the monument was an ionic column, of perhaps 3.6 m tall, supporting a figure.[356]

The fragmentary inscription has had many suggested restorations, and these depend heavily on the author's interpretation of the monument. For example, Hiller argues that the first line of the inscription was engraved before the battle of Marathon and the second line added later to commemorate Callimachus' death in the battle.[357] Wilhelm interprets the two lines as inscribed at the same time, after the battle of Marathon, by Callimachus' friends.[358] It has also been argued that the monument was originally dedicated to Athena by Callimachus before the battle of Marathon.[359] If the monument was originally commissioned by Callimachus then only the first couplet can have been intended for the dedication; the second couplet must have been composed after Callimachus' death due to the 'unambiguous reference' to Marathon.[360] It has been argued that if the letters 'mn', which begin the final word we have of the second inscription, are of the word '*mnēma*' (translated above as 'memorial') then the

---

[354] See *IG* I³ 784 where a date of 490-485 BC is suggested; trans. Bowie 2010: 203-204.
[355] Statue: Acropolis Museum nos. 228, 335, 424Y, 443, 690, 2523, and two fragments without numbers; Capital: Acropolis Museum nos. 3776, 3820, 3830, Θ312, and one fragment without a number; Column: no. EM 6339 fragments c-h.
[356] Raubitschek 1940: 53-56; West 1965: 24.
[357] See Hiller's (1926: no. 10) restoration.
[358] Wilhelm 1934: 112-115; see West 1965: 27-28. Also, Jacoby (1945: 158, n. 8) thinks the epigram may have been inscribed by Callimachus' brother.
[359] Raubitschek 1940: 53-56.
[360] Quote from Bowie 2010: 204, who also states that 'neither letter forms nor other considerations can help us pin down how soon after 490 BC this was done.'

monument may be interpreted as having been transformed from a private to public monument.³⁶¹ Callimachus' part in the battle of Marathon, his death, and the victory would then be portrayed as having been performed 'on behalf of the Greeks' (as restored in the second epigram).

This monument is understood here as a private monument which was transformed into a public monument at some point after the battle of Marathon. Due to the varied interpretations of the monument's intended meaning based on the inscriptional evidence, the monument may only be accepted tentatively.

11.   Engraved Marble Base

Epigram 1 -
[The fame] of these [dead] men [shines] forever... For fighting on land and... they kept all Greece from seeing the day of slavery.

Epigram 2 -
These men had unconquer[ed...] when they planted their spears before the gates by the sea to burn...the city, by force having turned back of the Persians...

Epigram 3 -
...[on f]oot and...on(?) the island...they threw.

Epigram 4 -
For the enclosure in front of...of Pallas...holding the richest point
*Peak of the calf-nourishing land, for these happiness giver of all bloom frequents.*³⁶²

These epigrams survive on four stone fragments referred to here as stone A I, stone A II, stone B, and stone C. Stone A I, made of pentelic marble, was found in the wall of a modern house in the Athenian agora in 1932 (see Figure 8).³⁶³ A larger fragment (stone A II) had been discovered in the 19th century and first published in 1855 (see Figure 9).³⁶⁴ This fragment, also of

---

[361] Bowie 2010: 204; this point of view is also attested by West 1965: 24-25 which resonates with Hiller's earlier argument (1926).
[362] *IG* I³ 503/504.
[363] Oliver 1933: 480; Clairmont 1983: 106.
[364] Rangabē 1855: 597, no. 784b.

Figure 8. Stone A I (I 303 a, Agora Excavations, The American School of Classical Studies at Athens).

pentelic marble, was found in the courtyard of a modern house on Hadrian Street in Athens.[365] A further smaller fragment, again of pentelic marble and referred to here as part of 'stone B', was reused as a door threshold in the library of Hadrian (see Figure 10).[366] The fragment was published by Peek, who was provided a description of the stone by Vanderpool.[367] More recently the largest fragment, referred to here as 'stone C', was discovered in 1973 built into a retaining wall of the ancient road leading from the Kerameikos to the Academy.[368] The stone was later rediscovered by Angelos Matthaiou in the Ephorate's storerooms.[369]

---

[365] Clairmont 1983: 106.
[366] Clairmont 1983: 102; see also Peek 1953: 305.
[367] See Peek 1953: 306.
[368] See Matthaiou 2003: 198.
[369] See Matthaoiu 1988, with images on pl. 17 and pl. 18.

THE MONUMENTS AND THE EVIDENCE

Figure 9. Stone A II (I 303 b, Agora Excavations, The American School of Classical Studies at Athens).

Figure 10. Stone B (after Clairmont 1983: pl.13, 7b. Reproduced by kind permission of BAR Publishing).

The inscribed fragments are envisaged to be the top level of a stepped base of a single monument, which had chiselled sockets to receive inserted objects, such as steles.[370] The discovery of stone C reveals further evidence of cuttings on top of the fragment which, it is believed, would have received the steles measured 70 cm wide and 20 cm deep; it is suggested the long base would have held multiple steles of a similar size to a number of other casualty list steles (e.g. see **no. 7**).[371] Following this restoration, then, the fragments would have been a part of a long base, consisting of at least four blocks, which carried a number of standing steles. The front side of each block was decorated with a band of horizontal stippling with smoothed marble bands above and below. Epigram 1 is inscribed on the upper smooth band of stone A. The upper band of stones B and C do not exist so it is not possible to say whether this epigram continues beyond stone A.[372] The stippled surface of the front of the front of the stones has been smoothed out (see below for the discussion on dating) to create space for epigrams 2 (on stone A), 3 (on stone B), and 4 (on stone C).

The letter forms have led to the inscriptions being dated to the 470s BC.[373] However, it is suggested that epigrams 1 (on the upper smooth band) was composed by a different hand to epigram 2 (on the stippled lower band).[374] The style of epigram 1 has been likened to that of the Hekatompedon inscription, dating to 485-484 BC and therefore may be

---

[370] Oliver 1936: 225-234; steles were suggested by Raubitschek 1940 as the inserted objects and these fragments are published as *IG* I³ 503/504; this contrasts with the theory that the sockets would have supported herms, suggested by Meritt 1956; *contra*. Clairmont (1983: 109) who argues, having examined stone A II, that there is no evidence to suggest that the cutting on top of the stone was made to receive a stele; Oliver (1940: 483) also states that that there is no way of telling whether the cutting was original or medieval; in contrast Raubitschek (1940: 56-59) suggested the cutting was made at the same time as epigram 2 for a stele bearing the names of Athenian casualties of a Persian attack at Phalerum after their defeat at Marathon; this, in turn, has been refuted by Oliver (1940: 483-484). For an image of a suggested restoration of the monument see Matthaiou 1988: 122.
[371] Matthaiou (2003: 195) offers several examples such as: *IG* I³ 1147 and 1147bis, the monument was composed of ten steles (one for each tribe), standing on a common base; *IG* I³ 1163, the base of the monument consists of three long adjoining blocks.
[372] Although Bowie (2010: 206) believes this to be probable.
[373] Petrovic 2013: 49; Jacoby 1945: 164; Page 1981: XX, 220.
[374] Oliver 1933: 484; Clairmont (1983: 108) believes the inscriptions are contemporaries.

by the same hand.³⁷⁵ Some argue that epigram 2 was inscribed up to 15 years after epigram 1.³⁷⁶ This theory has been refuted by Clairmont on the grounds that the inscriptions are not being assessed on stylistic evidence but on political grounds.³⁷⁷ The argument which dates epigram two to 15 years after epigram 1 is based on Kimon attempting to redress the wrong done to his father Miltiades after the failed expedition to Paros, and the eclipsing of Miltiades' fame by Themistocles. However, if the epigrams were inscribed at the same time, the question remains of why they are of different hands.³⁷⁸ Nevertheless, it has been stated that the time span between the upper and lower inscriptions cannot be judged.³⁷⁹

The matter of the monument's original location, due to the dispersed surviving fragments, has also been debated. It has been suggested that the monument was constructed in the Athenian agora, perhaps in the vicinity of the statue of the Tyrannicides.³⁸⁰ However, it has been argued that the discovery of stone C suggests the monument stood in the public cemetery, despite the fact that other fragments were found in the agora; fragments of monuments would often travel into the city for reuse but it was unlikely that fragments would be transported in the opposite direction.³⁸¹

Before a review of the interpretations begins, it is worthy of note that interpretations of these epigrams are numerous, as are the conclusions drawn as to which battle(s) the monument commemorates. Also, given the

---

[375] An idea put forward by Wilhelm (1898: 487-491) and later noted by Clairmont 1983: 108; the observation is based on the engraver's partiality for the punctuation mark of three vertical circles with dots in each (visible in epigram 1 on stone A II, see Figure 9) and for the vertical line of epsilon and lambda which extend slightly below the line (see also West 1965: 43).

[376] Peek 1953: 310 f; Meiggs 1966: 90 f; this is followed by Bowie (2010: 206-207).

[377] Clairmont 1983: 108.

[378] Oliver (1933) suggests that before 480 BC two separate stones existed, one bearing epigram 1 which was composed by Simonides, and the other bearing epigram 2 composed by Aeschylus. After 480 BC epigrams 1 and 2 were combined on a single monument.

[379] See Bowie 2010: 207;

[380] Clairmont 1983: 110.

[381] Arrington 2014: 45; see also Matthaiou 2003: 199; this location is also accepted by Bowie 2010.

amount of text missing, any interpretations of the text must be understood as tentative.[382]

Most scholarship supports the attribution of at least some of the extant inscribed text to Marathon, although multiple interpretations of the text have been put forward. For example, Hiller suggested epigram 1 referred to the battles of Salamis and Plataea.[383] Hiller's proposed restoration, which contained reference to ships was confirmed by the discovery of a fragment published in 1956 found imbedded in a modern wall east of the temple of Ares in the Athenian Agora, thought to be a 4th century BC copy of epigram 1.[384] If the late 4th century BC fragment was to be accepted as a faithful copy of epigram 1 then there is a clear reference to ships in the third line. However, as stated by Meritt, the phrase '*epi neon*' could be read as 'by the ships' as well as 'on the ships'.[385] Therefore, this reference may be interpreted as referring to the conflict on the beach at Marathon as the Persians fled the mainland to the safety of their fleet. The epigram could then be understood as contrasting the two parts of the battle: the conflict on the plain and the Persian rout by the ships.[386] Furthermore, albeit before the 4th century BC fragment was published, the epigrams were interpreted as referring to the battle of Marathon by Wilhelm who provides a restoration of the text which, instead of restoring a reference to ships in epigram 1, suggests a reference to Persian cavalry.[387]

---

[382] As noted by Arrington 2014: 44.

[383] Hiller (1934: 204-206) published a restoration of the text and interpreted a contrast drawn between a land and sea battle; Podlecki 1973 attributes epigram 1 to Salamis; Hammond (1973: 191f) agrees with Amandry (1960:1-8) that epigram 1 not only refers to Salamis but to the years 480-479 BC, which would have comprised of the battles of Salamis, Artemisium and Plataea. This is also followed by Clairmont (1983: 107); *contra.* Meritt (e.g. 1956), who argues that epigrams 1 and 2 deal solely with Marathon. Oliver agrees with this conclusion (1933: 480-494), as does Peek (1934: 339-343).

[384] Meritt 1956: 268-280; for a suggested restoration of this inscription see Meritt 1962: 296; see also Clairmont 1983: 106.

[385] Meritt 1956: 271-272; this fragment has only two letters in common with the 5th century BC epigram and its connection has recently been refuted on the grounds that the inscription may have adorned a private monument, see Matthaiou 2000-2003 and Petrovic 2013: 48, n. 13 for further references.

[386] West 1965: 44.

[387] Wilhelm 1934: 95 (for epigram 1) and 102 (for epigram 2); the attribution of both epigrams to commemorating Marathon is also put forward by Oliver 1933.

Epigram 2, on the other hand, has been attributed to the battle of Marathon.[388] The text references a battle outside the city gates which prevents the destruction of the city; however, the battle of Marathon wasn't fought at the gates of Athens.[389] 'The gates' have been interpreted as referring to the narrows at the southern end of the Marathonian plain, between Mount Agrieliki and the sea, through which led the road from the plain to Athens.[390] The Athenians commemorated by this epigram were therefore praised for blocking the Persian advance through the gates by the sea.

With regard to the stone B, bearing the fragmented epigram 3 which references foot-soldiers and an island, Clairmont argues it is to be understood in relation to the conflict between Athens and Aegina in the early 5th century BC.[391] Peek attributes this fragment to the battles of Salamis and Plataea on the basis that reference to men on foot and an island are mentioned.[392] However, it is noted by West that the evidence for the attribution of this monument is slight; even so, West includes the fragment in his collection of Athenian commemorations of the battle of Salamis.[393] The fragment is not fully preserved and, considering the general association of epigram 2 with the battle of Marathon, it has been suggested that the island could refer to Euboea which was devastated before the battle of Marathon rather than Salamis.[394]

It has been noted that demonstrative pronouns in both epigrams refer to the same lists of men (e.g. 'these men' in epigrams 1 and 2); therefore the second epigram, although inscribed later than the first, could not commemorate men who were not already mentioned on the original

---

[388] Hiller 1934: 204-206; Podlecki 1973: 37-39; see also Clairmont 1983: 106; West (1965: 44) states that this attribution is generally accepted.

[389] Another likely candidate as the subject of this commemoration is the battle of Plataea, but Athens would have already been sacked by the time the battle of Plataea was fought, see West 1965: 44.

[390] Matthaiou 2003; for a summary see Bowie 2010: 207.

[391] Clairmont (1983: 102) reconstructs the fragment to bear reference to horses.

[392] Peek 1953: 305-312.

[393] However, West (1965: 150-151) entitles the monument 'Small fragment...possibly commemorating Salamis and Plataea'.

[394] Bowie 2010: 207, n. 13; Arrington 2014: 45.

monument.[395] The adornment of further inscriptions on a monument already commemorating the Marathon dead would fit in with the continuous commemoration of the event throughout the 5th century BC.[396]

Epigram 4, on stone C, has been examined by Matthaiou, who interprets the enclosure mentioned in the first line as referring to the *temenos* of Heracles at Marathon, or possibly Athena (who is mentioned in the second line as 'Pallas').[397] In contrast, the second couplet of epigram 4, in referencing those who hold the peak of the calf-nourishing land, has been suggested as having a strong connection to Salamis.[398] An examination of word choice has been interpreted as referencing the tip (or toe) of Italy. One ship from this area fought at Salamis, under the command of Phayllos of Croton the Pythian victor, and so this epigram has been interpreted as referring to this naval battle alone.[399]

With regard to the monument as a whole, Oliver was the first to suggest the monument was a cenotaph which supported lists of the Athenian casualties.[400] The idea of a cenotaph may be contested on the grounds that a cenotaph may only be constructed if the casualties of a battle are not recovered (and the Marathon casualties were buried on the battlefield, see **nos. 1** and **2**).[401]

However, it has been observed by Matthaiou that later ephebic ceremonies involved a cenotaph in the *demosion sema* and a *polyandrion* on the Marathon battlefield.[402] An ephebic decree dated to 176/175 BC mentions a regular contest which took place at Marathon but also by the

---

[395] Arrington 2014: 45-46, who attributes both epigrams and the monument as a whole to Marathon.
[396] Arrington 2014: 46.
[397] Matthaiou 2003: 200-201; however, it has been pointed out that the role of a *temenos* of Athena is otherwise unattested at Marathon (Bowie 2010: 207).
[398] See Bowie 2010: 208-209; it should be noted that the dead of the battle of Salamis were buried on the promontory of the island of Salamis (see **no. 37**).
[399] Bowie 2010: 8-9; see Hdts. 8.47 for the reference of Phayllos at Salamis.
[400] Oliver 1933: 480; see also Matthaiou 2003 and Petrovic 2013: 49.
[401] See Jacoby 1945: 157-185, also on 176-177 Jacoby tentatively suggests the Marathon epigrams were a 'war memorial' in itself and did not support casualty lists; see also West 1965: 36; furthermore, see chapter section 4.2.1 where it is argued that the only consistent aspect in raising a cenotaph is the absence of bodies.
[402] Matthaiou 2003: 197-198.

polyandrion next to the city.⁴⁰³ This inscription is similar to one dating to the Hellenistic period, which describes behavioural commemoration being undertaken at the Marathon battlefield, at which young Athenians would offer a wreath and sacrifice specifically to the war dead.⁴⁰⁴ Both these inscriptions refer to organised sporting activity and a *polyandrion*. Matthaiou suggests that a cenotaph stood in the *demosion sema* and was known popularly as 'the *polyandrion*', and that only the dead of Marathon would have been famous enough to have a monument commemorating their victory referred to as 'the *polyandrion*'.⁴⁰⁵ A *polyandrion* would usually refer to a mass grave, however in this case the name may have been attributed to a cenotaph in absence of the bodies. While discussing the public cemetery both Thucydides and Pausanias specifically mention that the dead of Marathon were buried on the battlefield while not mentioning the dead of any other battle of the Persian Wars who were also absent from the *demosion sema*.⁴⁰⁶ It has been suggested that the cenotaph to the Marathon war dead erected at the *demosion sema* prompted these references to the Marathon war dead specifically.⁴⁰⁷ The ceremonies mentioned above support the idea of a monument in the *demosion sema* connected to Marathon, and the interpretations of epigram 2 which connect it with this battle. These connections allow a tentative conclusion that at least part of the monument explicitly commemorated the battle of Marathon.⁴⁰⁸

As the preceding discussion illustrates, the multitude of varying theories attests to the pliability of the limited, available evidence. Therefore, any conclusions drawn must be accepted tentatively. The

---

⁴⁰³ *IG 2³* 1313.
⁴⁰⁴ *IG 2²* 1006, 65-71.
⁴⁰⁵ Matthaiou 2003: 197-200; the monument has been associated with the elegiac inscription *IG 1³* 503/504. For further discussion on these fragments see Petrovic 2013 and '*Postscript*' on p.61 for further bibliography.
⁴⁰⁶ Thuc. 2.34.5; Paus. 1.29.4.
⁴⁰⁷ Arrington 2010: 506; see Arrington 2014: 46 for a suggestion that the monument was a *polyandrion-cum-cenotaph* of 490 BC, intended to commemorate all the Athenian dead from that year. This interpretation would allow the references to ships and islands to be attributed to conflicts with Aegina. Furthermore, the demonstrative pronouns would refer to the dead from one year, whose names would have been inscribed in steles above the epigrams. This would also provide a reason for why the monument was referred to as a '*polyandrion*' in later inscriptions, e.g. *IG II²* 1006, 22-23 (see also Arrington 2014: 46, n. 126).
⁴⁰⁸ Bowie 2010: 209.

proposed form of the monument suggests it was a structure that displayed casualty lists. Furthermore, on the basis of the holding of funeral contests in front of both the *polyandrion* at Marathon and the '*polyandrion*' in the city, the monument commemorated Marathon, at least in part. Therefore, this monument is attributed here to the battle of Marathon tentatively, although it is accepted that it is quite possible that the structure served as a commemorative monument to multiple, as yet undefined, conflicts.

12. Painting in Stoa *Poikile*

The painting within the stoa is mentioned by Aeschines:

> *And now pass on in imagination to the Stoa Poikile... What is it then, fellow citizens, to which I refer? The battle of Marathon is pictured there.*[409]

The monument is also mentioned in the pseudo-Demosthenic tirade against Neaera:

> *The Plataeans, men of Athens, alone among the Greeks came to your aid at Marathon... And even to this day the picture in the Painted Stoa exhibits the memorial of their valour*[410]

The painting in the Stoa is mentioned by Pausanias:

> *At the end of the painting are those who fought at Marathon; the Boeotians of Plataea and the Attic contingent are coming to blows with the foreigners.*[411]

This monument was painted in stoa at the north side of the Athenian Agora. The battle was depicted with key figures displayed prominently with heroes aiding the Greek side. It has been suggested that the manner in which the battle was depicted would have helped the development

---

[409] Aesch. *Against Ctesiphon* 186.
[410] [Dem.] *Against Neaera* 94.
[411] Paus. 1.15.3. The painting is also mentioned in numerous later sources, some of which are referenced below.

of the Marathon legend in Athens.[412] It is worthy of note that while describing the battle of Marathon Herodotus mentions the heroism of Callimachus, Stesilaus and Cynegeirus,[413] and tells the story of the blinding of Epizelus.[414] There is a strong correlation between these selected stories and what was depicted in the painting, which showed Callimachus, Cynegeirus, and Epizelus.[415] Herodotus' choice of stories to recount about the battle may have been influenced by those depicted in the painting.

The structure itself has been dated to the decade of the 460s BC due to the foundations of the building containing pottery fill belonging exclusively to this decade.[416] No consensus was reached in antiquity on who painted the depiction of the battle of Marathon which adorned the stoa's interior.[417] However, it is thought to have been painted soon after the construction of the building, between 470–450 BC.[418] The structure was originally called the 'Stoa Peisianaktos' after Peisianax, the brother in law to Kimon.[419] The dating of the picture is based on the connection between the construction and Kimon who was the leading Athenian politician between 470s and 460s BC. Furthermore the paintings themselves, both those focussed on real battles and the depictions of myth, are thought to parallel the circumstances of the defeating of the Persians by the Delian League under Kimon in the 470s and 460s BC.[420]

Based on the secure dating of the construction, the correlation between the reported painting and Herodotus' account of the battle, and modern interpretations of the paintings linking the works to the time of Kimon, this monument is accepted with confidence.

---

[412] West 1965: 47.
[413] Hdts. 6.114.
[414] Hdts. 6.117.
[415] For Callimachus and Cynegeirus being described in the painting: Ael. *On the Characteristics of Animals* 7.38, Pliny 35.57; for Epizelus: Ael. *On the Characteristics of Animals* 7.38.
[416] Shear 1984: 13-15 and 18; see also Castriota 2005: 90; this dating is also consistent with the architectural carving, see Stansbury-O'Donnell 2005: 81.
[417] West 1965: 47-48.
[418] See Castriota 2005: 90-91; Stansbury-O'Donnell 2005: 81.
[419] Plut. *Kimon* 4.5; Castriota 2005: 90.
[420] See Castriota 2005: 90, and for further references.

13. Temple of Eukleia

Pausanias mentions the Temple in the Athenian Agora:

> *Still farther on is a temple to Eukleia, this too being a thank-offering for the victory over the Persians, who had landed at Marathon. This is the victory of which I am of opinion the Athenians were proudest*[421]

Pausanias is our only source who relates the Temple for Eukleia with the battle of Marathon. Plutarch notes that Eukleia has altars and images set up in every market place in Boeotia.[422] However, the epithet Eukleia is not mentioned in known Athenian inscriptions until the 1st and 2nd centuries AD.[423] Due to the lack of evidence in support of the sole literary reference, it is only possible to accept this monument cautiously.

14. Sanctuary of Pan

Herodotus mentions the sanctuary to Pan:

> *While still in the city, the generals first sent to Sparta the herald Philippides, an Athenian and a long-distance runner who made that his calling. As Philippides himself said when he brought the message to the Athenians, when he was in the Parthenian mountain above Tegea he encountered Pan. Pan called out Philippides' name and bade him ask the Athenians why they paid him no attention, though he was of goodwill to the Athenians, had often been of service to them, and would be in the future. The Athenians believed that these things were true, and when they became prosperous they established a sacred precinct of Pan beneath the Acropolis.*[424]

Pausanias, when describing his descent from the Acropolis also mentions honours made to Pan:

> *On descending, not to the lower city, but to just beneath the Gateway, you see a fountain and near it a sanctuary of Apollo in a cave. It is here*

---

[421] Paus. 1.14.5.
[422] Plut. *Aristides* 20.6.
[423] *IG* 2^2 1035, 1.53; 3738; 4193A, 13; see also West 1965: 49.
[424] Hdts. 6.105.

that Apollo is believed to have met Creusa, daughter of Erechtheus.... when the Persians had landed in Attica Philippides was sent to carry the tidings to Lacedaemon. On his return he said that the Lacedaemonians had postponed their departure, because it was their custom not to go out to fight before the moon was full. Philippides went on to say that near Mount Parthenius he had been met by Pan, who told him that he was friendly to the Athenians and would come to Marathon to fight for them. This deity, then, has been honoured for this announcement.[425]

Herodotus states that the sanctuary is 'beneath' the Acropolis and the sanctuary of Pan is generally understood to be a cave on the northwest slope.[426] A sanctuary of Pan on the Acropolis is also mentioned by other 5th century BC authors.[427] Furthermore, a dedicatory epigram of a statue of Pan set up by Miltiades has been recorded in the Palatine Anthology.[428] Based on the literary evidence, the fact of Pan being worshipped by Athenians in the 5th century BC is not doubted.[429] On the strength of Herodotus' association of the sacred precinct of Pan with the battle of Marathon, this monument is accepted with confidence.[430]

15. Statue Group

Pausanias is the only ancient literary source who mentions this statue group that was set up at Delphi. The wooden horse mentioned is a monument dedicated by the Argives:

On the base below the wooden horse is an inscription which says that the statues were dedicated from a tithe of the spoils taken in the engagement at Marathon. They represent Athena, Apollo, and Miltiades, one of the generals. Of those called heroes there are Erechtheus, Cecrops, Pandion, Leos, Antiochus, son of Heracles by Meda, daughter of Phylas, as well as Aegeus and Acamas, one of the sons of Theseus. These heroes gave names, in obedience to a Delphic oracle, to tribes at Athens. Codrus however, the

---

[425] Paus. 1.28.4.
[426] West 1965: 50; Hurwit 2004: 229, see also Fig. 8.
[427] Eurip. *Ion* 938; Aristoph. *Lysistrata* 911.
[428] Pal. Anth. 232.
[429] West 1965:51.
[430] See chapter section 2.1 above for the confidence attributed to Herodotus as a source.

son of Melanthus, Theseus, and Philaios, these are not givers of names to tribes. The statues enumerated were made by Pheidias, and really are a tithe of the spoils of the battle.[431]

We are informed by Pausanias that this monument was made by Pheidias and therefore the monument has been dated to the 470s to 460s BC.[432] The attribution of the monument to Pheidias has been questioned on the grounds that if it commemorated Marathon it would probably have been constructed earlier and Pheidias would have been too young around 490 BC to have been offered such a prestigious commission.[433] However, other monuments commemorating Marathon were made possibly as late as 460 BC, such as the painting in the Stoa *Poikile* (see **no. 12**).

The statue group was situated on the south eastern corner of the precinct of Apollo.[434] The lower courses of the monument's base, consisting of limestone blocks, are still in position. There are dowel holes visible on the top surface of the upper course of blocks, which are slightly smaller and set back from the lower course.[435] None of the statue base remains in situ and no inscription relating to the statue group has been discovered.

The monument has been suggested as having commemorated the battle of Marathon where gods and heroes aided Miltiades and the Athenians in their victory.[436] As noted by Pausanias, seven of the ten heroes had Kleisthenic tribes named after them and instead of the three missing tribal heroes (Ajax, Oeneus, and Hippothous), Codrus, Theseus and Philaios are named. Due to Pausanias' statement that seven of the statues were eponymous heroes and in addition there were three more it is difficult

---

[431] Paus. 10.10.1-2; instead of the name Philaios, the Perseus Digital Library reports the name Neleus. For the textual emendation to Philaios see Vidal-Naquet 1986: 304-305.
[432] Morgan 1952: 314; West 1965: 53; Scott (2010: 97) also dates the monument to *c.* 460 BC; Jacquemin (1999: 315, no. 78) suggests a broader date of the second quarter of the 5th century BC.
[433] Furtwängler 1895: 55-57.
[434] For the location of the monument see Scott 2010: 102, Fig. 4.8 no. 142; the location is based on Pausanias' comment that the statue group was below the 'wooden horse', which has been interpreted as an Argive dedication (not commemorating the Persian Wars) that has been located on archaeological and inscriptional grounds. For this monument see Scott 2010: Appendix C, no. 182 and Jacquemin 1999: 313, no. 67 for further bibliography.
[435] See West 1965: 53 for a description.
[436] West 1965: 53-54.

to accept the conclusion that he was mistaken in the attributions, or the names were later altered by a careless scribe.[437] The replacement of the three of the eponymous heroes with these specific individuals has been interpreted as providing a stronger emphasis on the battle of Marathon.[438] Theseus and Philaios were ancestors of Miltiades and have been suggested as appropriate choices,[439] and Codrus has been interpreted as representing self-sacrifice as the last king who gave his life in defending Athens.[440] Through the juxtaposition of Miltiades and Codrus, it has been suggested that Kimon, who has been credited as the likely candidate for funding this public monument, would have been keen to present Miltiades (his father) as embodying the qualities necessary to die for one's country.[441]

This monument has been interpreted as part of a wider re-evaluation of the importance of the battle of Marathon by the Athenians in their own political identity, and as part of a wider set of monuments commemorating the battle raised in Athens and elsewhere at this time.[442] The monument is therefore accepted with confidence.

16. Bronze Statue of Athena

Demosthenes states clearly that the Athenians raised the statue of Athena on the Acropolis in connection with the Persian Wars:

> *Does anyone say that this inscription has been set up just anywhere? No; although the whole of our citadel is a holy place, and although its area is so large, the inscription stands at the right hand beside the great brazen Athene which was dedicated by the state as a memorial of victory in the Persian war, at the expense of the Greeks.*[443]

---

[437] As suggested by West 1965: 54.
[438] Jacquemin 1999: 191; see also Scott 2010: 97.
[439] Arrington 2014: 204; Plutarch (*Theseus* 35.5) also relates a tale that Theseus appeared as a phantom and fought at Marathon.
[440] Jacquemin 1999: 191; Arrington 2014: 204.
[441] Arrington 2014: 204; as for Miltiades' death, Herodotus (6.134, 6.136) informs us he died from a gangrenous wound he sustained (not in battle) during the siege of Paros.
[442] Scott 2010: 97; the other monuments include the Athena *Promachos* on the Acropolis (**no. 16**) and the Stoa *Poikile* in Athens (**no. 12**).
[443] Dem. *On the False Embassy* 272.

Pausanias, when describing the Athenian Acropolis, also mentions the statue on two occasions and attributes the work to Pheidias:

> In addition to the works I have mentioned, there are two tithes dedicated by the Athenians after wars. There is first a bronze Athena, tithe from the Persians who landed at Marathon. It is the work of Pheidias...[444]

Secondly:

> The Plataeans have also a sanctuary of Athena surnamed Warlike; it was built from the spoils given them by the Athenians as their share from the battle of Marathon. It is a wooden image gilded, but the face, hands and feet are of Pentelic marble. In size it is but little smaller than the bronze Athena on the Acropolis, the one which the Athenians also erected as first-fruits of the battle at Marathon; the Plataeans too had Pheidias for the maker of their image of Athena.[445]

The literary sources inform us of a colossal statue of Athena constructed on the Athenian Acropolis. However, the exact height of the figure is not stated. Pausanias does inform us that the statue's helmet crest and tip of the spear could be seen by sailors as they passed cape Sunium.[446] Furthermore, in the second of Pausanias' excerpts cited above, it is stated that the statue of Athena at Plataea (see **no. 70**) is smaller than that on the Acropolis. It has been suggested that a height of 7.5 m would have been sufficient to make the top of the statue visible from the sea.[447]

This monument is generally suggested to have been constructed in the 450s BC.[448] This conclusion is based on the survival and dating of construction accounts of the 5th century BC.[449] The accounts, which generally relate to expenditure on copper, tin and workforce wages, suggest the construction of a large bronze work, undertaken by the Athenians at public expense, and

---

[444] Paus. 1.28.2.
[445] Paus. 9.4.1.
[446] Paus. 1.28.2.
[447] Stevens 1936: 443 ff.; *contra.* Dinsmoor (1921: 118 ff.) who estimated a height of 16.36 m; it is argued that it is unlikely that this statue would be larger than the Parthenos and therefore Cullen Davison (2009: 279) and West (1965: 57) accept a height of between 7-10 m.
[448] West 1965: 58-59; Lewis 1994: 505; Cullen Davison 2009: 279-280.
[449] *IG* I^3 435.

raised on the Acropolis a little before 450 BC; the colossal bronze Athena suits this description.[450]

The poros foundations of the statue base have been located approximately 40 m east of the Propylaea, the foundations of which align almost exactly with the base.[451] Furthermore, two marble blocks, found on the Acropolis, bear a fragmentary inscription.[452] This inscription has been restored as 'The Athenians made the dedication from Median spoils'.[453] However any interpretation of the text must be seen as tentative as each block bears only three letters.[454]

In excerpts above, Pausanias states that the monument commemorates Marathon on two occasions. However Demosthenes, more generally, says the monument commemorates the defeat of the Persians. If the monument is of the 450s BC then it could be part of Kimon's efforts to embellish the Acropolis after the battle of Eurymedon, and the victory at Marathon was led by Kimon's father Miltiades.[455] Due to lack of consensus over the commemorative focus of this monument, it is attributed to the battle of Marathon tentatively.

17. 'Old' Parthenon

The Parthenon standing today was built on the foundations of an earlier temple, referred to here as the Older Parthenon.[456] It has been suggested by Dinsmoor, and subsequently followed by West, that the earlier structure was a monument to commemorate the battle of Marathon specifically.[457] Dinsmoor's general argument for attributing this structure to the commemoration of Marathon rests on the dating of the beginning of construction to just after 490 BC.[458]

---

[450] Cullen Davison 2009: 279; furthermore, a 5th century BC moulding pit has been found on the Acropolis, which would have provided a suitable site for the creation of the statue (see Zimmer 1990: 62-71).
[451] Cullen Davison 2009: 277.
[452] *IG* I^3 505.
[453] See Raubitschek and Stevens 1946: 107-114.
[454] See Cullen Davison 2009: 279-280.
[455] Cullen Davison 2009: 280.
[456] Boardman 1977: 39, and n. 3; see also Kousser 2009: 275-276.
[457] Dinsmoor 1934; West 1965: 62-63.
[458] This is followed by Kousser 2009:264, who states the building would have reached the height of the third column drum by the time of the Persian sack.

The dating for this temple is based on three main points. The building material for the structure is Pentelic marble, which became more readily available after the battle of Marathon. The potsherds found in the fill of the building's foundations date to the decade 490-480 BC specifically. Thirdly, there are traces of fire damage on this structures foundations and a layer of burned debris on top of the fill.[459] The temple is supposed to have been begun soon after Marathon and then destroyed, in an unfinished state in 480 BC. Furthermore, Dinsmoor relies on astronomical data to strengthen the case for dating the construction of this temple to the decade following the battle of Marathon. Aristides, as archon and 'overseer of public revenues',[460] may have begun the temple in 489/488 BC which would have coincided with the Panathenaic festival of 488 BC. The festival would have taken place in the month of Hecatombaion, and in 488 BC the sun rose exactly along the line of the temple's axis on the third day from the end of that month.[461]

While the evidence suggests the temple was constructed soon after Marathon, due to the lack of more affirmative evidence, this monument may only be accepted as a commemorative monument to Marathon tentatively.

18. Annual Sacrifice of 500 Kids to Artemis Agrotera

Aristophanes references the vow:

> *Agoracritus: So when I saw myself defeated by this ox dung, I outbade the fellow, crying, 'Two hundred!' And beyond this I moved that a vow be made to Diana of a thousand goats if the next day anchovies should only be worth an obol a hundred.*[462]

Xenophon also describes the vow and the alteration made after the conflict:

> *And while they had vowed to Artemis that for every man they might slay of the enemy they would sacrifice a goat to the goddess, they were unable to find goats enough; so they resolved to offer five hundred every year, and this sacrifice they are paying even to this day.*[463]

---

[459] See West 1965: 62.
[460] Plut. *Aristides* 4.2.
[461] Dinsmoor 1942: 202-206; see also West 1965: 63.
[462] Aristoph. *Knights* 658-662.
[463] Xen. *Anabasis* 3.2.12.

Plutarch's reporting of the vow, and the alteration, reaffirms the report of Xenophon:

> *For it is said that the Athenians made a vow to sacrifice so many kids to Diana Agrotera, as they should kill barbarians; but that after the fight, the number of the dead appearing infinite, they appeased the Goddess by making a decree to immolate five hundred to her every year.*[464]

Xenophon relates the form of the vow and states that it was still being repaid in his time. Despite Plutarch confirming Xenophon's details, it is Aristophanes' comedic reference to the vow which confirms the practice was instigated in the 5th century BC. On the strength of the literary evidence, this act of commemoration is accepted with confidence.

19. Temple of Nemesis with Statue of Nemesis

Pausanias is the sole literary reference for this monument:

> *About sixty stades from Marathon as you go along the road by the sea to Oropus stands Rhamnus. The dwelling houses are on the coast, but a little way inland is a sanctuary of Nemesis, the most implacable deity to men of violence. It is thought that the wrath of this goddess fell also upon the foreigners who landed at Marathon. For thinking in their pride that nothing stood in the way of their taking* **Athens***, they were bringing a piece of Parian marble to make a trophy, convinced that their task was already finished. Of this marble Pheidias made a statue of Nemesis, and on the head of the goddess is a crown with deer and small images of Victory.*[465]

The temple of Nemesis at Rhamnus has been dated to the 430s BC on grounds of architectural style.[466] The statue of Nemesis within this temple, according to Pausanias, was made from the stone brought to Marathon by the Persians. Pausanias states that the statue can be attributed to Pheidias but it has been asserted that it is more likely the work of his student Agoracritos of Paros and may not have been constructed until the

---

[464] Plut. *On the Malice of Herodotus* 26.
[465] Paus. 1.33.2-3.
[466] See Dinsmoor (1950: 181-183) who states the building shows the influence of the 'new' Parthenon and may the work of the architect who constructed the Hephaesteion in Athens.

420s BC.[467] The statue would have stood at about twice life size and stood on a pediment which bore relief sculpture on its sides.[468] The relief, also described by Pausanias, depicts Helen being led to Nemesis by her mother Leda; the action is being watched by others such as Tyndareus, the Dioscuri, Menelaus, Agamemnon, and Pyhrrus son of Achilles.[469]

These reliefs have been interpreted as Helen's homecoming after Troy and, furthermore, symbolically connected with the Persian Wars because it may be understood as Helen being led to Nemesis in retribution for the Persian invasion.[470] Herter cautiously believes that the statue and temple commemorate the battle of Marathon specifically, opposed to the Persian Wars in general.[471] This conclusion is drawn by combining the Persian Wars association of the relief and Pausanias' assertions about the statue's marble.

The association with Marathon is cast in some doubt considering the sole late literary reference and late dates for the temple and statue. However, monuments which commemorated Marathon were being constructed in the 460s BC. This monument is therefore accepted tentatively.

20. Statue of Arimnestos

Pausanias mentions this statue while describing what is inside the temple of Athena *Areia* at Plataea:[472]

> *In the temple are paintings. These paintings are on the walls of the foretemple, while at the feet of the image is a portrait of Arimnestos, who commanded the Plataeans at the battle against Mardonius, and yet before that at Marathon.*[473]

---

[467] Richter 1950: 240-242.
[468] West 1965: 69; a fragment of the statue's head is held in the British Museum, see Smith 1892: 1.264-265, no. 460 who catalogues the fragment under the sculptor 'Agoracritos of Paros' and attributes the fragment to him on stylistic grounds, material of fragment, and location of find; for discussion and images of the fragment see Despines 1971: 45-50 pl. 54-55 who also dates the statue to *c*. 430 BC on stylistic grounds.
[469] Paus. 1.33.8; for discussion and reconstruction of the base see Lapatin 1992, with further bibliography.
[470] Svoronos 1909: 1.167-179, nos. 203-214.
[471] Herter 1935: 2351-2352; this view is also followed by West 1965: no. 23.
[472] For the temple of Athena *Areia* see **no. 70**.
[473] Paus. 9.4.2.

Pausanias refers to Arimnestos as the leader of the Plataean forces at Marathon. However, Arimnestos is not mentioned as a commander at Marathon by either Plutarch or Herodotus, and is connected only with the battle of Plataea by these authors.[474] These references need not contradict Pausanias as his specific reference to Marathon may have been prompted by an inscription on the statue's base.[475] Furthermore, West suggests that during the 460s BC the Athenians constructed a statue group at Delphi which included their Marathon commander Miltiades (who did not die there), and around this time the Plataeans could have honoured their Marathon commander also at this time.[476]

Pausanias is our sole literary source for this monument. On the strength of Pausanias' statement, this monument is attributed to the commemorations of Marathon, but may have possibly served a dual commemorative focus by incorporating the later battle of Plataea. The lack of earlier literary evidence concerning the monument and the lack of references to connect Arimnestos with Marathon prevent attributing this monument with any confidence.

ARTEMISIUM

21. A Circle of Marble Steles with an Epigram

The monument was set up by Athenians in the precinct of Artemis *Proseoa* at Artemisium, as Plutarch describes:

> *It has a small temple of Artemis surnamed Proseoa, which is surrounded by trees and enclosed by upright slabs of white marble. This stone, when you rub it with your hand, gives off the colour and the odour of saffron. On one of these slabs the following elegy was inscribed:*
>
> *Nations of all sorts of men from Asia's boundaries coming,*
> *Sons of the Athenians once, here on this arm of the sea, Whelmed in a battle of ships, and the host of the Medes was destroyed;*
> *These are the tokens thereof, built for the Maid Artemis.*
> *And a place is pointed out on the shore, with sea sand all about it, which*

---

[474] Hdts. 9.72; Plut. *Aristides* 11.5.
[475] Suggested by West 1965: 73.
[476] West 1965: 73.

supplies from its depths a dark ashen powder, apparently the product of fire, and here they are thought to have burned their wrecks and dead bodies.[477]

Plutarch also mentions the inscription in his tirade against Herodotus:

Is then this a fellow fit to be believed when he writes of any man or city, who in one word deprives Greece of the victory, throws down the trophy, and pronounces the inscriptions they had set up to Artemis Proseoa (eastward-looking) to be nothing but pride and vain boasting?[478]

It is curious that Plutarch describes this dedication as a 'trophy'. This monument is not a trophy in the usual sense but is a circle of marble steles upon one of which an epigram is inscribed.[479] Since the steles do not stand over the graves of the fallen it cannot be considered an epitaph;[480] it is a dedicatory inscription, concerning the exploits of the Athenian sailors. To take Plutarch's phrase 'trophy' literally, Athens may have erected a temporary trophy that was later transformed into a permanent trophy (as Plutarch saw it). Neither side were defeated at Artemisium, so it is possible that both sides claimed the victory. It has been suggested that one of the steles may have been raised there originally and the others were added later for unknown reasons when the trophy was rebuilt;[481] however the date of the epigram is uncertain.[482]

Due to the lack of contemporary sources relating to battlefield monuments at Artemisium this monument may only be accepted cautiously.

---

[477] Plut. *Themistocles*. 8.2-3.
[478] Plut. *On the Malice of Herodotus*. 34. Plutarch quotes the inscription identically in both excerpts.
[479] West 1965: 145.
[480] See Jacoby 1945: 157, n. 3.
[481] West 1965: 145.
[482] Hiller (1926: 14) when relating the poem includes the date of 480/479 BC in the title, without further justification; the poem has also been published by Page 1981: XXIV, who does not discuss authenticity.

22. Shrine to Boreas

Herodotus mentions a shrine being constructed to Boreas for aid at Artemisium:

> I cannot say whether this was the cause of Boreas falling upon the barbarians as they lay at anchor, but the Athenians say that he had come to their aid before and that he was the agent this time. When they went home, they founded a sacred precinct of Boreas beside the Ilissus river.[483]

Pausanias mentions the tie between the Athenians and Boreas:

> The rivers that flow through Athenian territory are the Ilissus and its tributary the Eridanus, whose name is the same as that of the Celtic river. This Ilissus is the river by which Oreithyia was playing when, according to the story, she was carried off by the North Wind. With Oreithyia he lived in wedlock, and because of the tie between him and the Athenians he helped them by destroying most of the foreigners' warships.[484]

The two literary sources, one of which is from the 5th century BC, appear to complement one another, therefore on the strength of the literary evidence this monument is accepted here with confidence.

THERMOPYLAE

23. Epigram for the Spartiates

Herodotus describes how the Spartans have an inscription which commemorates them alone at the battlefield of Thermopylae:

> Go tell the Spartans, thou that passest by,
> That here obedient to their words we lie.[485]

This epigram is also quoted by Lycurgus and other later sources:

> Go tell the Spartans, thou that passest by,
> That here obedient to their laws we lie.[486]

---

[483] Hdts. 7.189.3.
[484] Paus. 1.19.5.
[485] Hdts. 7.228.2.
[486] Lyc. *Against Leocrates* 109; see also Diod. 11.33.2 and Strabo 9.4.16.

After recording the inscription, Herodotus states that the Amphictyons had the epigram inscribed.[487] The Herodotean version of this famous epigram differs somewhat from that related by Lycurgus, Diodorus and Strabo. Lycurgus *et al* mention 'laws' (*nomimois*), whereas Herodotus uses 'words' (*rēmasi*). West judges Herodotus' account of the inscription correct, but bases this on Herodotus having visited the battlefield, which is uncertain.[488] Herodotus does not state that he has seen this epigram himself, or the epigram to the Peloponnesians (**no. 24**). It has been argued that Herodotus relied on Spartan sources for the information regarding the battle of Thermopylae, and the recounting of solely Spartan and Peloponnesian epigrams represents information given by highly prejudiced informants.[489] It should be noted that Herodotus is 90 degrees out on his orientation of the battlefield, which he states runs north to south.[490] This mistake indicates that if he did visit the area he probably did not spend much time there.[491]

It is unclear whether Herodotus actually visited the battlefield; however he was, at least, informed about the existence of the epigrams which are confirmed by later sources (albeit containing slight amendments). Therefore, on the strength of the 5th century BC literary reference, and the general consensus of later authors, this monument is accepted with confidence.

24. Epigram for the Peloponnesians

Herodotus describes how all the Greeks who fell at Thermopylae were buried where they fell and reports a general inscription over the dead:

Four thousand warriors, flower of Pelops' land,
Did here against three hundred myriads stand.[492]

---

[487] Hdts. 7.228.4.
[488] West 1965: 183.
[489] Page 1981: 233.
[490] Hdts. 7.176.
[491] Whether Herodotus spent long enough at the battlefield to copy the inscriptions is not possible to prove; see West 1985: 289.
[492] Hdts. 7.228.1. See also Diod. 11.33.2; Aristides 49.380; and the *Pal. Anth.* 7.248.

After recording the inscription, Herodotus states that the Amphictyons had the epigram inscribed.[493] This epigram, and indeed all monuments memorialising this battle, was almost certainly erected after the battle of Plataea as the Thermopylae pass would have been under enemy control. The troop numbers cited (4000 Greeks) agrees with Herodotus' numbers and may be the source of his information while Herodotus' estimation of the Persian numbers is lower.[494] The Thespians, Thebans, Lokrians and Phokians are excluded in this general epigram. On the strength of Herodotus' assertion that the epigram stood on the battlefield at Thermopylae, this monument is accepted here with confidence (see **no. 23** for discussion on whether Herodotus visited the battlefield).

However, as the epigram does not mention the dead specifically, Wade-Gery says this inscription would not have been an epitaph, and that the inscription did not belong to a grave, it merely marked a battlefield.[495] At the conclusion of the battle, the Persians were left in control of the field, and it would have been a good deal later that the bodies were buried and later still that the Amphictyons erected monuments.[496]

25. Epigram for the Opuntian Locrians

Strabo, in describing the geography of the Opuntian gulf, mentions five steles and is the only reference for the Opuntian inscription. Strabo states the inscription is 15 stades from the sea, and 60 stades from the sea port.

> *Opoeis, metropolis of the Locrians of righteous laws,*
> *Mourns for these who perished in defence of Greece against the Medes.*[497]

Strabo is the only source for this epigram and the fact that five steles are present. Due to Herodotus' silence regarding this monument, it may have been a later addition to the site (see **no. 23** for discussion on whether Herodotus visited the battlefield). After fighting alongside the Spartans at Thermopylae, Opus surrendered to the Persians and, in constructing this

---

[493] Hdts. 7.228.4.
[494] Greek forces: Hdts. 7.202-203; Persian forces: Hdts. 7.185-186.
[495] Wade-Gery 1933: 72.
[496] See Wade-Gery 1933: 72; Macan 1908: 1.335.
[497] Strabo 9.4.2.

monument, may have attempted to emphasise their earlier efforts in the defence of Greece.[498]

According to Herodotus the Opuntians were present at the defence of the Thermopylae pass;[499] however Herodotus who describes other monuments at the site fails to mention this epigram. Therefore, due to the late date of the sole literary reference to this monument, it may only be accepted tentatively.

26. Epigram for the Thespians

Stephanus of Byzantium provides us with the Thespian epigram at Thermopylae:

> *Men that in life beneath the heights abode*
> *Of Helikon; whose pride makes Thespiai proud.*[500]

The epigram is attributed to the otherwise unknown Philaidas of Megara. The attribution to an obscure poet from Megara has been interpreted to suggest the poem was demonstrative rather than inscriptional, and preserved solely in an anthology.[501] If the poem were inscribed, the author most probably would not have signed it. Therefore it has been deemed unlikely, the otherwise unknown, Philaidas would have been the recognised author of the epigram in the sole source dating to some 1000 years after the battle of Thermopylae.[502]

Whether the poem was inscribed or not, it has been suggested that it is incomplete; Hiller believes that the epigram originally consisted of two distichs and the first one is missing.[503] Conversely, Page suggests that the lines as we have them read like a beginning and at least one couplet would have certainly followed.[504] No consensus may be drawn where the distich we have would have fitted in to the poem as a whole.

---

[498] Medising: Hdts. 7.132, 8.66, 9.31; see also West 1965: xxxvi.
[499] Hdts. 7.203.1.
[500] Steph. Byz. s.v. *Thespeia*; translation in Wade-Gery 1933: 76.
[501] Page 1981: I, 78.
[502] Page 1981: I, 78.
[503] Hiller 1926: 19.
[504] Page 1981: I, 78.

The sole reference for this monument is late and the epigram is attributed to an otherwise unknown source. Furthermore, the poem itself appears to be incomplete. Therefore, it is not possible to accept this monument with any confidence.

27. Stone Lion

Herodotus provides us with a vague positioning for the stone lion:

> *This hill is at the mouth of the pass, where the stone lion in honour of Leonidas now stands.*[505]

Herodotus states that the stone lion, which stood in honour of Leonidas, was erected upon the hillock to which the Spartans retreated to make their last stand on realisation they were surrounded. It is not clear who erected the monument but it would be safe to assume it was the Spartans. However, it could also have been the Amphictyons as they had erected the stele for the Spartans in general (**no. 23**). Leonidas was buried on the battlefield and Pausanias informs us that in c. 440 BC (40 years after battle) his remains were reburied at Sparta (see **no. 29** for discussion on this dating).[506] It has been suggested that Herodotus' phrase '*epi Leōnidē*' should be read as 'over Leonidas' grave' which allows for the, arguably more practical, interpretation that the monument was only erected after Leonidas' body was moved.[507]

On identifying the mound upon which the Greek forces at Thermopylae made their last stand, Clarke mentions traces of a pedestal which may have served as the base for a monument.[508] Foundations of Leonidas' monument has been identified as the partial remains of a rectangular foundation on Stahlin's 'Hill 1'.[509] The north and north-west sides are missing but the south side is 14m long and the east side is 11.55 m long, built of large stones 0.4 m high, 1.1 m long and 0.57 m thick. The wall is primarily of limestone with a mixture of breccia and sandstone and, as it is not joined with mortar,

---

[505] Hdts. 7.225.2.
[506] Paus. 3.14.1.
[507] West 1965: 185.
[508] Clarke 1818: 7.305-310.
[509] Kroll and Mittelhaus 1934: 2414.

could well be 5th century BC. The disappearance of the stone lion set up for Leonidas has been put down to structural developments undertaken upon the kolonos in the Roman and Byzantine periods.[510] However, it is worth noting that no sources reference this specific monument at Thermopylae after Herodotus.

Herodotus' reference to a monument in the 5th century BC provides a certain level of confidence for attribution (however, see **no. 23** for discussion on whether Herodotus visited the battlefield), which is further confirmed by the identification of a suitable monument base at the site. Therefore, this monument is accepted with confidence.

28. Burial Mound

The hillock upon which the Spartans made their last stand was identified by Dodwell as a 'green hillock, with a house upon its summit, which was once a *derveni*, or custom house.'[511] The topographical information presented in Dodwell's description is vague but the stone foundations present on the hillock today may have served as those of the custom house. In addition, Dodwell presumes the hillock would have acted as the Greek sepulchre as it is probable they were buried where they fell.[512] In contrast to Dodwell, Clarke, who also describes visiting the site of Thermopylae and identifying the hillock, mentions the remains of some pedestal which may have served as a foundation for a monument but makes no mention of an extant building, it is probable that Clarke wrote of a different mound.[513] William Leake, on travelling through the Thermopylae pass mentions, in no great detail, the hillock upon which the Greeks were thought to have made their last stand against the Persians. Leake refers to the hillock as a 'remarkable rock' upon which are the 'remains of ancient monuments'.[514]

In 1929, excavations were undertaken at Thermopylae by Spyridon Marinatos which led to the identification of the hillock being moved from the western end of the pass, by the Phokian wall, to the eastern end; this idea contrasted with earlier unsuccessful excavations at the western end

---

[510] Robertson 1939: 200; Luce *et al.* 1939: 700.
[511] Dodwell 1819: 2.67.
[512] Dodwell 1819: 2.68.
[513] Clarke 1818: 7.305-310.
[514] Leake 1835: 5; see also Gell 1827: 238-239.

of the pass.[515] Upon the hill, known as the *kolonos* today, many arrow heads were discovered and have been compared to the finds unearthed at the Marathon *soros* and are nearly all dated to the 5th century BC.[516] In addition to the multitude of arrow heads, which goes some way to confirming Herodotus' account of the final Persian assault one Persian spear head was found and a Greek spear butt strengthening the identification of the *kolonos*.[517] No bones were recovered as the 5th century BC stratum is below water level.[518] Remains of fortifications were located on the hillock and are thought to have been the result of multiple building programs dating to the Hellenistic period. Coins and masses of pottery dating to a similar period were also found.[519] During the Roman and Byzantine periods the hill was used for dwelling with the remains of houses, tiles and tombs being visible.[520] The remains of fortifications and houses visible to Marinatos could validate the observations made by Dodwell and Leake and further support the claim that Clarke was indeed describing a separate hill.

On the strength of the archaeological evidence, which connects the *kolonos* with the hill of the Greeks' last stand, and that Herodotus informs us the Greeks were buried where they fell;[521] this monument is accepted here with confidence.

29. Tomb of Leonidas

Pausanias mentions this tomb when describing Sparta:

> *On going westwards from the market-place is a cenotaph of Brasidas the son of Tellis. Not far from it is the theatre, made of white marble and worth seeing. Opposite the theatre are two tombs; the first is that of Pausanias, the general at Plataea, the second is that of Leonidas. The bones of Leonidas were taken by Pausanias from Thermopylae forty years after the battle.*[522]

---

[515] Robertson 1939: 200; Luce *et al.* 1939: 700.
[516] Robertson 1939: 200; Luce *et al.* 1939: 700.
[517] Final Persian assault: Hdts. 7.225.3; Persian spear head: Robertson 1939: 200; Luce *et al.* 1939: 700; spear butt: Robertson 1939: 200.
[518] See Kraft *et al.* 1987, for the geological changes to the Thermopylae area.
[519] Luce *et al.* 1939: 700.
[520] Robertson 1939: 200; Luce *et al.* 1939: 700.
[521] Hdts 7.228.1.
[522] Paus. 3.14.1.

Pausanias states that Leonidas' body was returned to Sparta some 40 years after the battle of Thermopylae, which is *c.* 440 BC. Pausanias, the author, notes that the body was brought back to Sparta by Pausanias. This Pausanias (the Spartan) may be interpreted as the son of Pleistoanax, who ruled as King between 408–394 BC.[523] However Pausanias (the Spartan), when very young, also held kingly power between 445–426 BC, when his father Pleistoanax was banned from kingship for an unsuccessful Attic campaign.[524] If Pausanias (the author) is correct in dating the removal of Leonidas' body to 40 years after the battle of Thermopylae, this would coincide with the Spartan Pausanias' early reign in place of his father. It should be noted, however, that the Spartan Pausanias was still a minor in 427 BC as Cleomenes, his uncle, led the Spartan forces as regent during the campaign of that year.[525] Pausanias' young age, particularly around 440 BC therefore, conflicts with Pausanias' statement that the bones were 'taken by' him. It has been suggested that the '40 years' was a late corruption of Pausanias' text which had originally read 'four years'.[526] The removal of Leonidas' body four years after Thermopylae would place the move within the lifetime of the Spartan general Pausanias, who led the Spartans at Plataea.

Herodotus does not mention Leonidas' tomb although it is likely he visited Sparta and saw a list of names of those who fought at Thermopylae (see **no. 30**). However, it is possible Herodotus visited Sparta before 440 BC and so would have missed Leonidas' reburial. A cult of Leonidas was later developed, which would have included athletic contests.[527]

In lieu of any firm evidence to contradict Pausanias' dating of the repatriation of Leonidas' bones, and the suggested dating coinciding with Pausanias' (the Spartan) initial reign in place of his father, the date of *c.* 440 BC is accepted here. However, the date of Leonidas' body being removed from the battlefield is not beyond doubt, and the literary reference to the monument is late, therefore this allows for only tentative acceptance of this monument.

---

[523] West 1965: 119.
[524] Thuc. 2.21; 5.16.
[525] Thuc. 3.26; West 1965: 120.
[526] See Macan 1908: 1.352.
[527] As attested in the late 1st century AD inscription *IG* 5^1 658.

30. List of Spartans Who Fought at Thermopylae

Pausanias, when describing the area in Sparta near the theatre, mentions the inscribed list:

There is set up a slab with the names, and their fathers' names, of those who endured the fight at Thermopylae against the Persians.[528]

Pausanias' description of this stele follows directly on from his mentioning Leonidas' tomb, and so may be interpreted as having been erected nearby. Herodotus does not mention this stele but claims to know the names of each of the 300 Spartans and so may have seen this stele when in Sparta.[529]

However, it is possible that this list of names was constructed at a later date.[530] If this monument was a construction of, perhaps, the Roman period it would stand as a testament to the surviving commemorative tradition of the Thermopylae war dead. Furthermore, honouring the war dead as a collective (the '300') and as individuals (being named) within the Spartan urban centre was unique amongst the Spartan monuments represented in this study. The combination of public commemoration and individualisation afforded to the Thermopylae war dead was more than was usually available to the Spartan war dead.[531] Therefore if this monument was a later construction, the anomalous practice of individualising collective war dead commemorations at Sparta may also have developed later.

The acceptance of this monument is tentative because we are reliant solely on one late source and the type of monument is anomalous to the otherwise attested Spartan commemorative practices.

---

[528] Paus. 3.14.1.
[529] Hdts. 7.224.1.
[530] See Low 2011: 6; for example the interest in the Persian Wars during the Roman period is well attested, see Alcock 2002: 74-86.
[531] Individual commemorations at Sparta were scattered and associated with private commemorations, while collective war dead commemorations would focus on the mass, effacing the individual (see Low 2011: 6).

31. Shrine of Maron and Alpheius

Pausanias describes this shrine:

> There is also a sanctuary of Maron and of Alpheius. Of the Lacedaemonians who served at Thermopylae they consider that these men distinguished themselves in the fighting more than any save Leonidas himself.[532]

Pausanias states that this shrine was situated on the Aphetaid road leading from the market, upon which were many shrines, sanctuaries and tombs.[533] Herodotus agrees with Pausanias that Maron and Alpheius distinguished themselves at Thermopylae but does not mention the shrine.[534]

The particular mention awarded to these two warriors is consistent in the literary sources, of both the classical period and later, however the date of the monument itself is uncertain. Due to the sole literary reference to this monument being late and the uncertainty of the date, it may only be accepted tentatively.

32. Hero-cult Practices for the Fallen

Diodorus is our sole reference for this poem:

> And, speaking in general terms, these men alone of the Greeks down to their time passed into immortality because of their exceptional valour. Consequently not only the writers of history but also many of our poets have celebrated their brave exploits; and one of them is Simonides, the lyric poet, who composed the following encomium in their praise, worthy of their valour:
>
> 'Of those who perished at Thermopylae
> All glorious is the fortune, fair the doom;
> Their grave's an altar, ceaseless memory's theirs
> Instead of lamentation, and their fate
> Is chant of praise. Such winding-sheet as this

---

[532] Paus. 3.12.9.
[533] See Paus. 3.12.8-9; West 1965: 121.
[534] Hdts. 7.227.

> Nor mould nor all-consuming time shall waste.
> This sepulchre of valiant men has taken
> The fair renown of Hellas for its inmate.
> And witness is Leonidas, once king
> Of Sparta, who hath left behind a crown
> Of valour mighty and undying fame.'[535]

Diodorus states this poem is the work of Simonides, and it has been suggested that it was produced in the decade following the culmination of the Persian Wars.[536] It has further been suggested that '[t]heir grave's an altar' may indicate that the poem is performed away from Thermopylae and the actual tomb of the dead, and the tomb is therefore represented by an altar.[537] If this is an accurate reading of the text, the performance would have been most appropriate near the tomb of Leonidas, with the stele bearing the names of the 300 nearby.[538]

While Diodorus attributes this poem to Simonides, the late date of the sole reference to the poem, and the lack of supporting evidence, allows for a tentative acceptance of the monument here.

33. Epigram for Leonidas

This epigram is recorded in the Palatine Anthology:

> *Leonidas, King of spacious Sparta, illustrious are they who died with thee and are buried here.*
> *They faced in battle with the Medes the force of multitudinous bows and of steeds fleet of foot.*[539]

The epigram addresses Leonidas himself, and it has therefore been suggested that the poem may have been inscribed on Leonidas' tomb itself in Sparta.[540] The poem also references the other Spartans who died at Thermopylae; the practice of commemorating the war dead in the Spartan

---

[535] Diod. 11.11.6.
[536] Bowra 1933: 277-281; see also West 1965: 122 for further references.
[537] West 1965: 123.
[538] West 1965: 123.
[539] Pal. Anth. 7.301.
[540] West 1965: 124.

urban centre would fit in with the general Spartan commemorative practice of honouring the dead within this site type (see **no. 30**, which may have been situated close by). However it has also been suggested, on the strength of the references to the war dead, there is no reason why it could not have stood at Thermopylae.[541] The monument is believed here (albeit tentatively) to have been raised in Sparta due to the explicit reference to Leonidas whose body was, apparently, repatriated some time during the 5th century BC (see **no. 29**).

The Palatine Anthology attributes this poem to Simonides; however we cannot be certain of the author. Furthermore, it has been suggested that due to the epigram being of 'mediocre' quality, it is probably from the later Hellenistic period.[542] There is no physical evidence to confirm the accuracy, original location, or indeed existence of this epigram and, therefore, this monument may not be accepted with confidence.

SALAMIS

34. Trophy on the Island of Psyttaleia

Plutarch, in describing the hoplite assault on the Persian troops stationed on Psyttaleia, says a trophy was erected on the island because the most strenuous part of the fighting was in the region:

> *For the greatest crowding of the ships, and the most strenuous part of the battle, seems to have been in this region. And for this reason a trophy was erected on Psyttaleia.*[543]

Pausanias, in stark contrast, makes the point that Psyttaleia has no commemorative structure but only some crude statues:

> *The island [Psyttaleia] has no artistic statue, only some roughly carved wooden images of Pan.*[544]

---

[541] See Molyneux 1992: 181; *contra*. Page 1981: VII, who states that there would be no room for the inscribed stele bearing this epigram considering Strabo's statement (9.4.2) that there were only five inscribed steles on the battlefield.
[542] See Page 1981: VII.
[543] Plut. *Aristides* 9.2.
[544] Paus. 1.36.2.

Wallace and Vanderpool obtained permission to investigate the north side of this island.[545] On investigating the promontory which juts out towards Cynosoura, at the very extreme point where the island and Cynosoura are closest, the pair uncovered the remains of a foundation which would have been capable of holding a stone monument of similar proportions to that at Marathon. Wallace concedes that, taken alone, this evidence is not enough to indicate that the monument stood at this spot; however, considering the possible position of the Salamis trophy across the narrowest point in the stretch of water (see **no. 35**), one may surmise the Athenians were aware of the importance the geography of the area played in their victory over the Persians.[546] Furthermore, if Plutarch's statement is accepted, that the most strenuous part of the battle took place off the island of Psyttaleia, then the construction of a trophy on the coastline would correspond with the practice of constructing trophies on the nearest shore to the naval conflict.[547]

Considering the inconclusive archaeological evidence, and the conflicting literary sources, this monument may only be accepted tentatively.

35. Trophy on the Island of Salamis (Cynosoura)

Pausanias mentions the existence of a trophy:

In Salamis...is a sanctuary of Artemis, and also a trophy erected in honour of the victory which Themistocles, the son of Neocles, won for the Greeks.[548]

In addition to Pausanias' reference, Plutarch also mentions the trophy by relating how, on being asked to move wings by the Spartans before Plataea, the Athenians are persuaded to face the Persians.[549] Plutarch depicts the Athenians spreading the word that the coming battle at Plataea would not only be for land and city but for the trophies at Marathon and Salamis. The soldiers are thus reminded that the earlier victories against the Persians were not only Miltiades' victories, but Athens'. Also, as mentioned above in reference to the Marathon trophy (see **no. 3**), Plato mentions the trophy

---

[545] Wallace 1969.
[546] Wallace 1969: on the debate over the island Psyttaleia see 293-299; on the discovery of foundation stones see 302.
[547] Pritchett 1974: 2.260; see also the discussion on trophies in chapter section 4.2.2.
[548] Paus. 1.36.1.
[549] Plut. *Aristides* 16.3-4.

during a justification of not sending aid to the Persian King in fear of disgracing the trophies of Marathon, Salamis and Plataea.[550]

A trophy certainly existed in Pausanias' time and therefore if an immediate degradable trophy, possibly in the form of a trireme, was erected immediately after the battle, as was the custom, it must have been rebuilt in stone.[551] It has been argued that the restored, permanent monument was erected in the town of Salamis;[552] 'en Salamini' could be interpreted both 'on' and 'in Salamis'. However the publication of two 18th century travellers presents a testimony which certainly supports the view that the *tropaion* stood on Cynosoura:

> Some fragments of an ancient column of white marble, which are yet remaining on Punto Barbaro and promontory of Salamis, at the entrance to the straights which separate that island from the continent of Attica. They are probably the remains of a trophy erected for the victory at Salamis. These fragments are yet very discernible from Athens, and must have been much more so when the column was entire. The monument of and victory, which had established the liberties of Greece, and in which the Athenians had acquired the greatest glory, must have been to them a most pleasing and a most interesting object; and we may for that reason conclude, that they placed it in and part of the island, where those who viewed it from Athens, might see it to the greatest advantage; which intention this situation perfectly answers.[553]

Chandler also attests to examining some worked stones and a 'fragment or two of marble' while exploring Cynosoura and supposed they belonged to the monument erected at the defeat of the Persian forces.[554]

The remains found by the 18th century travellers can be attested by Wallace and Vanderpool who were given special permission to examine the promontory. Wallace reported that nearing the extreme end of Cynosoura a cutting in the bedrock was discovered, measuring c. 1.8m². Other worked stone blocks lay strewn around the area (see Figure 11) with evidence of the removal of many. Wallace suggests that this space, with its near proximity to the

---
[550] Plato *Menexenus* 245a.
[551] Possibly the trireme dedicated to Ajax on Salamis, Hdts. 8.121; see West 1969: 16.
[552] Hammond 1956: 53-54.
[553] Stuart and Revett 1762: ix.
[554] Chandler 1776: 202; see also Gell 1827: 303.

Figure 11. Squared block on Salamis (author's own photograph).

extremity of the promontory and so as close to Athens and Psyttaleia as possible, could have been the site of Themistocles' trophy.[555] Cynosoura was to become known as Cape *Tropaia* evidently, it seems, due to the monument constructed at its tip. It is suggested by West that the Salamis trophy was transformed from a perishable trophy to a permanent monument in the 5th century BC possibly before the Peloponnesian War.[556] In Book One of Thucydides, Marathon and Salamis are singled out as the decisive battles of the Persian Wars.[557] The land battle at Plataea where Sparta played the leading role is apparently side-lined in Athenian victorious self-representation. Thus, with Salamis playing a central role alongside Marathon as key Athenian victories, one may infer that permanent monuments were erected at these sites of conflict.

Due to the consensus of later literary sources that a trophy stood at Salamis, in addition to Thucydides' assertion that Salamis played a central role in 5th century BC Athenian self-representation, and the remnants of an ancient structure at the tip of the Cynosoura, this monument is accepted with confidence.

---

[555] To further contrast with Hammond's point of view see Wallace 1969: 302.
[556] West 1969: 17.
[557] Thuc. 1.73.2-73.4.

36. Gravestone with Epitaph for the Corinthians Buried on Salamis

The epigram is mentioned by Plutarch:

> *And in Salamis they had permitted them to bury the dead near the city, as being men who had behaved themselves gallantly, and to write over them this elegy:*

> *Well-watered Corinth, stranger, was our home;*
> *Salamis, Ajax's isle, is now our grave;*
> *Here Medes and Persians and Phoenician ships*
> *We fought and routed, sacred Greece to save.*[558]

The epigram survives and is currently held in the Athens Epigraphical Museum.[559]

The preserved stele is inscribed with the first couplet only. The identification of this inscription has been the cause of some debate. It has been argued that the first couplet is considered ancient while the second is probably a forgery and possibly a late, literary addition.[560] Jeffery, on the other hand, states the date for this inscription is beyond question (480/479 BC).[561] Carpenter, in his otherwise flattering review of Jeffery's work on the local scripts of archaic Greece, strongly contests the identification of this inscription. It is argued that as the closing couplet has been identified as a literary addition and was never inscribed on the stone, the object bears no reference to the battle of Salamis and need not have any connection to it.[562]

The poem, as recounted by Plutarch, has been argued by Page to have once been inscribed on the surviving stele.[563] The stone is smoothly finished well below the area which is inscribed today, which provides enough space to have held another couplet. Furthermore, it has been suggested that it is fairly common (although not invariable) for epitaphs to state the cause of death of, or

---

[558] Plut. *On the Malice of Herodotus* 39.
[559] EM 22. Image provided *LSAG* pl. 21, Corinth 29. See also *IG* I³ 1143; *SEG* 10.404a. See also a translation by Bowra 1938: 189.
[560] Bowra 1938: 189; *GHI* 16.
[561] *LSAG* 120.
[562] Carpenter 1963: 81-82, who also argues that the style of the lettering suggests a 7th century BC date.
[563] See Page 1981: XI.

Figure 12. Corinthian epitaph from Salamis (author's own photograph).

the specific enemies fought by, the men that are being honoured.[564] Although a specific date is not offered by Page, the distinction between the Persians and the Medes, 'points to the early date' for the second couplet.[565]

Despite the inscribed stone having been discovered, the authenticity is not beyond doubt. The lack of the second distich, as reported in the literary evidence, has caused some difficulty in accepting the monument with confidence. Furthermore, no consensus has been reached about either the date of the inscription or indeed the original existence of a second distich. Due to the inconsistencies between the archaeological and literary evidence, therefore, this stele may only be accepted tentatively as a monument commemorating the Persian Wars.

---

[564] See **nos. 6, 7, 21, 24, 25** and **52**, for examples of inscriptions also raised on the battlefield referencing the specific enemy fought and/or the Greek dead.

[565] Page 1981: XI, 202 and 204, argues that the later the composition the greater the improbability of a writer using the same term 'within the same breath'. Aeschylus only twice uses 'Mede' as a synonym for 'Persian' (*The Persians* 236, 791). Furthermore, Herodotus generally calls the invaders 'Medes' and distinguishes between them and 'Persians' only when it is necessary (e.g. 7.211, 9.31) or convenient (8.89, 9.40).

37. Burial Mound

In a short chapter discussing the island of Salamis, primarily in the context of the Persian conflict there in 480 BC, Gell mentions seeing a tumulus at the base of the Cynosoura but fails to identify it as the Greek burial mound.[566] Frazer also noted the tumulus but identified this mound as prehistoric whereas, only a few years later, the eminent German topographer, Milchhoefer identified the tumulus as that of the Greeks who died during the sea battle at Salamis.[567] Pritchett, on examining the site, was unable to find any prehistoric sherds to confirm Frazer's theory and so, while having agreed the mound is artificial, discounted the suggestion of such an early date and tentatively followed Milchhoefer's identification.[568]

There is no literary evidence for the mass burial of Greek soldiers after the battle of Salamis. However, a 1st century AD inscription concerning the

Figure 13. Burial Mound on Salamis (author's own photograph).

---

[566] Gell 1827: 303.
[567] Prehistoric dating: Frazer 1965: 2.478; period of the Persian Wars: Milchhoefer 1904: Heft VII-VIII, 28-29.
[568] Pritchett 1965: 1.96.

restoration of sanctuaries in Attica mentions the Salamis promontory on which is situated the trophy of Themistocles and a *polyandrion*.[569]

Due to the lack of affirmative evidence this monument may not be accepted confidently. However, the structure that is today marked as a commemorative monument to Salamis is an artificial mound in the proximity of the site of conflict, which would accord with treatment of the war dead from other battles of the Persian Wars. The monument is therefore accepted tentatively.

38. Tomb of Themistocles

Thucydides praises Themistocles heavily and mentions his bones were brought home from Persian territory after his death:

> *His bones, it is said, were conveyed home by his relatives in accordance with his wishes, and interred in Attic ground. This was done without the knowledge of the Athenians; as it is against the law to bury in Attica an outlaw for treason.*[570]

Plutarch describes a structure thought to be the tomb of Themistocles:

> *Diodorus the Topographer, in his work 'On Tombs,' says, by conjecture rather than from actual knowledge, that near the large harbour of the Piraeus a sort of elbow juts out from the promontory opposite Alcimus, and that as you round this and come inside where the water of the sea is still, there is a basement of goodly size, and that the altar-like structure upon this is the tomb of Themistocles.*[571]

Thucydides describes Themistocles' burial in Attica as a private matter without the knowledge of the Athenian people. Therefore the burial, initially at least, was a private affair. However, Plutarch's reference, while noting his apparent scepticism, seems to describe a tomb of a more substantial nature, having been adorned with an altar-like structure. This may be interpreted as a development from a private burial to a more public monument. Plutarch also references Plato *Comicus* to support the reference of Diodorus and so tradition would have Themistocles' tomb (in its public form) in the Piraeus

---

[569] *IG* 2^2 1035, 33; see Pritchett 1985: 4.129-131 for further bibliography; the inscription is published by Culley 1975; for the date see *SEG* 26.121.
[570] Thuc. 1.138.5-6.
[571] Plut. *Themistocles* 32.4.

by the late 5th or early 4th century BC.[572] Pausanias also states the presence of Themistocles' tomb by his time, the 2nd century AD:

> Even up to my time there were docks there, and near the largest harbour is the grave of Themistocles. For it is said that the Athenians repented of their treatment of Themistocles, and that his relations took up his bones and brought them from Magnesia.[573]

The ancient references to the monument all agree, at least, that the bones were brought back to Attica.

According to Dodwell, after the repentance of the Athenians the bones may well have been afforded a public burial.[574] Dodwell, in his exploration of the Athenian ports, mentions a sarcophagus placed in a cavity on the shore line which was regularly flooded and difficult to examine and states that '[s]ome have supposed this to be the sepulchre of Themistocles'.[575] The contents of the sepulchre had disappeared by the time of Dodwell's visit but it is clear that a particular place, by some at least, was held to be Themistocles' tomb in the early 19th century. In addition, the significance of the tomb's location was not lost on Dodwell:

> And what locality could be more appropriate for the reception of his venerable ashes, than the same shore which had witnessed his triumph, and which still overlooks the Psytalian and Salaminian rocks, and the whole extent of the Saronic gulph?[576]

---

[572] Plut. *Themistocles* 32.5 quotes the comic poet Plato
'Thy tomb is mounded in a fair and sightly place;
the merchantmen shall ever hail it with glad cry'; see also West 1965: 142.
[573] Paus. 1.1.2.
[574] Dodwell's suggestion on this point is speculative (1819: 1.424). He points out that Thucydides' assertion that Themistocles was buried privately was hearsay, and this account contradicts later sources such as Diodorus, Plutarch, and Pausanias (all mentioned in this discussion).
[575] Dodwell 1819: 1.423.
[576] Dodwell 1819: 1.424.

Gell mentions as a boat sails out of the Piraeus on the left are large column pieces which lie in ruins, thought to be erected in memory of Themistocles, who apparently 'certainly had a monument near this spot'.[577]

No ancient source explicitly connects the burial of Themistocles with the commemoration of the battle of Salamis specifically. In fact, West attributes this to the commemoration of the Persian Wars in general.[578] However, the possible development of this tomb from a private burial to public monument in the late 5th or early 4th century BC and the specific location selected to honour Themistocles (overlooking the Salamis straight), suggest it was intended to recall the victory at Salamis. The conclusions drawn here are based on speculation and therefore dictate the tomb may only be accepted with caution.

39.– 41. Thank-Offering of Three Triremes (Isthmus, Sunium and Salamis)

Herodotus mentions the three ships:

As for the Greeks, not being able to take Andros, they went to Carystus. When they had laid it waste, they returned to Salamis. First of all they set apart for the gods, among other first-fruits, three Phoenician triremes, one to be dedicated at the Isthmus, where it was till my lifetime, the second at Sunium, and the third for Ajax at Salamis where they were.[579]

The triremes dedicated at the Isthmus and Sunium were most probably dedicated to Poseidon, who was the protecting divinity at the battle of Salamis, while Ajax was honoured at Salamis as the local hero to where the battle was fought.[580] If these triremes were spoils from the battle of Salamis, although this is not certain, then it may be suggested that these triremes were dedicated at some point within the decade following the battle.[581]

---

[577] Gell 1827: 100.
[578] West 1965: 140-142.
[579] Hdts. 8.121.1.
[580] West 1965: 91-92; Macan 1908: 548 suggests Athena and Poseidon to be recipients of the dedicated triremes at Sunium and Isthmus respectively.
[581] West (see 1965: lxv, Table 4, no. 28) suggests a dedication of these ships in the decade following the battle, and counts the dating of these examples as 'probable'.

Triremes, or more frequently the beaks of the ships, were appropriate thank-offerings for naval victories.[582] However, whole ship dedications set within sanctuaries have been deemed exceedingly rare, and this has been put down to the amount of space required, the logistics of hauling a ship into a *temenos*, and the challenges of constructing a building around an installed ship.[583]

These monuments are accepted with a certain degree of confidence due to the monuments being mentioned by a 5th century BC source, and Herodotus' remark that specifically points out that the trireme at the Isthmus was still there in his lifetime, which suggests he may have seen it, although this is not certain.[584]

42. Statue of Apollo Holding the Beak of a Ship

Herodotus mentions this statue standing at Delphi:

After that, they divided the spoils and sent the first-fruits of it to Delphi; of this was made a man's image twelve cubits high, holding in his hand the figurehead of a ship. This stood in the same place as the golden statue of Alexander the Macedonian.[585]

Pausanias also mentions the monument:

The Greeks who fought against the king...dedicated also an Apollo at **Delphi**, *from spoils taken in the naval actions at* **Artemisium** *and* **Salamis**.[586]

There are discrepancies between Herodotus' and Pausanias' accounts of the statues they describe at Delphi; Herodotus describes a statue of a man holding the beak of a ship while Pausanias mentions a statue of Apollo. However, it is generally agreed that these sources are referencing the same

---

[582] Rouse 1902: 103.
[583] Westcoat 2005: 154-155, and n. 3 for examples of this practice; see also Pritchett 1979: 3.281-285 for discussion on naval spoils and ship models.
[584] Macan (1908: 548) describes this remark as 'curious' and questions why Herodotus would include the comment unless he had either seen the trireme or had more information about that specific monument over the other two.
[585] Hdts. 8.121.2.
[586] Paus. 10.14.5.

statue.[587] Pausanias attributes the monument to Salamis and Artemisium, and although he does not mention the beak of the ship it has been suggested this aspect of the statue may have prompted this statement.[588]

The discovery of a fragmented base immediately north of the foundations of the serpent column (**no. 80**) has led to the location of this statue being identified as the east temple terrace.[589] The statue would have stood at a height of 5.91 m and therefore dominated the area.[590] Cuts on the top of the stone reveal the positioning of the statue's feet which, it has been suggested, resemble the pose of an archaic *kouros*.[591] The statue base was adorned with a dedicatory inscription which only survives in fragments, and has been dated to the 5th century BC.[592] The inscription appears to have '*Hellenes*' as the subject, which is the only use of this term defining a dedicatory group in a dedicatory inscription at Delphi; this terminology mirrors Herodotus in his description of the alliance of states that fought at Salamis.[593]

This monument is accepted with confidence based on its identification in literary sources, inscriptional interpretation and archaeological evidence.

43. Tomb of Eurybiades

Pausanias mentions this tomb when describing Sparta:

> *Opposite the temple is the tomb of Theopompus son of Nicander, and also that of Eurybiades, who commanded the Lacedaemonian warships that fought the Persians at Artemisium and Salamis.*[594]

---

[587] Frazer 1965: 1.309; West 1965: 92-93; Scott 2010: Appendix C, no. 103.
[588] West 1965: 93.
[589] Scott 2010: 83, Fig. 4.3 no. 103; Bommelaer 1991: 169.
[590] Following Herodotus' estimated height, Scott 2010: 83.
[591] Bommelaer 1991: 169, no. 410b.
[592] For restorations of the fragmented base, see Jacquemin and Laroche 1988: Figs. 7, 8 and 10; Bommelaer 1991: 169, Fig. 71; the base was also published as inv. 1198 in *FD* II 282, Fig. 287; for dating the inscription see Jacquemin and Laroche 1988: 246; the monument is more specifically dated to after 480 BC by Jaquemin 1999: no. 309; West (see 1965: lxv, Table 4, no. 29) counts this monument among 'probable' examples dating to 480-470 BC.
[593] The alliance was described as 'the Greeks', see Hdts. 8.96 and 121; Scott 2010: 84.
[594] Paus. 3.16.6.

Pausanias is the only literary source we have for this tomb. Eurybiades may well have been honoured with a tomb in the urban centre as we learn from Herodotus that he was awarded a crown of olive as an award for excellence at Salamis.[595]

The particular mention awarded to Eurybiades is consistent in the literary sources, of both the classical period and later, however the date of the monument itself is uncertain. Due to the sole literary reference to this monument being late and the uncertainty of the date, it may only be accepted tentatively.

44. Painting of Salamis Holding the Beak of a Ship

Pausanias, when describing the temple of Zeus at Olympia, mentions the painting:

> *Of these screens the part opposite the doors is only covered with dark-blue paint; the other parts show pictures by Panaenus. Among them is Atlas, supporting heaven and earth, by whose side stands Heracles ready to receive the load of Atlas, along with Theseus; Perithous,* **Hellas,** *and* **Salamis** *carrying in her hand the ornament made for the top of a ship's bows; then Heracles' exploit against the Nemean lion, the outrage committed by Ajax on Cassandra, Hippodameia the daughter of Oenomaus with her mother, and Prometheus still held by his chains, though Heracles has been raised up to him. Last in the picture come Penthesileia giving up the ghost and Achilles supporting her; two Hesperides are carrying the apples, the keeping of which, legend says, had been entrusted to them.*[596]

The painting of Salamis holding the beak of a ship is one of a group of nine paintings, however the remaining eight mythological scenes are not understood to be related to the painting of Salamis.[597] Pausanias names the painter as Panaenus, who he says is the brother of Pheidias and also the artist who painted the scene of Marathon in the Stoa *Poikile*.[598]

---

[595] Hdts. 8.124.2.
[596] Paus. 5.11.5-6.
[597] West 1965: 149.
[598] Paus. 5.11.6.

The sanctuary at Olympia, which was administered by the city-state Elis, has been identified as a site primarily for the Peloponnese.[599] Despite this Peloponnesian focus, the presence of images of Athenian heroes such as Theseus, and depictions of victories which were led by Athenian generals, being painted on screens at Olympia has been seen as redolent of a more pro-Athenian stance at Elis during the 5th century BC.[600] Therefore, this monument is accepted tentatively due to the late literary reference describing unusual imagery of Athenian symbolism being utilised at Olympia during the 5th century BC.

45. Sanctuary of the Hero Cychreus

Pausanias mentions the sanctuary when describing Salamis:

There is also a sanctuary of Cychreus. When the Athenians were fighting the Persians at sea, a serpent is said to have appeared in the fleet, and the god in an oracle told the Athenians that it was Cychreus the hero.[601]

The sanctuary to Cychreus on Salamis is only attested by Pausanias. However, we are told by Plutarch that Cychreus was worshipped by the Athenians.[602] Cychreus was an old local hero of Salamis, and the sanctuary therefore may have existed before the battle of Salamis.[603] Furthermore, other local heroes of the island are honoured in connection with the Greek victory at this naval battle (see **no. 41** for the dedication of a trireme to Ajax at Salamis). Given the precedent of honouring local heroes there is no reason to doubt Pausanias. However, due to a lack of evidence confirming the classical establishment of the sanctuary, this monument is accepted tentatively.

---

[599] Scott 2010: 185-186.
[600] Although these suggestions are speculative, see Raschke 1988: 46-47; Scott 2010: 185-186.
[601] Paus. 1.36.1.
[602] Plut. *Theseus* 10.2.
[603] West 1965: 150; according to Plutarch, Solon travelled to Salamis to sacrifice to Cychreus, an act perhaps performed within the sanctuary (Plut. *Solon* 9.1).

46. Epigram Engraved on a Cenotaph

Plutarch cites this epigram:

> *And their honorary sepulchre at the Isthmus has on it this epitaph:*
> *When Greece upon the point of danger stood,*
> *We fell, defending her with our life-blood.*[604]

Plutarch states that the Corinthians set up a 'cenotaphion' at the Isthmus and inscribed an epigram upon it.[605] The epigram is recorded by Plutarch and the Palatine Anthology as a single distich, and is regarded 'in accordance with the simplicity of the early 5th century'.[606] Aristides Aelius also records the epigram but quotes an expanded version of three distichs; the additional distichs are:

> *But we bound many pains in the hearts of the Persians, memories of the harsh naval battle.*
> *Salamis holds our bones. But our country, Corinth, has erected this monument in return for our good deeds.*[607]

The additional two distichs are understood as a literary addition which add only clarifying detail to the first two lines.[608] No archaeological evidence has been unearthed to corroborate the literary evidence and so we must rely solely on the late literary sources, which vary in their detail. Therefore, this monument is accepted tentatively.

47. Bronze Mast with Three Gold Stars

Herodotus describes this monument:

> *Having sent the first-fruits to Delphi, the Greeks, in the name of the country generally, made inquiry of the god whether the first-fruits which he had received were of full measure and whether he was content. To this he said*

---

[604] Plut. *On the Malice of Herodotus* 39.
[605] This epigram is also cited, identically to Plutarch, in the Palatine Anthology (7.250).
[606] West 1965: 167.
[607] Aristides *Orations* 28.66, trans. Behr 1986: 2.120-121.
[608] West 1965: 167-168.

that he was content with what he had received from all other Greeks, but not from the Aeginetans. From these he demanded the victor's prize for the sea-fight of Salamis. When the Aeginetans learned that, they dedicated three golden stars which are set on a bronze mast, in the angle, nearest to Croesus' bowl.[609]

According to Herodotus, the Aeginetans were prompted by the Delphic oracle to provide their own commemorative monument for the battle of Salamis.[610] This monument form is unique among the examples presented in this study and Herodotus does not offer an explanation on its design. The form of the monument has been interpreted as representative of natural phenomena or symbolic of nautical skill.[611] The location of the monument has been suggested in the region of the entrance to the temple of Apollo, given that Herodotus states it is situated near Croesus' bowl.[612] Again based on Herodotus' reference the monument is thought to have been raised in the decade following the battle of Salamis.[613] This monument is therefore accepted with confidence based on the literary evidence.

48. Pedimental Sculptures of the Temple of Aphaea

The temple of Aphaea, on the island of Aegina, was completed around 490 BC.[614] The pedimental sculptures of both the west and the east sides were almost identical and represented combat at Troy. However, three sets of pedimental sculptures are preserved, when only two pediments ordained the temple.[615] Dinsmoor suggests that the west pediment is older in style than the east pediment, the original of which may have been damaged during a Persian raid when the Greeks and Persians fought at

---

[609] Hdts. 8.122.
[610] Scott 2010: 84 adds that the Aeginetans' individual monument would be understandable given the close relationship between the polis, the cult of Apollo *Pythieus*, and Delphi.
[611] Natural phenomenon (St. Elmo's fire): Rouse 1902: 135; nautical skill: West 1965: 186.
[612] Herodotus (1.51.1) earlier states that Croesus sent two bowls to Delphi, which stood either side of the temple entrance; see Scott 2010: 83, Fig. 4.3 no. 105 for the monument's proposed position.
[613] Scott 2010: Appendix C, no. 105 dates the monument to 480 BC.
[614] West 1965: 186;
[615] The pediment sculptures were recovered in 1811 and purchased by Ludwig I of Bavaria and are now on display in the Glyptothek in Munich; see Darling 2004: 174.

Salamis;[616] the east pediment was then replaced with new sculpture while the damaged example was set up east of the temple as a memorial.[617]

The attribution of the pedimental sculptures as a commemorative monument of Salamis is understood here to be extremely tentative due the lack of affirmative evidence.

PLATAEA

49.– 51. Trophies

While describing the division of the war booty, Plutarch references the trophies raised at Plataea:

> *then the Lacedaemonians set up a trophy on their own account, and the Athenians also for themselves.*[618]

Pausanias provides us with some vague information regarding the positioning of a trophy.

> *The trophy which the Greeks set up for the battle at Plataea stands about fifteen stades from the city.*[619]

In addition, 4th century BC orators also reference a trophy at Plataea,[620] but Herodotus describes the monuments on the Plataean battlefield with no reference to a trophy.[621] For a trophy to be visible in the 2nd century AD, when Pausanias travelled to Plataea, the monument standing may have been made of stone.[622] The text preceding Plutarch's reference to

---

[616] It is worthy of note that we are informed by Herodotus (8.93) that the Aeginetans were considered most courageous in this battle, which may have prompted their desire to commemorate the conflict.

[617] See Dinsmoor 1950: 107, who dates the west pediment to 'before 490 BC' and the replacement east pediment to 'just after 480 BC'; Darling (2004: 172) dates the structure to the early 5th century BC; see also **no. 85** for another example of displaying fragments of destroyed temples as commemorative monuments.

[618] Plut. *Aristides* 20.3.

[619] Paus. 9.2.6.

[620] Plato, *Menexenus* 245a; Isoc. *Plataicus* 59.

[621] Hdts. 9.85.

[622] Pritchett 1957: 12. Pritchett found a concentrated deposit of sherds along a road upon which Pausanias reported monuments stood; however, secure evidence of a permanent

the trophies suggest the setting up of the Spartan and Athenian trophies was an act carried out soon after the culmination of battle.[623] It is possible that Plutarch describes perishable trophies set up by the Athenians and Spartans to commemorate their specific efforts in the battle, probably placed on their respective wings where their actions took place. Pausanias, on the other hand, may be describing a more permanent, pan-Hellenic monument.

Hunt claims that if the trophy, mentioned by Pausanias (**no. 49**), stood where the battle raged hottest it would be by the temple of Demeter.[624] Hunt has identified this area to be to the south-west of the city of Plataea near a Byzantine church which is estimated to be out about 15 stades from the entrance to the city. However, according to regular practice, the trophy should be where the battle turned. Grundy, seemingly in agreement with Hunt, states that the battle would have turned just south of the hill where the ruined church of St. Demetrius stands.[625] This site happens also to be about two miles or 15 stades from Plataea, a distance which accords with Pausanias' assertion, and may in fact be the same site mentioned by Hunt. Two inscriptions were discovered amongst a pile of stones beside an 'ancient well' at the base of mount Cithaeron to the east of modern day Erythres,[626] a settlement that has been identified as the site of the ancient town Hysiai.[627] These inscriptions, which were found separately but have since been re-joined, allude to the worshipping of Demeter and very probably contain the name Tesamenos, an Elean who acted as the Spartan diviner at the battle of Plataea.[628] These inscriptions may denote the location of the temple of Demeter, around which the Spartans routed the engaged Persian forces.[629]

Plutarch, in excerpt above, attributes separate trophies to Athens and Plataea (**nos. 50** and **51**) and describes their construction at the culmination of the battle. The act of setting up trophies after the culmination of battle

---

trophy eludes archaeologists to this day.
[623] See Plut. *Aristides* 19.7-20.3.
[624] Hunt 1890: 468; see also Hdts. 9.62-65.
[625] Grundy 1901: 496.
[626] *IG* 7 1670 and 1671.
[627] Pritchett 1957: 12-15; Pritchett 1965: 1.104-106.
[628] Hdts. 9.33-36.
[629] Hdts. 9.62-65.

is well attested in the 5th century BC.⁶³⁰ In addition, the setting up of more than one trophy for a battle in the classical period was not unheard of.⁶³¹ Due to the frequency of these references, trophies are understood here as a regular post-battle commemorative act. Therefore, the Athenian and Spartan trophies, set up immediately after the conflict are accepted here with confidence.

The third trophy (**no. 49**), that mentioned by Pausanias (which was probably stone) in the excerpt above, is accepted here with less confidence. Pausanias attributes the monument to 'the Greeks' and so one may assume he interpreted the monument as 'pan-Hellenic', which is how it is interpreted here. However, the date for the monument is unclear and Pausanias does not provide any information as to when this trophy was constructed. Therefore, due to the lack of archaeological evidence, this monument is accepted here tentatively.

52. Epigram for the Athenians

The epigram is recorded in the Palatine Anthology:

The Sons of Athens who wholly destroyed the Persian array,
*Thrust slavery's bitter yoke from their fatherland far away.*⁶³²

It has been suggested that this epigram may be dated to the 5th century BC, based on its 'curtness and brevity of style'.⁶³³ It has further been suggested that this epigram was erected over the Athenian grave at Plataea.⁶³⁴ If this epigram did stand over the grave at Plataea it may have been the '*elegeia*' attributed to Simonides and mentioned by Pausanias.⁶³⁵

---

[630] Thucydides records fifty eight examples of the construction of trophies and these range from minor skirmishes to major battles, see Pritchett 1974: 2.264-266, Table 9 for a tabulation of examples from Thucydides.
[631] E.g. Thuc. 5.3.4, 7.24.1, 7.45.1, 7.54.1.
[632] *Pal. Anth.* 7.257; or Way 1939: no. 258.
[633] West 1965: 159; see also Weber 1929: 46.
[634] Weber 1929: 45-47.
[635] Paus. 9.2.5; as suggested by West 1965: 160.

However the authenticity of the epigram is not certain and therefore, without further evidence, may not be accepted with confidence.[636]

53. Epigram for the Spartans

This epigram is recorded in the Palatine Anthology:

> *These, who have wreathed with unfading renown their country's story,*
> *Over their own heads flung death's luridly-dark cloud-pall,*
> *They died – they are not dead! Valour, the giver of deathless glory,*
> *Hath stooped from high to bring these upward from Hades' Hall.*[637]

This epigram is attributed to Simonides in the Palatine Anthology which would date it to the 5th century BC, although this attribution is not supported by further evidence. The epigram directly references the war dead and so this inscription may have been an epitaph. Herodotus provides us with an epigram honouring the Spartans at the battlefield of Thermopylae, so this poem may refer to the Spartans who died at the battle of Plataea.[638] A lack of further evidence in support of both a speculative connection to Plataea, and the sole reference in the Palatine Anthology prevents this monument being accepted with confidence.

54. Epigram for the Corinthians

Plutarch relates a poem for the Corinthians who fought at Plataea, which he attributes to Simonides:

> *I' th' midst were men, in warlike feats excelling*
> *Who Ephyre, full of springs, inhabited,*
> *And who in Corinth, Glaucus' city, dwelling,*
> *Great praise by their great valor merited;*

---

[636] *Contra.* Jacoby 1945: 185, n. 107, who states that the monument is 'probably late and literary'. This comment is made at the end of a discussion concerning the choice of word used to describe the Persians; Simonides (to which this current epigram is attributed) uses '*Mēdoi*' in the one epigram that Jacoby deems securely attributed to the poet (Hdts. 7.228.3), while the current epigram uses '*Persōn*'.
[637] *Pal. Anth.* 7.251, translation provided by Way 1939.
[638] West (1965: 125-126) connects this monument to the battle of Plataea; Pausanias states (9.2.5) that the Spartan tomb was adorned with an elegiac verse composed by Simonides.

> *Of which they to perpetuate the fame,*
> *To th' Gods of well-wrought gold did offerings frame.*[639]

Plutarch is the only source for this poem and gives no indication that it was inscribed on a monument; however, the frequent reference to the dead may indicate the poem is an epitaph, but this is not certain.[640] It is unlikely the full three distichs would be inscribed on a stele, but the first two are complete and it has been suggested they alone would serve as an inscription if the reason for the dead receiving 'great praise' was understood.[641] If this poem was inscribed it may have stood over the tomb on the battlefield, but Herodotus does not say the Corinthians had a 'full' tomb.[642] However, it is possible that the Corinthians, after the battle, may have set up an empty grave, as other cities did (see **nos. 56-62** for discussion on burial on the Plataean battlefield).

Due to Plutarch's assertion that the poem commemorated the battle of Plataea and it was attributed to a 5th century BC source, it may be accepted tentatively. However, it may not be accepted confidently as an epigram because there is no archaeological evidence to support the claim or literary evidence stating it was ever inscribed.

55. Epigram for the Tegeans

This epigram is recorded in the Palatine Anthology and is attributed to Simonides:

> *Through these men's valour it was that the smoke of Tegea's burning*
> *Up from her fair wide meads ascended not to the sky.*
> *To bequeath to their children a city prospering free were they yearning,*
> *And accounted it well that themselves in the forefront of battle should die.*[643]

This epigram may have stood over the Tegean grave on the battlefield as Herodotus states the Tegeans had a full grave there, and there is particular

---

[639] Plut. *On the Malice of Herodotus* 42.
[640] West 1965: 168.
[641] West 1965: 169.
[642] Hdts. 9.85.
[643] *Pal. Anth.* 7.512. Translation provided by Way 1939.

reference to those who are buried.⁶⁴⁴ The epigram appears to be in the form of an epitaph with direct reference to those who are buried. It probably dates to the 5th century BC as the phrase '*tōnde di anthrōpōn*' suggests '*andron tond' arete*' of an epigram inscribed for the Athenian dead at (possibly) Marathon dated to the early 5th century BC (see **no. 11**).⁶⁴⁵ However, lack of further evidence in support of both a speculative connection to Plataea, and the sole reference in the Palatine Anthology prevents this monument being accepted with confidence.

56.– 62. Burial Mounds

Herodotus lists the tombs in which the dead were buried after the distribution of the booty:

> *But the Greeks, when they had divided the spoils at Plataea, buried each contingent of their dead in a separate place. The Lacedaemonians made three tombs; there they buried their 'irens,' among whom were Posidonius, Amompharetus, Philocyon, and Callicrates. In one of the tombs, then, were the 'irens,' in the second the rest of the Spartans, and in the third the helots. This, then is how the Lacedaemonians buried their dead. The Tegeans, however, buried all theirs together in a place apart, and the Athenians did similarly with their own dead. So too did the Megarians and Phliasians with those who had been killed by the horsemen. All the tombs of these peoples were filled with dead; but as for the rest of the states whose tombs are to be seen at Plataea, their tombs are but empty barrows that they built for the sake of men that should come after, because they were ashamed to have been absent from the battle. There is one there called the tomb of the Aeginetans, which, as I learn by inquiry, was built as late as ten years after, at the Aeginetans' desire, by their patron and protector Cleades son of Autodicus, a Plataean.*⁶⁴⁶

---

⁶⁴⁴ Hdts. 9.85; West 1965: 192; *contra*. Hiller (1926: 39), who argues this epigram may refer to the battle between Tegea and Sparta in 473/472 BC.
⁶⁴⁵ *IG* I³ 503/4; see also West 1965: 192.
⁶⁴⁶ Hdts. 9.85.

Herodotus contradicts himself when relating how the Aeginetans erected an empty tomb because they were not present, as he names them as contributing 500 men to the Greek forces.[647]

Pausanias provides us with some information regarding the positioning of the graves:

> *Roughly at the entrance into Plataea are the graves of those who fought against the Persians. Of the Greeks generally there is a common tomb, but the Lacedaemonians and Athenians who fell have separate graves, on which are written elegiac verses by Simonides.*[648]

Pausanias' statement contradicts that of Herodotus' description of the burials. However, it is possible that a reworking of the commemorative landscape took place between the 5th century BC and the 2nd century AD.

Gell, approaching the site of ancient Plataea from the north, identified what he describes as 'vestiges of tombs' to the right of the walls: that is on the western side of the ancient city.[649] Leake, on visiting the site of the ancient city, believed he had located the eastern gate to the city of Plataea. Directly outside this eastern gate, Leake tentatively suggests that the tombs of the dead Greek participants in the battle of Plataea are marked 'by a ruined church near the right bank of the torrent, on the left bank of which, nearly opposite to the chapel, are the foundations of a gate'.[650] Leake's suggestion of the positioning of the Greek tombs would place them on the opposite side of the ancient city to Gell's identification.

On the strength of the 5th century BC literary evidence, and the fact that communal burials were practised on the battlefields of other conflicts of the Persian Wars (see **nos. 1, 2, 28** and **37**), these monuments are accepted with confidence.

---

[647] Hdts. 9.28.6; the burial of the dead was also included as part of the first clause of the Oath of Plataea. For discussion on the oath see **no. 63**.
[648] Paus. 9.2.5.
[649] Gell 1827: 111.
[650] Leake 1835: 366-367.

63. Ruins of Sanctuaries as Memorial of Persian Impiety

Lycurgus describes the Oath of Plataea, apparently made before the battle of Plataea, a part of which was the agreement to leave ruined sanctuaries untouched:

> *It was for this reason, gentlemen of the jury, that all the Greeks exchanged this pledge at Plataea, before taking up their posts to fight against the power of Xerxes. The formula was not their own but borrowed from the oath which is traditional among you. It would be well for you to hear it; for though the events of that time are ancient history now we can discern clearly enough, in these recorded words, the courage of our forbears. Please read the oath.*
> *'Oath. I will not hold life dearer than freedom nor will I abandon my leaders whether they are alive or dead. I will bury all allies killed in the battle. If I conquer the barbarians in war I will not destroy any of the cities which have fought for Greece but I will consecrate a tenth of all those which sided with the barbarian. I will not rebuild a single one of the shrines which the barbarians have burnt and razed but will allow them to remain for future generations as a memorial of the barbarians' impiety.'*[651]

Diodorus also mentions the oath which references leaving sanctuaries unrepaired:

> *And when the Greek forces were assembled at the Isthmus, all of them agreed that they should swear an oath about the war, one that would make staunch the concord among them and would compel them nobly to endure the perils of the battle. The oath ran as follows: 'I will not hold life dearer than liberty, nor will I desert the leaders, whether they be living or dead, but I will bury all the allies who have perished in the battle; and if I overcome the barbarians in the war, I will not destroy any one of the cities which have participated in the struggle; nor will I rebuild any one of the sanctuaries which have been burnt or demolished, but I will let them be and leave them as a reminder to coming generations of the impiety of the barbarians.'*[652]

---

[651] Lyc. *Against Leocrates* 80-81.
[652] Diod. 11.29.2-3.

Pausanias notes how certain temples were not repaired:

> The treatment that the god at Abae received at the hands of the Persians was very different from the honour paid him by the Romans. For while the Romans have given freedom of government to Abae because of their reverence for Apollo, the army of Xerxes burned down, as it did others, the sanctuary at Abae. The Greeks who opposed the barbarians resolved not to rebuild the sanctuaries burnt down by them, but to leave them for all time as memorials of their hatred. This too is the reason why the temples in the territory of Haliartus, as well as the Athenian temples of Hera on the road to Phalerum and of Demeter at Phalerum, still remain half-burnt even at the present day. Such, I suppose, was the appearance of the sanctuary at Abae also, after the Persian invasion, until in the Phocian war some Phocians, overcome in battle, took refuge in Abae. Whereupon the Thebans gave them to the flames, and with the refugees the sanctuary, which was thus burnt down a second time. However, it still stood even in my time, the frailest of buildings ever damaged by fire, seeing that the ruin begun by the Persian incendiaries was completed by the incendiaries of Boeotia.[653]

According to the excerpts presented above there was a tradition in the ancient sources that the Greeks swore an oath before the battle of Plataea, a part of which was to leave the destroyed sanctuaries unrepaired as a memorial to Persian impiety. Pausanias, in the excerpt above, mentions a number of examples of ruined sanctuaries which suggest the oath was made. However, no 5th century BC source mentions the oath specifically and Theopompus (who was writing in the 4th century BC) calls the oath Athenian fiction.[654]

A stele was discovered in 1932 which is inscribed with what is understood to be a version of the Oath of Plataea.[655] The inscribed stele was originally erected in a religious shrine within Acharnae that was one of the demes which constituted the Athenian *polis*.[656] The lettering on the stele has been

---

[653] Paus. 10.35.2-3; the oath is also referenced by Cicero (*On the Republic* 3.8.15).
[654] Theo. *The Philippica* frag.153.
[655] The inscription is published in *RO* 88.23-46; Robert 1938: 302-316; West 1965: 99.
[656] Cartledge 2013: 6; the document is a dedication by Dio, priest of the cult Ares and Athena Areia at Acharnae, see *RO* 88; see also Parke 1948: 82.

dated to 350-325 BC.[657] With slight variations, the oath is quoted by both Lycurgus and Diodorus in the excerpts above and the clause about not rebuilding damaged sanctuaries is only mentioned by the literary sources.

The oath of Plataea has been divided into three provisions by West:[658] For provision 1 there is general agreement between the sources (for discussion on burial of the dead see **nos. 56-62**). For provision 2, Lycurgus and Diodorus both make a general statement about the inviolability of Greeks cities who fought together to protect Greece and Lycurgus goes on to mention the punishment of the Medising city-states (for discussion on the tithing of Medising Greeks see **no. 64**).[659] The Acharnae stele, however, specifically mentions Athens, Sparta and Plataea as cities to be preserved and Thebes as a city to be tithed. This has been interpreted as 4th century BC anti-Theban bias which may have been added to the 5th century BC oath.[660] Provision 3 is only attested in the literary sources and is not mentioned on the Acharnae stele. In addition the Acharnae stele states the oath was sworn by the Athenians while Lycurgus and Diodorus state it was sworn by all Greeks. The version of the text on the stele has been interpreted as a 4th century BC compilation due to the specific anti-Theban references; furthermore the variations in the literary texts, and the fact that the sources are late (of the 4th century BC at the earliest), indicates that the exact oath has not been accurately preserved.[661]

With specific reference to provision 3, Plutarch describes a proposed deliberation, called for by Pericles, over whether to rebuild the sanctuaries destroyed by the Persians. If the Greeks had sworn an oath after the battle of Plataea then Pericles' congress of city-states has been deemed an appropriate course of action before rebuilding.[662] Furthermore, the Athenian Acropolis was left in ruins until the rebuilding under Pericles; this inaction for over a

---

[657] See Cartledge 2013: 6, 3-7 for an overview of the document, and Fig. 1.1 for an image; *RO* (88) date the inscription to the middle of the 4th century BC.

[658] West 1965: 100.

[659] It has been suggested by Meiggs (1972: 504) that Diodorus does not include reference to tithing because the source he relied on had followed Herodotus who records the oath to tithe shortly before Thermopylae (7.132).

[660] West 1965: 101; Meiggs 1972: 505.

[661] West 1965: 99, 101.

[662] See Dinsmoor 1950: 150-151; West 1965: 103.

Table 21. Provisions of the Oath of Plataea

No.	Provision	Reference
1	Resolution to fight to one's utmost, to consider freedom more valuable than life, not to leave one's post and to obey orders, and to bury the dead.	Acharnae stele, lines 23-31; Lycurgus, lines 1-4; Diodorus, lines 1-4.
2	Resolution to tithe cities which had sided with the Persians.	Acharnae stele, lines 31-36; Lycurgus, lines 4-7.
3	Resolution not to rebuild ruined sanctuaries.	Lycurgus, lines 7-10; Diodorus, lines 6-9.

generation suggests some form of prohibition.[663] It is this point that has been said requires 'special explanation' which, it could be interpreted, is provided by the Oath of Plataea.[664] While the evidence discussed above suggests the probable existence of the Oath of Plataea, the lack of secure 5th century BC evidence allows only tentative acceptance of this monument.

64. Tithing of Medising Greeks

Herodotus mentions an oath to tithe Medising Greek states:

> Among those who paid that tribute were the Thessalians, Dolopes, Enienes, Perrhaebians, Locrians, Magnesians, Melians, Achaeans of Pythia, Thebans, and all the Boeotians except the men of Thespiae and Plataea. Against all of these the Greeks who declared war with the foreigner entered into a sworn agreement, which was this: that if they should be victorious, they would dedicate to the god of Delphi the possessions of all Greeks who had of free will surrendered themselves to the Persians. Such was the agreement sworn by the Greeks.[665]

Herodotus does not state where this oath was sworn but according to the sequence of the narrative it would appear it was sworn before the battle of Thermopylae while Xerxes was encamped at Tempe.[666] However, it has been suggested that the oath mentioned by Herodotus may be associated

---

[663] West 1965: 103.
[664] Meiggs 1972: 507, and see 597 for additional discussion which further complicates the issue of authenticity, without a certain conclusion.
[665] Hdts. 7.132.
[666] As noted by West 1965: 102.

with the Oath of Plataea; this association is based on Herodotus' inclusion of punishable groups such as Locrians and Thebans who did not Medise until after the battle of Thermopylae.[667] The Oath of Plataea did include a provision calling for the tithing of Greek states that sided with the Persians (for discussion on the oath see **no. 63**) but was apparently sworn before the battle of Plataea.[668]

The presence of the threat of tithing in the oath mentioned by Herodotus and the Oath of Plataea may not be enough to relate these two specific examples. However, Herodotus' statement does indicate that this practice in dealing with Medisers was utilised in the 5th century BC.[669] Therefore this vow is accepted with confidence.

65. *Eleutheria*

Diodorus mentions the *Eleutheria*:

> *When Mardonius and his army had returned to Thebes, the Greeks gathered in congress decreed to make common cause with the Athenians and advancing to Plataea in a body, to fight to a finish for liberty, and also to make a vow to the gods that, if they were victorious, the Greeks would unite in celebrating the Festival of Liberty on that day and would hold the games of the Festival in Plataea.*[670]

Strabo also mentions the *Eleutheria*:

> *I have already said that the Asopus flows past Plataeae. Here it was that the forces of the Greeks completely wiped out Mardonius and his three hundred thousand Persians; and they built a temple of Zeus Eleutherius, and instituted the athletic games in which the victor received a crown, calling them the Eleutheria.*[671]

---

[667] Parke 1948: 93.
[668] The provision is mentioned on the Acharnae stele where it is states the oath was sworn before the fight with the barbarians: *RO* 88.31-36; the provision is also mentioned by Lycurgus who states the oath was sworn before battle with Xerxes' forces commenced: *Against Leocrates* 80-81; Diodorus (11.29.2-3) states the oath was sworn at the Isthmus.
[669] West 1965: 102-103.
[670] Diod. 11.29.1.
[671] Strabo 9.2.31.

Plutarch mentions the proposal to celebrate the *Eleutheria* every fourth year:

After this, there was a general assembly of the Hellenes, at which Aristides proposed a decree to the effect that deputies and delegates from all Hellas convene at Plataea every year, and that every fourth year festival games of deliverance be celebrated—the Eleutheria; also that a confederate Hellenic force be levied, consisting of ten thousand shield, one thousand horse, and one hundred ships, to prosecute the war against the Barbarian; also that the Plataeans be set apart as inviolable and consecrate, that they might sacrifice to Zeus the Deliverer in behalf of Hellas.[672]

Games called the *Eleutheria* were instituted at the behest of Aristides according to Plutarch and are included in Plutarch's description of the Covenant of Plataea. The Covenant of Plataea is not considered here as a monument in itself, but rather a document indicating items of commemorative significance.[673] The covenant, as reported by Plutarch, consists of four clauses:

1. 'Deputies' and 'Delegates' were to assemble at Plataea every year.
2. A victory festival, the *Eleutheria*, was to be celebrated at Plataea every four years.
3. A pan-Hellenic force of 10,000 men, 1000 horse, and 100 ships was to be levied, in order to continue to the war against Persia.
4. Plataea was to be kept inviolate and sacrosanct, so that the Plataeans might offer sacrifices to Zeus on behalf of all the Greeks.[674]

The authenticity of the covenant has been disputed; the most serious objection that has been put forward is that there are no clear references to the covenant at the two instances where it would have been most pertinent: the trial of the Plataeans after their surrender in 427 BC, as depicted by Thucydides, and Isocrates' *Plataicus* which was written after

---

[672] Plut. *Aristides* 21.1.
[673] West (1965: 110) is followed here on this understanding of the Covenant of Plataea.
[674] Regarding clause 4, West (1965: 1907) interprets the covenant to stop at the end of Plut. *Aristides* 21.1, whereas Meiggs (1972: 507) includes the beginning of Plut. *Aristides* 21.2 (which outlines annual rites carried out at the communal graves by Plataeans) as an addition to the clause. West's definition of the fourth clause is followed here because Plutarch appears to conclude his description of the covenant before continuing, and therefore treats the annual rites practised by the Plataeans as a separate monument, see **no. 68**.

Plataea's destruction in 373 BC.⁶⁷⁵ However, Thucydides does have the Plataeans plead for the Spartans to 'be not unmindful of the oaths which your fathers swore, and which we now plead', but this has been dismissed as 'indefinite'.⁶⁷⁶ In favour of the Covenant of Plataea, it has been suggested that if (albeit late) attestations regarding the covenant hadn't survived 'it would be necessary to postulate something of this kind'.⁶⁷⁷ For example, Pausanias' campaign in 478 BC suggests an official decision to continue the conflict and formal arrangements, it is assumed, would have to have been made regarding the tending of the graves at Plataea.⁶⁷⁸ However, while the covenant may be based on an authentic agreement of some kind, it has been claimed that the covenant, as presented by Plutarch, is probably a propagandistic creation of the 4th century BC.⁶⁷⁹ Clause 1 is included in the discussion of **no. 68** and clause 4 is included in the discussion of **no. 66**. Clause 3 is interpreted here as not of commemorative significance but as a means to continue the conflict. Nevertheless, the details of this clause have been interpreted as further evidence for the oath's inauthenticity. The numbers outlined in the oath have been suggested as not well suited to continuing the war with Persia, as there are too many hoplites and not enough ships.⁶⁸⁰

Considering clause 2 (the *Eleutheria* festival), Zeus *Eleutherios* was apparently honoured at Plataea from the culmination of battle; we are informed by Thucydides that the honouring of Zeus *Eleutherios* took place soon after the battle in the Plataean agora.⁶⁸¹ In addition, an altar was raised at Plataea (see **no. 67**) and sacrifices were to be made to Zeus by the Plataeans. Sacrifices are reported by Plutarch to have been carried out down to his time, in addition to the Hellenic council assembled at Plataea.⁶⁸²

---

[675] See Meiggs 1972: 507. Thuc. 3.53-67; Isoc. *Plataicus*; see also Cartledge 2013: 127-130 for a brief overview of the covenant.
[676] Thuc. 3.59.2; dismissal on the grounds that it is unclear what oaths are being referred to: Meiggs 1972: 507.
[677] Larsen 1940: 179.
[678] Meiggs 1972: 508.
[679] See West 1965: 107.
[680] Meiggs 1972: 507, who also states the proposed numbers bear little resemblance to the forces led by Pausanias in 478 BC.
[681] Thuc. 2.71.2.
[682] Plut. *Aristides* 19.7; see also Raaflaub 2004: 102-117; Mikalson 2003: 99-101; Pritchett 1979: 3.173-83 for treatment of the pan-Hellenic altar and cult of Zeus *Eleutherios*.

It is not until the early 3rd century BC, however, that a reference to the freedom festival at Plataea emerges; the comic poet Poseidippos describes Plataea, and thus provides the earliest literary evidence of the foundation for the *Eleutheria* festival on a pan-Hellenic scale:

It has two temples, a stoa, and its name,
a bath and the fame of Serambos.
Most of the time it is fallow,
and only at the festival of the Eleutheria
does it become a city.[683]

This illustrates the obscurity of Plataea when celebrations are not recalling the prominent (physical) position of the city during the final land battle of the Persian Wars on mainland Greece. Schachter believes the fragment by Poseidippos implies the existence of an official cult.[684] Whether or not Schachter's claim may be supported, Poseidippos' fragment offers a *terminus ante quem*, of around the early 3rd century BC, for the instigation of *Eleutheria* festival.

It should be noted that Philip II of Macedon is said to have vowed to restore Plataea after the battle of Chaeronea in 338 BC.[685] In addition, Alexander the Great, after he was proclaimed King of Asia, also made special mention of plans to restore Plataea 'because their ancestors had furnished their territory to the Greeks for the struggle in behalf of their freedom'.[686] It has been suggested, based on Plutarch's texts, that the site of Plataea and the restoration of the city would have provided an ideal pretext for an increase in the grandeur of the celebrations of the Greek triumphs over the barbarian.[687]

---

[683] Edmonds 1961: Fragment 29.
[684] Schacter does not immediately justify why this fragment implies 'an official cult with all the administrative trappings'. However, the fragment states the name of the festival as the *Eleutheria* which is attested as an organised event until the 3rd century AD (see Schacter 1994: 139, n. 6 where a roughly chronological list of inscriptions relating to the *Eleutheria* is presented dating from the late 3rd century BC to the 3rd century AD). The fragment by Poseidippos, dated to the early 3rd century BC, is therefore understood here to be the earliest reference to this festival.
[685] Paus. 4.27.10; 9.1.8.
[686] Plut. *Alexander* 34.1; cf. Plut. *Aristides* 11.9.
[687] Schachter 1994: 130.

The Monuments and the Evidence

Figure 14. Drawing of boundary stone (after Skia 1917: 161).

It is not until the end of the 4th century BC, until material evidence emerges which arguably relates to cult activity with reference to Zeus Eleutherios (Figure 14).[688]

The boundary stone fragment pictured in Figure 14 can be seen to bear the inscription 'O(ros) El(eutheriou Dios)'.[689] It appears that by the end of the 4th century BC, an area was being specially demarcated by a stone possibly bearing Zeus' epithet 'Eleutherios'.

By the middle of the 3rd century BC, however, material evidence emerges that clearly signifies pan-Hellenic celebrations at Plataea: an inscription put up in honour of Glaucon the Athenian. This famous decree mentions games of a pan-Hellenic nature being held at Plataea.

> [Glaucon] has enriched the sanctuary with dedications and with revenues which must be safeguarded for Zeus Eleutherios and the Concord of the Greeks; and he has contributed to making more lavish the sacrifice in

---
[688] See Skia 1917: 160-161.7 where the stone is dated on letter form.
[689] Alternatively 'El(lēnōn)? See Schachter 1994: 131, n. 1.

honour of Zeus Eleutherios and Concord and the contest which the Greeks celebrate at the tomb of the heroes who fought against the barbarians for the liberty of the Greeks; therefore all may know that the federal assembly of the Greeks repays thanks worthy of their benefactions...[690]

This inscription, then, presents the most definitive references to competitive games, the *Koinon* (collective group of Greek cities regularly meeting at Plataea), the sanctuary of Zeus *Eleutheria*, the joint worship of Zeus and *Homonoia* (goddess representing unanimity and collectively being of one mind) with accompanying joint altar and sacrifices.[691]

The existence of a 5th century BC *Eleutheria* festival is far from beyond doubt. Therefore, due to the lack of evidence concerning the date of instigation, this monument may only be accepted with caution.

66. Inviolability of Plataea

Thucydides, in describing how the Plataeans are pleading that the Spartans not destroy them, mentions that Plataea is inviolable:

> *Pausanias, son of Cleombrotus, your countryman, after freeing Hellas from the Medes with the help of those Hellenes who were willing to undertake the risk of the battle fought near our city, offered sacrifice to Zeus the Liberator in the market-place of Plataea, and calling all the allies together restored to the Plataeans their city and territory, and declared it independent and inviolate against aggression or conquest. Should any such be attempted, the allies present were to help according to their power.*[692]

Plutarch also mentions that Plataea be set apart as inviolable:

> *After this, there was a general assembly of the Hellenes, at which Aristides proposed a decree to the effect that deputies and delegates from all Hellas convene at Plataea every year, and that every fourth year festival games of deliverance be celebrated—the Eleutheria; also that a confederate Hellenic force be levied, consisting of ten thousand shield, one thousand horse, and*

---

[690] *SEG* 40.412, trans. Austin 2006: no. 63; see also Etienne and Piérart 1975.
[691] For discussion on the Glaucon Decree, see Etienne and Piérart 1975: 51-75.
[692] Thuc. 2.71.2.

one hundred ships, to prosecute the war against the Barbarian; also that the Plataeans be set apart as inviolable and consecrate, that they might sacrifice to Zeus the Deliverer in behalf of Hellas.[693]

The inviolability of Plataea is included in Plutarch's description of the Covenant of Plataea (see **no. 65** for discussion on the covenant). Plataea was in fact sacked twice after the Persian Wars, once by Sparta in 427 BC and once by Thebes in 373 BC. The destruction of a city, twice, which has apparently been deemed inviolable, makes the authenticity of Plataea's inviolability seem unlikely. However, Thucydides has the Plataeans clearly state, in the excerpt above, that the Spartan general Pausanias made Plataea inviolate from attack. Furthermore the Spartans charge the Plataeans with having 'departed from the common oath',[694] the implication being that the Spartans would be permitted to attack. Plataea's desertion of the covenant is described by Thucydides in book 3 when the Thebans are debating with the Plataeans in 427 BC.[695] It is suggested that the Plataeans' breach of covenant was their alliance with Athens and thus their joining in subjugating Greek city-states who were also covenanters such as Aegina, Euboea, and Potidaea.[696] By the aggressive behaviour Plataea displayed by allying with Athens, the Spartans, as described by Thucydides, felt released from the binds of the covenant.[697]

Thucydides clearly states that Plataea was deemed inviolate after the battle of Plataea by Pausanias. Furthermore it is stated that Plataea breached the agreement of the covenant which left the city vulnerable to attack in recompense. The clause of the Covenant of Plataea which allocated Plataea inviolable is therefore accepted here with confidence.

67. Altar of Zeus *Eleutherios* with Epigram

Plutarch mentions the altar:

Lastly they set up an altar, on which was engraven this epigram:

---

[693] Plut. *Aristides* 21.1.
[694] Thuc. 2.74.2.
[695] Thuc. 3.64.2-3 and 3.63.
[696] Meritt *et al.* 1953: 3.102-103.
[697] Meritt *et al.* 1953: 3.103.

> *The Greeks, by valour having put to flight*
> *The Persians and preserved their country's right,*
> *Erected here this altar which you see,*
> *To Zeus, preserver of their liberty.*[698]

Pausanias also mentions the altar:

> *Not far from the common tomb of the Greeks is an altar of Zeus, God of Freedom. This then is of bronze, but the altar and the image he made of white marble.*[699]

Leake, in the same passage as suggesting a position for the tombs of the Greek dead at Plataea, suggests the 'temple' of Zeus *Eleutheria* is also directly outside the eastern gate of the city and marked in his day by a ruined church; it is also noted that the 'temple' was reduced to an altar by Pausanias' time.[700] Rouse mentions an inscription by Simonides,[701] which is identical to Plutarch's epigram noted above, and states that this is the only altar dedicated for a feat of war, that he has uncovered, until Mummius dedicates an altar to the gods at Thebes (in the 2nd century BC).[702]

The altar has been understood as connected to the fourth clause of the Covenant of Plataea, where Plataea is to sacrifice to Zeus on behalf of all Greeks (see **no. 65** for discussion on the covenant).[703] Thucydides states that the Spartan Pausanias made a sacrifice to Zeus in the Plataean agora which may have initiated a cult for which the altar was shortly built.[704] The existence of the altar is accepted here on the grounds that Pausanias sacrificed to Zeus, specifically, after the battle and the existence of an altar accords with clause 4 of the covenant.

---

[698] Plut. *On the Malice of Herodotus* 42.
[699] Paus. 9.2.5.
[700] Leake 1835: 366.
[701] *Pal. Anth.* 6.50.
[702] Rouse 1902: 125.
[703] West 1965: 113.
[704] West 1965: 113-114, see also lxv, Table 4 where West suggests a date of 480-470 BC for the monument.

68. Annual Rites Performed at the Greek Tombs

Thucydides mentions these rites when he depicts the Plataeans appealing to the Spartans who are about to let them be destroyed by the Thebans:

> Look at the sepulchres of your fathers, slain by the Medes and buried in our country, whom year by year we honoured with garments and all other dues, and the first fruits of all that our land produced in their season, as friends from a friendly country and allies to our old companions in arms! Should you not decide aright, your conduct would be the very opposite to ours.[705]

The rites are also reported by Plutarch:

> the Plataeans undertook to make funeral offerings annually for the Hellenes who had fallen in battle and lay buried there.[706]

Isocrates, in his *Plataicus* written after 373 BC,[707] states that the Plataeans mention the reinstitution of this tomb cult when requesting Athens to restore their city after the Theban destruction in 373 BC:

> that we, who fought at your side for freedom, alone of the Greeks, have been driven from our homes, and that the graves of their companions in peril do not receive the customary funereal offerings through the lack of those to bring them[708]

The implication here is that no other city-state would have taken over the commemorative activity at the site of the tombs on the Plataean battlefield in the interim period while the city of Plataea was uninhabited.

Immediately prior to mentioning the annual rites paid to the war dead by the Plataeans, Plutarch outlines what has become known as the Covenant of Plataea (see discussion of the covenant in **no. 65**).[709] In clause 1 of the covenant ('Deputies' and 'Delegates' were to assemble at Plataea every

---

[705] Thuc. 3.58.4.
[706] Plut. *Aristides* 21.2, the rites are then described in some detail (21.2-5).
[707] Steinbock 2013: 157.
[708] Isoc. *Plataicus* 61.
[709] Plut. *Aristides* 21.1; for discussion on the Covenant of Plataea see West 1965: 106-110.

year) the 'Deputies' and 'Delegates' have been translated from '*theoroi*' and '*probouloi*', respectively. It has been suggested that the yearly festival described by Thucydides in the excerpt above would have required the presence of *theoroi*.[710] Although we have no direct 5th century BC reference of annual meetings of representatives at Plataea, it has been suggested that clause 1 may be interpreted in connection with the yearly festival mentioned by Thucydides.[711] Despite the annual rites being carried out until Plutarch's time,[712] the meeting of the *theoroi* and *probouloi* at Plataea may never have taken place; the meetings at Plataea were replaced with meetings at Delos when the Delian League was formed in 478 BC and it became clear that Athens was leading the war against Persia instead of the Spartans.[713]

The graves of the war dead from the battle of Plataea would have been close to Plataea itself (see **nos. 56-62**) and so it would be practical for Plataeans to tend to the honouring of the dead. Furthermore, on the strength of Thucydides' reference to the Plataeans carrying out rites at the graves of the dead the rites are accepted here with confidence. However, the association of these rites with the Covenant of Plataea is understood as questionable.

69. Tomb of Mardonius

Pausanias, before describing the uncertain fate of Mardonius' body, briefly mentions his tomb:

> Returning to the highway you again see on the right a tomb, said to be that of Mardonius. It is agreed that the body of Mardonius was not seen again after the battle, but there is not a similar agreement as to the person who gave it burial. It is admitted that Artontes, son of Mardonius, gave many gifts to Dionysophanes the Ephesian, but also that he gave them to others of the Ionians, in recognition that they too had spent some pains on the burial of Mardonius.[714]

---

[710] West 1965: 108; Meritt *et al.* 1953: 3.101; *theoroi* was the official title given to a city's representative at another city's festival, see *OCD* '*theoroi*', for a definition see Dimitrova 2008: 9-14; *probouloi* was a term used for officials in various Greek states (*OCD* '*probouloi*') but whose powers and responsibilities are unclear, see Kagan 1987: 5.
[711] West 1965: 108; Meritt *et al.* 1953: 3.101.
[712] Plut. *Aristides* 21.5.
[713] Thuc. 1.96.2; see West 1965: 108; Meritt *et al.* 1953: 3.101.
[714] Paus. 9.2.2.

It is generally agreed that Mardonius' body disappeared after the battle but without consensus on who buried him; Pausanias probably follows Herodotus in his account of attributing the burial to Dionysophanes the Ephesian, as he received gifts from Artontes, Mardonius' son, for burying his father.[715]

On the hill to the west, close to a church of the Anargyri, Pritchett noted among the underbrush a number of large, squared blocks.[716] These blocks rested on what looked like foundation walls but this is unverified by other sources. Pritchett was informed that the church was originally to be built on these ruins; however, as they were identified as the tomb of Mardonius by community seniors the site of the church was moved slightly, to the southeast of the city's walls. The inhabitants of Plataea even into the 20th century believed his tomb to be in the near vicinity, whether it was or not.[717]

The tomb of Mardonius was a site famous in antiquity and was pointed out to later travellers such as Pausanias.[718] Although the burial of Mardonius has not been recorded, the grave (whether authentic or not) was important enough to note by Pausanias which may be interpreted as the monument having obtained public importance on some level, at least by Pausanias' time. However, the lack of evidence concerning the monument's authenticity, location, or public commemorative relevance, prevents the monument being accepted with confidence.

70. Temple and Statue of Athena *Areia*

Plutarch links the construction of the temple to the battle of Plataea:

> *To this proposal Aristides was first to agree on behalf of the Athenians, then Pausanias on behalf of the Lacedaemonians. Thus reconciled, they chose out eighty talents of the booty for the Plataeans, with which they rebuilt the sanctuary of Athena, and set up the shrine, and adorned the temple with frescoes, which continue in perfect condition to the present day; then the Lacedaemonians set up a trophy on their own account, and the Athenians also for themselves.*[719]

---

[715] Hdts. 9.84.
[716] Pritchett 1957: 14-15.
[717] West 1965: 191.
[718] West 1965: 191.
[719] Plut. *Aristides* 20.3.

Contrastingly, Pausanias attributes the construction of the sanctuary and statue to the commemorations of Marathon:

> The Plataeans have also a sanctuary of Athena surnamed Warlike; it was built from the spoils given them by the Athenians as their share from the battle of Marathon. It is a wooden image gilded, but the face, hands and feet are of Pentelic marble. In size it is but little smaller than the bronze Athena on the Acropolis... the Plataeans too had Pheidias for the maker of their image of Athena. In the temple are paintings: one of them, by Polygnotus, represents Odysseus after he has killed the wooers; the other, painted by Onasias, is the former expedition of the Argives, under Adrastus, against Thebes.[720]

When describing the statue of Athena for Pellene in Achaea, Pausanias infers that the statue of Athena *Areia* in Plataea and the bronze Athena on the Acropolis **(no. 16)** are contemporaries, or at least near contemporaries.[721] The statue, therefore, may have been made in the 450s BC.[722] This later date would suit the attribution of the statue to Pheidias, rather than immediately after the battle of Marathon, in the 480s BC for example, as Pheidias would have been too young.[723]

Neither Plutarch nor Pausanias provides the dimensions for the statue but Pausanias compares this statue with that of the bronze Athena on the Acropolis, also attributed to Pheidias. Although smaller than the Athena statue on the Acropolis, Pausanias' comment suggests the statue to Athena *Areia* was colossal.[724] According to Pausanias, the temple was adorned with paintings by Polygnotus and Onasias. These works have been interpreted as symbolically representing the battles of Marathon and Plataea. Onasias' work of the Seven Against Thebes has been said to represent fighting

---

[720] Paus. 9.4.1-2.
[721] Paus. 7.27.2; see also West 1965: 73.
[722] West 1965: 73.
[723] Cullen Davison 2009: 39; Cullen Davison suggests several elements of the description of the sanctuary which support the idea that Pheidias constructed the temple statue, such as the use of mythological scenes and the juxtaposition between historical figures and deities (2009: 40).
[724] The statue stood inside the temple and therefore it is believed it could not have been more than 10 m tall (Cullen Davison 2009: 40).

against imposed tyranny from outside, while Polygnotus' work of Odysseus could represent the punishment of invaders.[725]

There is a discrepancy between the two literary sources that reference the construction of the temple; Plutarch attributes the temple to commemorations of the battle of Plataea while Pausanias attributes it to Marathon. Plutarch's attribution is followed here as he is generally considered correct on this point.[726] However, due to discrepancies in the sources this attribution is not beyond doubt. For example it has been suggested that the cult of Athena *Areia* at Plataea was established after the battle of Marathon,[727] and Plutarch states that the temple was 'rebuilt' from the booty of Plataea. Therefore, it is possible that the temple of Athena *Areia* was established from the spoils of Marathon and later refurbished from the spoils from Plataea. The temple and statue are therefore accepted here tentatively as commemorating the battle of Plataea.

71. Tomb of Pausanias

Pausanias, describing the area in Sparta near the theatre, mentions this tomb:

> *Opposite the theatre are two tombs; the first is that of Pausanias, the general at Plataea, the second is that of Leonidas.*[728]

When recounting the death of Pausanias the Spartan, Thucydides states that upon his death the Spartans were planning to throw him into the Kaiadas, where they throw the bodies of criminals. However, Pausanias was interred elsewhere and only on the order of the oracle at Delphi was the tomb moved to the place where he died, near to the temple of the goddess of the Brazen House in Sparta.[729] Due to the manner in which Pausanias died

---

[725] Francis 1990: 74-75; these interpretations are necessarily tentative and the paintings have also been suggested as representative of domestic conflict, with Thebes specifically (Höcker and Schneider 1993: 51).

[726] West (1965: 72) argues that Plutarch's interest in Boeotian antiquities suggests he is correct on this point; Frazer (1965: 5.21) believes Plutarch better informed on the origins of the sanctuary due to the circumstantiality of Plutarch's account of the dispute over the assigning of the 80 talents; see also Cullen Davison 2009: 39; Steinbock 2013: 111.

[727] Farnell 1896: 1.356-357.

[728] Paus. 3.14.1.

[729] Thuc. 1.134.1-4.

and the ill feeling the Ephors bore him, it would be unlikely he was honoured immediately after his death for his role in the Persian Wars. However, despite the existence of the tomb being accepted here with confidence, the uncertainty concerning the immediate commemorative relevance of Pausanias' tomb dictates the monument is accepted tentatively.

72. Persian Spoils Displayed in the Parthenon

Demosthenes charges Timocrates with stealing treasures from the Acropolis:

> *Was it not he who, being appointed treasurer at the Acropolis, stole from that place those prizes of victory which our ancestors carried off from the barbarians, the throne with silver feet, and Mardonius's scimitar, which weighed three hundred darics?*[730]

Dio Chrysostom also mentions the sword of Mardonius specifically:

> *Therefore, he said, I am envious of the Athenians for the expense and lavish display around the city and sanctuaries of as many deeds they have accomplished previously. For they have the sword of Mardonius, and the shields of the Spartans captured on Pylos, a more revered and better dedication than the propylaia of the Acropolis and that at Olympia worth more than ten thousand talents.*[731]

Pausanias lists noteworthy examples of votive offerings:

> *The votive offerings worth noting are, of the old ones, a folding chair made by Daedalus, Persian spoils, namely the breastplate of Masistius, who commanded the cavalry at Plataea, and a scimitar said to have belonged to Mardonius. Now Masistius I know was killed by the Athenian cavalry. But Mardonius was opposed by the Lacedaemonians and was killed by a Spartan; so the Athenians could not have taken the scimitar to begin with, and furthermore the Lacedaemonians would scarcely have suffered them to carry it off.*[732]

---

[730] Dem. *Against Timocrates* 129.
[731] Dio Chr. *Orations* 2.36.
[732] Paus. 1.27.1.

Harpocration also mentions a silver footed throne which was included in the spoils:

> *That of Xerxes, and who as a warrior, presided and sat upon it, as he watched the naval battle. It is kept in the Parthenon of Athena.*[733]

The literary excerpts noted above are generally consistent with their references to the spoils.[734] In particular, the sword of Mardonius is mentioned by Demosthenes,[735] Dio Chrysostom and Pausanias, and Xerxes' throne is mentioned by Demosthenes and Harpocration.

We learn from Herodotus that the Greek forces amassed a great deal of spoils after the battle of Plataea.[736] Furthermore, the consensus that Mardonius' sword is displayed as spoils connects the dedication to the battle of Plataea, as does the breastplate from Masistius mentioned by Pausanias. The existence of this monument is accepted with confidence, and is accepted as a commemorative monument of Plataea. However, it is probable that the Athenians would also have amassed spoils from the battle of Marathon, and the references to Xerxes' throne, from which Harpocration tells us he watched 'the naval battle', indicates the spoils may have related to more than one battle.[737]

73. Odeum

Plutarch describes the Odeum at Athens:

> *The Odeum, which was arranged internally with many tiers of seats and many pillars, and which had a roof made with a circular slope from a single peak, they say was an exact reproduction of the Great King's pavilion, and this too was built under the superintendence of Pericles. Wherefore Cratinus, in his 'Thracian Women,' rails at him again:*

---

[733] Harp. s.v. *argyropos diphros*.
[734] The Persian spoils were also included in Pericles' account of Athens' wealth at the beginning of the Peloponnesian War (Thuc. 2.13.4).
[735] West (1965: 152) dates this speech to 353 BC.
[736] Hdts. 9.80.
[737] West (1965: 152-154) nevertheless interprets the spoils as commemorating the battle of Plataea solely.

The squill-head Zeus! lo! here he comes,
The Odeum like a cap upon his cranium,
Now that for good and all the ostracism is o'er.[738]

Pausanias places the structure in the area of the sanctuary of Dionysus:

Near the sanctuary of Dionysus and the theatre is a structure, which is said to be a copy of Xerxes' tent.[739]

Vitruvius also mentions the Odeum when describing colonnades:

Such places, for instance, are the colonnades of Pompey, and also, in Athens, the colonnades of Eumenes and the fane of Father Bacchus; also, as you leave the theatre, the music hall which Themistocles surrounded with stone columns, and roofed with the yards and masts of ships captured from the Persians.[740]

Plutarch quotes a 5th century BC source, Cratinus, who mentions the Odeum.[741] Vitruvius is the only source who states that Themistocles roofed the structure with beams taken from captured Persian ships, perhaps from Salamis. However, the Odeum has been dated to the last quarter of the 5th century BC which would be too late to attribute to Themistocles.[742] Excavations undertaken at the Odeum site have revealed that there were both stone columns and wood used in the monument's construction, but there is no way of determining whether the structure was built by Themistocles, or indeed Pericles as described by Plutarch in the excerpt

---

[738] Plut. *Pericles* 13.5-6.
[739] Paus. 1.20.4.
[740] Vitr. 5.9.1.
[741] Plutarch is trusted by West 1965: 155 as a reliable source for dating the structure to the 5th century BC due to this reference.
[742] Dinsmoor 1951: 1.317-318; this date is suggested in connection with the westward shift of the 'theatre of Nicias' (otherwise known as the theatre of Dionysus). The Odeum, dated to *c.* 425 BC and therefore constructed before the stone theatre (completed in 415 BC, see Dinsmoor 1951: 1.329-330), prevented its eastward expansion. See Camp 2001: 224 for the spatial relationship between the theatre and the Odeum.

above.⁷⁴³ It has been suggested that Themistocles did some building on the Odeum and Pericles later rebuilt or repaired the original building.⁷⁴⁴

The Odeum is understood here as a commemorative monument of Plataea because, according to Plutarch and Pausanias, it was constructed as a replica of Xerxes' tent which was left to Mardonius at Plataea and may well have fallen into Athenian hands after the conflict.⁷⁴⁵ Despite the Odeum remaining mostly unexcavated,⁷⁴⁶ the monument is accepted here with confidence due to the agreement in the literary sources of a 5th century BC Odeum existing in Athens, and its connection with the Persian Wars.

74. Shields Hung on Temple Architraves

Aeschines mentions the shields:

> Now it was reported to us by one and another who wished to show friendship to our city, that the Amphissians, who were at that time dominated by the Thebans and were their abject servants, were in the act of bringing in a resolution against our city, to the effect that the people of Athens be fined fifty talents, because we had affixed gilded shields to the new temple and dedicated them before the temple had been consecrated, and had written the appropriate inscription, 'The Athenians, from the Medes and Thebans when they fought against Hellas.'⁷⁴⁷

Pausanias also mentions the monument when describing the temple of Apollo:

> There are arms of gold on the architraves; the Athenians dedicated the shields from spoils taken at the battle of Marathon, and the Aetolians the arms, supposed to be Gallic, behind and on the left. Their shape is very like that of Persian wicker shields.⁷⁴⁸

---

[743] Davison 1958: 34-35; the structure has only been partially excavated and the details of the building plan are obscure, see Camp 2001: 101.
[744] See Davison 1958: 34-35; West 1965: 156-157.
[745] Hdts. 9.82.1.
[746] Camp 2001: 255.
[747] Aesch. *Against Ctesiphon* 116.
[748] Paus. 10.19.4.

Early in the 4th century BC the temple of Apollo at Delphi was destroyed, either by fire or earthquake.[749] During the rebuilding, the Athenians hung gilded shields of the Persian type and erected an inscription nearby stating they were taken from the Persians and Thebans. French excavators found one slab form the outer surface of a metope upon which the outline of a shield is visible due to the difference in weathering, which supports the literary evidence.[750]

The dedication of the shields in the 4th century BC has been suggested as a rehanging of an original dedication of Persian spoils immediately following the Persian Wars in the early 5th century BC; many of the original shields may have dislodged in the destruction of the temple in *c.* 373 BC.[751] Furthermore the inscription, as quoted by Aeschines, has been suggested as being a repetition of original phrases engraved on the spoils at their first dedication with an added Theban reference due to the anti-Theban sentiment amongst Athenians at the time.[752]

Pausanias states the shields were dedicated from the spoils of Marathon but, according to the inscription reported by Aeschines, the battle concerned involved fighting against Persians and Thebans. The only battle at which the Thebans fought alongside Persia was at Plataea and therefore this monument is understood here to be dedicated from the spoils of Plataea.[753] While the archaeological evidence supports the literary assertions describing the hanging of the shields in the 4th century BC, the suggestion that this dedication replaced an earlier dedication referencing Persians solely is speculative and therefore accepted here tentatively.

---

[749] See Parke 1939: 71-72.
[750] See an image of the metope in *FD* II 1 Fig. 18; Parke 1939: 72.
[751] Parke 1939: 71-72.
[752] Parke 1939: 72; West (1965: 158) states this copying of inscriptions as 'doubtless' but does not qualify his certainty. For the emphasis on Theban Medism in Athenian political discourse see Steinbock 2013: 119-127
[753] See Parke 1939: 71-78; West 1965: 159; Scott 2010: 77, n. 11 dates the monument to either 490 or 479 BC due to the inconsistent references in the literary sources.

75. Bronze Statue of Artemis the Saviour

The sole literary reference for this Megarian statue is provided by Pausanias:

> Not far from this fountain is an ancient sanctuary, and in our day likenesses stand in it of Roman emperors, and a bronze image is there of Artemis surnamed Saviour. There is a story that a detachment of the army of Mardonius, having over run Megaris, wished to return to Mardonius at Thebes, but that by the will of Artemis night came on them as they marched, and missing their way they turned into the hilly region. Trying to find out whether there was a hostile force near they shot some missiles. The rock near groaned when struck, and they shot again with greater eagerness, until at last they used up all their arrows thinking that they were shooting at the enemy. When the day broke, the Megarians attacked, and being men in armour fighting against men without armour who no longer had even a supply of missiles, they killed the greater number of their opponents. For this reason they had an image made of Artemis Saviour.[754]

Pausanias relates a story of Artemis confusing the Persian forces. This study presents various monuments commemorating the intervention of deities and heroes alike, such as Pan (**no. 14**), Cychreus (**no. 45**), and Theseus (**no. 12**). Pausanias goes on to mention that the statue was made by Strongylion.[755] The date for this sculptor is not known but it is thought that he may have been of the late 5th century BC.[756] Due to the lack of further evidence to support Pausanias' statement, this monument may only be accepted tentatively.

76. Bronze Statue of Artemis the Saviour

Pausanias is our only literary reference for this monument:

> As you go to Pagae, on turning a little aside from the highway, you are shown a rock with arrows stuck all over it, into which the Persians once shot in the night. In Pagae a noteworthy relic is a bronze image of Artemis surnamed Saviour, in size equal to that at Megara and exactly like it in shape.[757]

---

[754] Paus. 1.40.2-3.
[755] Paus. 1.40.3.
[756] See Richter 1950: 245-246.
[757] Paus. 1.44.4.

This monument commemorates the same skirmish which is commemorated by the statue of Artemis in Megara (**no. 75**).⁷⁵⁸ Due to a lack of supporting evidence this monument may also only be accepted tentatively.

77. Grave of Euchidas with Engraved Stele

Plutarch describes the grave and inscription to Euchidas:

> *There he purified his person by sprinkling himself with the holy water, and crowned himself with laurel. Then he took from the altar the sacred fire and started to run back to Plataea. He reached the place before the sun had set, accomplishing thus a thousand furlongs in one and the same day. He greeted his countrymen, handed them the sacred fire, and straightway fell down, and after a little expired. In admiration of him the Plataeans gave him burial in the sanctuary of Artemis Eukleia, and inscribed upon his tomb this tetrameter verse:*
>
> *Euchidas, to Pytho running, came back here*
> *the selfsame day.*⁷⁵⁹

Euchidas, who was a Plataean, was honoured by his countrymen for bringing the sacred fire from Delphi on the same day as the victory at Plataea; this act has been interpreted as an act of purification.⁷⁶⁰ The distance, calculated to about 114 miles, has been deemed physically impossible.⁷⁶¹ Due to the, possibly, exaggerated details of the feat, and reference to the grave surviving in only a single literary source, this monument may only be accepted tentatively.

78. Statue of an Ox

Pausanias mentions the statue when describing monuments at Delphi:

> *The Plataeans have dedicated an ox, an offering made at the time when, in their own territory, they took part, along with the other Greeks, in the defence against Mardonius, the son of Gobryas.*⁷⁶²

---

⁷⁵⁸ West 1965: 189.
⁷⁵⁹ Plut. *Aristides* 20.5.
⁷⁶⁰ West 1965: 190.
⁷⁶¹ Cartledge 2013: 131.
⁷⁶² Paus. 10.15.1.

The meaning of statues of oxen is disputed. It has been suggested that dedicated statues of oxen may be intended to represent an agricultural state or possibly the strength of the dedicator.[763] Alternatively, Pausanias believes that the oxen represent the victory over the barbarian and therefore the securing of the land which would now be free to plough.[764] Whereas Rouse suggests the dedication of an animal statue may be representative of the entire act of sacrifice, including the procession.[765]

The location of this monument has been suggested as somewhere on the east temple terrace.[766] This placement is based on Pausanias' description of the surrounding area and monuments before and after mentioning the Plataean ox statue.[767] Furthermore, it is on the strength of Pausanias' attribution of this statue to the battle of Plataea that the monument has been dated to 479 BC.[768] However, due to a lack of further evidence, the monument may only be accepted here tentatively.

79. Contents of the Manger of Mardonius Dedicated to Athena *Alea*

Herodotus is our sole literary source for this dedication:

> *The first to enter were the Tegeans, and it was they who plundered the tent of Mardonius, taking from it besides everything else the feeding trough of his horses which was all of bronze and a thing well worth looking at. The Tegeans dedicated this feeding trough of Mardonius in the temple of Athena Alea.*[769]

We learn from Herodotus that the Greek forces amassed a great deal of spoils after the battle of Plataea.[770] Other cities would have taken spoils from the battle and dedicated them in their own ways (e.g. **no. 72**). On the strength of Herodotus' statement and the likelihood of Greek contingents claiming spoils from the defeated Persians at Plataea, this monument is accepted with confidence.

---

[763] West 1965: xlviii.
[764] Paus. 10.16.6.
[765] Rouse 1902: 145.
[766] See Scott 2010: 83, Fig. 4.3, no. 112.
[767] Paus. 10.14.7-15.2.
[768] Scott 2010: Appendix C, no. 112; Jacquemin 1999: no. 412 who dates the monument based solely on the literary evidence.
[769] Hdts. 9.70.3.
[770] Hdts. 9.80.

GENERAL

80. Serpent Column

Herodotus mentions the Serpent Column at Delphi:

> *Having brought all the loot together, they set apart a tithe for the god of Delphi. From this was made and dedicated that tripod which rests upon the bronze three-headed serpent*[771]

Thucydides also mentions this monument and mentions the original inscription inscribed by Pausanias before its removal by the Spartans:

> *it was remembered that he had taken upon himself to have inscribed on the tripod at Delphi, which was dedicated by the Hellenes as the first-fruits of the spoil of the Medes, the following couplet:—*
> *'The Mede defeated, great Pausanias raised*
> *This monument, that Phoebus might be praised.'*
> *At the time the Lacedaemonians had at once erased the couplet, and inscribed the names of the cities that had aided in the overthrow of the barbarian and dedicated the offering.*[772]

The monument and original inscription is also mentioned by Pseudo-Demosthenes:

> *Pausanias, the king of the Lacedaemonians, puffed up by this, inscribed a distich upon the tripod at Delphi, which the Greeks who had jointly fought in the battle at Plataea and in the sea-fight at Salamis had made in common from the spoils taken from the barbarians, and had set up in honour of Apollo as a memorial of their valour. The distich was as follows:*
>
> *'Pausanias, supreme commander of the Greeks, when he had destroyed the host of the Medes,*
> *dedicated to Phoebus this memorial.'* [773]

---

[771] Hdts. 9.81.
[772] Thuc. 1.132.2-3.
[773] [Dem.] *Against Nearea* 97.

Diodorus mentions the monument and is the sole reference for this additional epigram:

The Greeks, taking a tenth part of the spoils, made a gold tripod and set it up in Delphi as a thank-offering to the God, inscribing on it the following couplet:

This is the gift the saviours of far-flung Hellas upraised here, Having delivered their states from loathsome slavery's bonds.[774]

Pausanias also mentions the monument and provides information about Phocian plundering of Delphi:

The Greeks in common dedicated from the spoils taken at the battle of Plataea a gold tripod set on a bronze serpent. The bronze part of the offering is still preserved, but the Phocian leaders did not leave the gold as they did the bronze.[775]

The literary sources above are generally consistent in describing this monument as dedicated to Apollo at Delphi and consisting of a tripod set on three bronze serpents. The base of the monument is in situ and the monument was placed on top of the old *peribolos* wall, of pre-548 BC, on the east temple terrace.[776]

Pausanias describes the removal of gold aspects of the monument by the Phocians, which has been interpreted as taking place between 355-346 BC, in the third Sacred War.[777] The monument is no longer in situ but a large fragment of the column has survived and is currently displayed in the Hippodrome in Istanbul. The removal of the column has been dated to the 4th century AD and attributed to Constantine.[778] After being covered by soil

---

[774] Diod. 11.33.2.
[775] Paus. 10.13.9.
[776] For the monument's location see Scott 2010: 83, Fig. 4.3 no. 109; see Jaquemin 1999: 336, no. 310 for a select bibliography.
[777] Bengston 1960: 303; see also Scott 2010: 124, and for further references.
[778] For discussion of the evidence on the date of the monument's removal see Madden 1992: 112-116.

and debris over time, the column was reported in Newton's documented travels in 1865.[779]

The preserved column is made up of 29 coils and stands at a height of about 5.5 m; the coils represent the intertwined bodies of three snakes, but the column was cast as a single piece.[780] The heads and the tails of the serpents are missing from the column but the upper part of one of the heads was found during an excavation in 1848.[781]

The column bears an inscription and is engraved on successive coils of the column. The inscription runs from the thirteenth coil to the third from the bottom and consists of a list of cities. The list is preceded by a brief sentence: 'The following fought in the war', which is understood to refer to the events of the second Persian invasion of 480-479 BC.[782] The coil is inscribed with the names of 31 cities which correspond exactly with Plutarch's number of cities who fought against the Persians.[783] It has been noted that this monument may have been the source of information for Plutarch's statement.[784] Furthermore, the list inscribed on this monument may have been an official list;[785] Herodotus informs us that the Tenians were added to the list specifically because of their services before the battle of Salamis, and Thucydides has the Plataeans appeal to the list's authority when threatened with destruction by the Spartans.[786]

Herodotus, in the excerpt above, is describing the loot taken from the battle of Plataea from which this monument was originally made and dedicated. According to Thucydides, in the excerpt above, the monument was originally inscribed by Pausanias who claimed to have defeated the Persians. However, the original inscription displeased the Spartans who had it erased and replaced with a list of cities that took part in the war. With the re-inscribing of the monument, its commemorative focus was changed from a monument specifically commemorating the battle of Plataea to the

---

[779] Newton 1865: 2.25-35.
[780] West 1965: 79.
[781] As noted by Frazer (1965: 5.302).
[782] *Syll.*³ 31, trans. West 1965: 81, and 80 where Salamis and Plataea are cited for the battles commemorated.
[783] Plut. *Themistocles* 20.3-4.
[784] See West 1965: 81, n. 6.
[785] Meritt *et al.* 1953: 3.95; see also West 1965: 84.
[786] Tenian addition: Hdts 8.82; Plataean appeal: Thuc. 3.57.

defeat of Xerxes' invasion generally.[787] Diodorus is the sole reference for an additional epigram, which may have been inscribed on the monument's base.[788] However, due to the numerous other references to the monument with no mention of the epigram this aspect of the monument is questionable.

Due to the general agreement of this monument's form and commemorative meaning, which is largely corroborated by the extant archaeological and inscriptional evidence, the Serpent Column is accepted here with confidence.

81. Bronze Statue of Zeus

Herodotus mentions this statue:

> *Having brought all the loot together, they set apart a tithe... for the god of Olympia, from which was made and dedicated a bronze figure of Zeus, ten cubits high*[789]

Pausanias also mentions the monument on three occasions:

> *As you pass by the entrance to the Council Chamber you see an image of Zeus standing with no inscription on it, and then on turning to the north another image of Zeus. This is turned towards the rising sun, and was dedicated by those Greeks who at Plataea fought against the Persians under Mardonius. On the right of the pedestal are inscribed the cities which took part in the engagement: first the Lacedaemonians, after them the Athenians, third the Corinthians, fourth the Sicyonians, fifth the Aeginetans; after the Aeginetans, the Megarians and Epidaurians, of the Arcadians the people of Tegea and Orchomenus, after them the dwellers in Phlius, Troezen and Hermion, the Tirynthians from the Argolid, the Plataeans alone of the Boeotians, the Argives of Mycenae, the islanders of Ceos and Melos, Ambraciots of the Thesprotian mainland, the Tenians and the Lepreans, who were the only people from Triphylia, but from the Aegean and the Cyclades there came not only the Tenians but also the Naxians*

---

[787] West 1965: 82; the monument cannot commemorate solely Plataea because city names included in the list, such as the Ceans, Melians, Tenians, Naxians, Cythians, and Syphnians, were not present at the battle of Plataea according to Herodotus' count (9.28 and 30); Scott (2010: 86) also believes the monument commemorated the Persian Wars generally.
[788] This epigram is accepted by Frazer (1965: 5.300).
[789] Hdts. 9.81.1.

and Cythnians, Styrians too from Euboea, after them Eleans, Potidaeans, Anactorians, and lastly the Chalcidians on the Euripus.[790]

After Iccus stands Pantarces the Elean, beloved of Pheidias, who beat the boys at wrestling. Next to Pantarces is the chariot of Cleosthenes, a man of Epidamnus. This is the work of Ageladas, and it stands behind the Zeus dedicated by the Greeks from the spoil of the battle of Plataea.[791]

The Greeks who fought against the king, besides dedicating at Olympia a bronze Zeus, dedicated also an Apollo at Delphi, from spoils taken in the naval actions at Artemisium and Salamis.[792]

A monument base, discovered at Olympia, has been suggested as supporting this statue of Zeus mentioned by Pausanias and Herodotus.[793] This monument base is situated on the south east side of the temple of Zeus about 5 m from the Altis wall.[794] However Frazer notes that the identification of the stone and its connection to this statue of Zeus is primarily based on Pausanias' route through the Altis, but his route is too uncertain for a confident identification.[795]

Herodotus is describing the loot taken at the battle of Plataea when mentioning the statue. Furthermore Pausanias, in two of the excerpts above, states that the statue is paid for by the spoils of the battle of Plataea. However, the names of the cities inscribed on the pedestal of the statue include a number of cities who did not take part in the battle of Plataea (e.g. Ceos, Melos, Tenos, Naxos and Cythnos).[796]

West suggests that when the names were inscribed on the pedestal, the meaning of the monument was altered from a commemoration of Plataea

---

[790] Paus. 5.23.1-2.
[791] Paus. 6.10.6.
[792] Paus. 10.14.5.
[793] See Wiesner 1939: 152.
[794] See also Hyde 1921: 345; Eckstein 1969: 23; See Scott 2010: 166, Fig. 6.7 for the positioning of the 'Plataian Zeus'.
[795] Frazer 1965: 3.631; it should be noted that the identification of the stone was also based on a cutting on the top of the stone which may have held a stele mentioned by Pausanias (5.23.4), see Eckstein 1969: 23.
[796] According to the forces present at Plataea outlined by Herodotus (9.28 and 30).

to a more general commemoration.⁷⁹⁷ Due to the inclusion of a broad collection of city-states in the inscription, beyond those who fought at Plataea, West's suggestion of a more general commemorative intention is followed here. This monument is included with confidence considering the consistent references in the literary sources; however the identification of the extant base is still uncertain.

82. Bronze Statue of Poseidon

Herodotus is our only literary source for this statue:

> *Having brought all the loot together, they set apart a tithe... for the god of the Isthmus, from which was fashioned a bronze Poseidon seven cubits high.*⁷⁹⁸

This statue was part of the original pan-Hellenic dedication made from the loot from the battle of Plataea, the two other parts being the statue of Zeus at Olympia and the serpent column at Delphi (see **nos. 80** and **81**). A list of cities who took part in the entire conflict was inscribed on the serpent column and the statue of Zeus which transformed those monument's meanings into more general commemorative monuments. Therefore, this statue is considered in the same light.⁷⁹⁹ However, while this monument is accepted here with confidence on the strength of Herodotus' assertion, there is no evidence that this statue bore such an inscribed list.

83. Persian Stoa in Sparta

This monument is described by Vitruvius:

> *Likewise the Lacedaemonians under the leadership of Pausanias, son of Agesipolis, after conquering the Persian armies, infinite in number, with a small force at the battle of Plataea, celebrated a glorious triumph with the spoils and booty, and with the money obtained from the sale thereof*

---

⁷⁹⁷ West 1965: 89, and it is further suggested that this list of cities may have been an imperfect copy of an official list which was inscribed more faithfully on the serpent column in Delphi (see **no. 80**).
⁷⁹⁸ Hdts. 9.81.1.
⁷⁹⁹ As it is by West (1965: 89-90).

built the Persian Porch, to be a monument to the renown and valour of the people and a trophy of victory for posterity. And there they set effigies of the prisoners arrayed in barbarian costume and holding up the roof, their pride punished by this deserved affront, that enemies might tremble for fear of the effects of their courage, and that their own people, looking upon this ensample of their valour and encouraged by the glory of it, might be ready to defend their independence. So from that time on, many have put up statues of Persians supporting entablatures and their ornaments, and thus from that motive have greatly enriched the diversity of their works.[800]

Pausanias also describes the Persian Stoa:

The most striking feature in the marketplace is the portico which they call Persian because it was made from spoils taken in the Persian wars. In course of time they have altered it until it is as large and as splendid as it is now. On the pillars are white-marble figures of Persians, including Mardonius, son of Gobryas. There is also a figure of Artemisia, daughter of Lygdamis and queen of Halicarnassus. It is said that this lady voluntarily joined the expedition of Xerxes against Greece and distinguished herself at the naval engagement off Salamis.[801]

The form of this monument and its elaborateness, in the 5th century BC, is uncertain as Thucydides claims that Spartans were less interested in constructing magnificent monumental landscapes than other *poleis*.[802] Pausanias, in the excerpt above, does state that the structure was elaborated over time so it is possible the initial monument was less ornate. Furthermore, it has been suggested that this monument should be identified with archaeological remains discovered on the north-west side of the Spartan agora.[803]

Vitruvius specifically mentions the battle of Plataea above, and it is quite possible that the Stoa was paid for from the sale of the booty from this

---

[800] Vitr. 1.1.6.
[801] Paus. 3.11.3.
[802] Thuc. 1.10; as noted in Low 2011: 3.
[803] See Waywell 1999: 14, who is tempted to make this connection, although is tentative due to no sign of the statues of the Persians; see Low 2011: 10, Fig. 1.4 for the proposed positioning of the monument.

battle.⁸⁰⁴ However, we are informed by Pausanias that the statues built to hold up the roof of the Stoa included Artemisia, who distinguished herself at Salamis. It may be assumed that the Stoa, instead of commemorating the battle of Plataea alone, came to be a monument for the Persian Wars in general.⁸⁰⁵ In the absence of secure dating for this monument it is considered here tentatively as a monument of the classical period.

84. Athenian Portico Displaying Spoils

The inscription can still be read on the portico's stylobate today:

> The Athenians dedicated the stoa and the cabl[es a]nd the ship's ornaments, having taken them from the en[em]y⁸⁰⁶

Herodotus mentions that the Athenians dedicated cables from the Persian bridge over the Hellespont:

> This done, they sailed away to Hellas, carrying with them the cables of the bridges to be dedicated in their temples, and all sorts of things in addition. This, then, is all that was done in this year.⁸⁰⁷

Pausanias mentions the dedication but associates it with another conflict:

> The Athenians also built a portico out of the spoils they took in their war against the Peloponnesians and their Greek allies. There are also dedicated the figure-heads of ships and bronze shields. The inscription on them enumerates the cities from which the Athenians sent the first-fruits: Elis, Lacedaemon, Sicyon, Megara, Pellene in Achaia, Ambracia, Leucas, and Corinth itself. It also says that from the spoils taken in these sea-battles a sacrifice was offered to Theseus and to Poseidon at the cape called Rhium. It seems to me that the inscription refers to Phormio, son of Asopichus, and to his achievements.⁸⁰⁸

---

⁸⁰⁴ The spoils of this battle were rich (Hdts. 9.80 and 81) and Sparta would have taken a large share, having commanded the forces.
⁸⁰⁵ West 1965: 118.
⁸⁰⁶ *Syll*³ 29; author's trans.
⁸⁰⁷ Hdts. 9.121.
⁸⁰⁸ Paus. 10.11.6.

The stoa of the Athenians was discovered in 1880 by French excavators and is situated against the polygonal wall beneath the south temple terrace.[809]

Pausanias states that spoils from the naval victories of the Athenian general Phormio were displayed in the portico. Pausanias also states that the portico itself was built from the spoils taken in these conflicts. However, the letter forms in the surviving inscription have been judged as too early to agree with Pausanias' dating, and should not be dated later than 470 BC, and may be as early as 510 BC.[810] The lettering is in an archaic Attic alphabet which was utilised in the 6th century BC but was gradually discarded in the 5th century BC. However, conclusive dating cannot be made on the inscriptional evidence alone because different letters of the archaic alphabet were retained longer than others.[811]

The structure itself is difficult to date with certainty due to a lack of similar structures with which to compare it.[812] The architectural remains have been analysed and it has been suggested that the structure could be dated to the 6th century BC, or may support a 5th century BC date if the structure is accepted as bearing 'archaising tendencies'.[813] The strongest argument against a 6th century BC date is the use of Pentelic marble in the construction of the columns. This material did not become into use in Athens until after the Persian Wars.[814] Furthermore, it has been suggested that the use of Ionic columns suggest a 5th century BC date for the structure; while Ionic columns had been used in Athenian architecture from the time of the Pisistratids, it was only in the middle of the 5th century BC that

---

[809] Haussoullier 1881: 7-19; for the location of the portico see Scott 2010: 83, Fig. 4.3 no. 133.

[810] See *ML* 25; varying dates have been suggested in collections of Greek historical inscriptions such as: 460/459 BC for an Athenian victory over the Aeginetans (*MGHI* 20), and 480 BC as a thank-offering for victory at Salamis (*GHI* 18).

[811] See West 1965: 131 for discussion on letter forms; see also Walsh 1986: 324-326, who argues that a date as late as 450 BC cannot be excluded when analysing the letter forms.

[812] West 1965: 130.

[813] Quote from West 1965: 130; for analysis of the archaising architectural features see *FD* II 92-101. These features include: the ratio between the height of the column and the lower diameter of the shaft (which vary between 7.88 and 8.48 in the Athenian portico) resembling an archaic figure of about 7-8. While in the classical period the ratio exceeds 9; and the ratio of the height of the base to the diameter of the shaft at the point of intersection with the base (which is 0.52 in the Athenian portico) contrasts with later classical ratios of 0.485-0.38.

[814] West 1965: 131.

they became prominent.[815] Based on the architectural remains and the inscriptional evidence a date of close to 480 BC has been suggested.[816]

It has been suggested that the portico was constructed in order to house (and display) the cables of Xerxes' bridge over the Hellespont and ornaments from some of the ships.[817] This idea supports the account provided by Herodotus, who uses the word *'hopla'* to describe the cables from the Persian bridge over the Hellespont, as does the inscription noted above. While the wide column spaces suggest it was designed for display, the material on show has also been disputed. For example, the term *'hopla'* has been suggested to refer to arms taken in battle rather than parts of a bridge.[818] Furthermore even the term *'helontes'*, which appears in the inscription adorning the portico, has come under scrutiny. The term may be understood to refer to seizure of goods, whereas the cables of Xerxes' bridge were initially removed to Kardia when the bridge was broken up and handed to the Greeks at Sestos.[819]

In contrast to the attribution of the monument to commemorations of the Persian Wars, it has been suggested that the monument did not refer to one specific conflict but all Athenian victories over a range of conflicts.[820] The vague reference to 'enemies' without specifying any one people supports this suggestion. Furthermore, the fact that the Persians are not mentioned in the inscription has been interpreted as evidence that the monument was not intended to commemorate victory in the Persian Wars at all.[821]

Based on the tentative dating of the structure, which is deduced from the archaeological and inscriptional evidence, and the apparent purpose of the structure complementing Herodotus' account, this stoa is cautiously accepted here as a monument of the Persian Wars. The lack of literary evidence attributing the structure to the commemorations of the Persian

---

[815] Walsh 1986: 332.
[816] *FD* II 108; this period is agreed with by Hansen (1989: 133); Walsh (1986) prefers a later date of construction, around the 450's BC.
[817] Amandry 1946: 1-8; see also *FD* II 1 5 91-121.
[818] See Walsh 1986: 322-323.
[819] Hdts. 9.115; Walsh 1986: 322; see also *ML* 25.
[820] Hansen 1989: 133-134.
[821] See Walsh 1986: 321, who goes on to argue that the spoils would have been taken from Greeks.

Wars, the lack of a specific enemy mentioned in the inscription and the general debate concerning the date of construction prevent accepting this monument with confidence.

85. North Wall of the Acropolis

The north wall of the Acropolis contains fragments of the unfinished Older Parthenon and the temple of Athena *Polias* which were destroyed during the Persian sacking of Athens (see **no. 17**).[822] The ostentatious display of aspects of Persian destruction has led Kousser to interpret the wall as commemorating Athenian victory over the Persians.[823] Two main stretches of the rebuilt Acropolis walls display destroyed building fragments: parts of the temple of Athena Polias' entablature are positioned north-west of the Erechtheion, and column drums from the Old Parthenon are displayed to the north-east of the Erechtheion (see Figures 15 and 16). The column drums have been said to be too unwieldy to have been selected for pragmatic reasons, as they weigh about seven tons each and there are 27 of them.[824] The entablature, too, is carefully arranged and is considered a purposeful selection; for example the architrave, the metope frieze and cornice appear just as they would have appeared on the temple of Athena *Polias*. Plenty of other plain rectangular blocks would have been available for use, instead the most temple-like fragments were selected: the column drums were lined up in a row and the entablature was extended to a distance similar to that of the original temple.[825]

Due to the lack of evidence confirming the construction as commemorative, Kousser's interpretation is followed here only tentatively. The construction of the wall is suggested as being a symbol of power and pride which enabled the Athenians of the 5th century BC to collectively recall the eventual repulsion of the Persians.[826]

---

[822] Dinsmoor 1950: 150.

[823] See Kousser 2009: 270-271; this idea is also suggested by West (1965: 134) who includes the wall as a monument to the Persian Wars; *contra.* Steskal (2004: 210-211) who argues the selection of material from destroyed buildings was an economic choice after a costly war.

[824] Hurwit 1999: 142; Kousser 2009: 271.

[825] See Kousser 2009: 271 for this argument and further bibliography; Hurwit (2004: 70) interprets the Acropolis wall construction discussed here as purposeful and describes it as 'an eternal lament'.

[826] Kousser 2009: 271.

Figure 15. Section of Acropolis wall displaying Temple of Athena Polias' entablature (after Kousser 2009: 270. Reproduced by kind permission of Professor Rachel Kousser).

Figure 16. Section of Acropolis Wall displaying column drums of the Older Parthenon (after Kousser 2009: 271. Reproduced by kind permission of Professor Rachel Kousser).

86. 'New' Parthenon

The construction of the 'New' Parthenon was initiated in 447 BC.[827] The New Parthenon was constructed directly on the site of the Old Parthenon (see also **no. 17**), and recycled much of the original building materials in the new structure.[828] The only aspects of the original that were not reused were the column drums too damaged by thermal fracture which were in turn transformed into their own commemorative monument, built into the north wall of the Acropolis (see **no. 85**). The reuse of building materials in the new temple has been analysed in economic terms,[829] however it has also been suggested that Athenians of the 5th century BC would have understood the structure as representing a 'rebirth' of the ruined sanctuary.[830] Furthermore, the connection between the Parthenon and the Persian Wars are thought to have been portrayed symbolically through myth.[831] The Persians may be associated with negative mythological exemplars such as the Centaurs and the Amazons who battle the Greek figures on the metopes. On a number of the metopes, depicting Greeks fighting both Amazons and Centaurs the humans appear in mortal danger.[832] The artistic impression is then one depicting the price of victory rather than its effortless achievement. It has been suggested that the presenting of the Persian Wars through myth allowed the Athenians to re-write the past and remember the initial defeats as the precursor to eventual victory, as the Greeks always win in the battles portrayed on the Parthenon's metopes.[833]

The Parthenon frieze has been the focus of much scholarly debate and has prompted numerous suggestions for its meaning and significance.[834] The frieze has been interpreted in connection with the battle of Marathon

---

[827] Kousser 2009: 269, 275, for further references for building accounts see n. 59; for discussion of the building accounts see also Pope 2000.
[828] See Boardman 1977: 39, and n. 3; Neils 2001: 27.
[829] Pope 2000: 65-66.
[830] Hurwit 2004: 72-76.
[831] As suggested by Kousser 2009: 276-277.
[832] It has also been argued that the subject of the west metopes on the Parthenon is a fight between Greeks and Persians, not Amazons, see Brommer 1967: 191-195.
[833] Kousser 2009: 277.
[834] E.g. the inaugural Panathenaic procession during the reign of Cecrops, first legendary king of Athens: Kardara 1964: 115-158, for objections see Neils 2001: 177-178, Boardman

in particular.[835] John Boardman has argued that the frieze represents the Great *Panathenaia* which took place on 28 Hecatombaion, six weeks before the battle of Marathon, an event which the *Marathonomachoi* would probably have attended.[836] The 192 dead Athenian war dead from Marathon were numbered at 192 by Herodotus,[837] and this number has been calculated as being represented on the frieze.[838] The war dead are interpreted by Boardman to have been heroised and therefore represented as knights on horseback or warriors in chariots.[839] These individuals have been suggested as the only mortal Athenian citizens who earned the right to be portrayed in the company of the gods, who are also represented on the frieze.[840]

Boardman's theory has been refuted.[841] Due to missing parts of the frieze it is difficult to calculate the exact number of individuals, therefore any conclusions based on figure numbers would be extremely questionable. However, a more serious objection has been raised about exactly who is counted on the frieze to make up the supposed 192 Marathon dead.[842] For example neither the charioteers nor the men who carry the cult equipment and lead the sacrificial animals are counted, while the marshals who direct the cavalcade and the young attendants who hold the horses' reins are counted. Furthermore, the lack of hoplites (even considering Boardman's explanation of heroisation) has been interpreted as a serious problem, as the battle of Marathon was a hoplite

---

1984: 210, Boardman 1977: 43; the east frieze depicting the actions preliminary to human sacrifice: Connelly 1996, for objections see Neils 2001: 178-180.

[835] Boardman 1977, 1984, 1999.

[836] See Boardman 1977: 47-48; the presence of the *peplos* on the east frieze has been regarded as evidence that the procession of the Great Panathenaia is depicted, e.g. Jenkins 1994: 24-25.

[837] Hdts: 6.117.1.

[838] For the calculation of the numbers see Boardman 1977: 48-49; Boardman 1984: 214-215; Boardman returns to this theory in 1999: 328-329.

[839] The connection between horses and heroes is deemed commonplace by Boardman, for discussion on the connection see Boardman 1977: 45.

[840] Boardman 1977: 43.

[841] E.g. Spence 1993: 267-71; Simon 1983: 59-60; Neils 2001: 180-181; Jenkins 1994: 26.

[842] Neils 2001: 180; Jenkins 1994: 26.

battle which did not feature Greek cavalry, who are also unarmed as depicted on the frieze.[843]

By 447 BC, when the construction of the 'New' Parthenon was initiated, Athens had defeated the Persians a number of times since the battle of Plataea, most notably at the battle of Eurymedon, and they had become the most formidable naval power in Greece.[844] The conjunction between a fiercely democratic political system within the city and an imperialistic foreign policy encouraged the building of the Parthenon; this monument has been said to document and celebrate these achievements as a victory monument.[845] It has been suggested that the new Parthenon was as much a monument thanking Athena for Athenian victory over Persia as it was a monument to the success and power of the Athenian state under Pericles.[846] Plutarch references the funds utilised to construct the Parthenon in a depiction of a debate over the building project on the Acropolis.[847] In this debate Pericles' political enemies argue over his aim of utilising funds amassed from the Delian League to pay for the building program. Pericles' response to his critics was that as long as Athens used necessary funds to continue the war then any surplus may be used to beautify the city and pay the workforce. It has been suggested, therefore, that the structure was closely related to Athens' position as *hegemon* in the ongoing war against Persia.[848] Plutarch's writing, while connecting the Parthenon with conflict between Athens and Persia, references the continuous and ongoing war, opposed to the Persian Wars as defined within this study.

---

[843] Neils 2001: 180 and 181, where Neils concludes that the frieze may commemorate Marathon in a general way but probably does not show the individuals who died during the battle.

[844] Kousser 2009: 275.

[845] See Kousser 2009: 275, who interprets the Parthenon as commemorating past suffering, the Persian sack of the Acropolis in particular, and that it was against this darker backdrop that the more recent triumphs of the Athenian Empire could be contrasted; Hurwit 1999: 228-232; Neils 2001: 173-201; Petsalis-Diomidis 2003: 191-196.

[846] Castriota 1992: 132.

[847] Plut. *Pericles* 12.1-4.

[848] Castriota 1992: 136.

Any argument concerning the Parthenon's meaning based on interpretations of the frieze are 'not capable of proof'.[849] Therefore, the inclusion of this structure as a monument is based on its physical placement (on the foundations of the 'Old' Parthenon) and the reuse of physical aspects of the 'Old' Parthenon. The interpreted allusion to conflict between Greek and Persian forces in the design (such as the metopes) may refer to the ongoing conflict between Athens and Persia as much as the Persian Wars. Furthermore, the funding of the building comes largely from Delian League tributes which again cannot be credited to the conflicts included within this study. The monument is included here tentatively as a general monument because it is likely that the monument commemorated the Persian Wars generally, at least in part.

87. Statue of Zeus *Eleutherios*

Isocrates mentions the statue as a topographical marker in the Athenian agora:

> *In gratitude we honoured them with the highest honours and set up their statues where stands the image of Zeus the Saviour, near to it and to one another, a memorial both of the magnitude of their benefactions and of their mutual friendship.*[850]

Pausanias also mentions the statue:

> *Here stands Zeus, called Zeus of Freedom, and the Emperor Hadrian, a benefactor to all his subjects and especially to the city of the Athenians.*[851]

Harpocration is the only source to report a connection between the monument and the Persian Wars:

> *Hyperides: 'Now to Zeus, O men of the jury, a title has been given which proclaims freedom because freedmen built the stoa which is near him.' Didymus says that the orator is wrong. For he was called eleutherios*

---

[849] Boardman 1977: 48, although it is also stated that such arguments are not capable of disproof either.
[850] Isoc. *Evagoras* 97.
[851] Paus. 1.3.2.

> because the Athenians were freed from the Medes. Because he is inscribed Soter, he is named Eleutherios, as Menander shows.[852]

The connection between the monument and the Persian Wars is made only by Didymus and reported by Harpocration. Harpocration here is contesting a statement made by the orator Hyperides, who claimed the *Eleutherios* Stoa was so named because it was built by freemen.[853]

According to Pausanias' description of the statue, it stood directly in front of a stoa identified as the Stoa of Zeus *Eleutherios*, which has been dated to the decade 430-420 BC due to architectural fragments and pottery found in its construction fill.[854] A circular base situated in front of the Stoa of Zeus *Eleutherios*, traces of which are visible today, is thought to be the location of the statue; it has been suggested that due to the positioning of the statue base, which lies directly on the east to west axis of the stoa, the stoa and statue were constructed concurrently.[855]

This monument is accepted with confidence on the strength of consistent literary references concerning the existence of the statue from the 4th century BC and the dating of the structure with which the statue base aligns.

88.– 89. Statues of Miltiades and Themistocles

Pausanias mentions statues of Miltiades and Themistocles when describing the Athenian agora:

> For the likenesses of Miltiades and Themistocles have had their titles changed to a Roman and a Thracian.[856]

Demosthenes states that Miltiades and Themistocles did not have statues:

> Take first Themistocles, who won the naval victory at Salamis, Miltiades, who commanded at Marathon, and many others, whose achievements

---

[852] Harpocration s.v. *Eleutherios Zeus*.
[853] See West 1965: 136-137.
[854] Camp 1992: 106.
[855] West 1965: 137; for an impression of the structure and statue positioning see Camp 1992: 106-107.
[856] Paus. 1.18.3.

were not on a level with those of our commanders today. Our ancestors did not put up bronze statues of these men, nor did they carry their regard for them to extremes.[857]

Aristotle informs us that Harmodius and Aristogeiton were the first to receive portrait statues in the Athenian agora,[858] while Demosthenes informs us that Conon was the first man to be honoured in this way after them.[859] The excerpt quoted from Demosthenes above is understood here to state there was no statue of Miltiades in the 5th century BC; the reference to ancestors not constructing statues is a description of Athenian practices specifically before his own time. Demosthenes also states that there was no statue of Themistocles in the 5th century BC; however he must have meant no statue constructed specifically in the Athenian agora because statues of Themistocles were set up privately elsewhere.[860] West suggests that due to the fact that Themistocles died in exile it is hardly likely he would have been honoured by the Athenians with a statue in the agora by the middle of the 5th century BC. However, by the end of the century or even some time in the 4th century BC his reputation may have been restored and a statue constructed.[861] If the 4th century BC sources are accepted that Conon's statue was the first raised after Harmodius and Aristogeiton for the victory at Knidos in 394 BC, we are provided with a *terminus post quem* for the statues of Miltiades and Themistocles.

Throughout the 5th century BC, within Athenian public space, individuals were not publicly honoured by the setting up of portrait statues; however it has been noted that the practice of erecting portrait statues to individuals in public places became comparatively common from the 4th century BC onwards.[862] Up until the beginning of the 4th century BC,

---

[857] Dem. *Against Aristocrates* 196.
[858] Arist. *Rhetoric* 1.9.38; fragments of an inscribed base, thought to be from this monument, has been found during excavations of the agora, see *IG* I³ 502. See also Geagan 2011: 4-5, A1 for further bibliography.
[859] Dem. *Against Leptines* 70; this statue is also mentioned by Isocrates (*Evagoras* 56-57), who states it was in honour of the naval victory off Knidos in 394 BC; see also Pausanias 1.3.2.
[860] For a statue of Themistocles in the temple of Artemis *Aristoboule*: Plut. *Themistocles* 22.1-2.
[861] West 1965: 139.
[862] Richter 1965: 1.5; West 1965: 138-139; Dillon 2006: 11, 101-102; see also Paus. 1.21.1, who states that in the Athenian theatre, by his time, undistinguished individuals may have portrait statues constructed; the material evidence for the Athenian agora is gathered in

individual military achievement was not usually held in higher regard than the accomplishments of the citizen soldiers.[863] For example, the Athenians who were victorious at the battle of Eion, of 476 BC, were permitted only to erect the modest herm monument in the agora at Athens.[864] Aeschines describes the monument and states that a great honour was given to them by receiving the right to set up three stone herms on the condition that they did not inscribe their own names on them, so the inscription would be perceived as belonging to the people and not only the generals.[865]

According to Lycurgus, who was writing in the 4th century BC, Athens was set apart from other cities by erecting statues of successful generals in their agora.[866] However, the development of portrait statuary as a public honour in public spaces in the 4th century BC is only to be understood in the Athenian urban context, and did not restrict private dedications within sanctuaries or the setting up of such statues outside of Athens.[867] For example, statues of Xanthippus and Pericles were set up on the Acropolis, a statue of Miltiades was raised at Delphi in commemoration of the battle of Marathon by the Athenians, and a painted portrait of Themistocles was dedicated in the Parthenon by his son.[868]

As noted above, Conon is said to have been the first individual to be honoured with a portrait statue after Harmodius and Aristogeiton. This honour was bestowed for the victory at the battle of Knidos in 394 BC and

---

Geagan 2011; agoras were used as sites to erect honorific statues throughout the Hellenistic period with a particularly dense development in the later Hellenistic period (see Ma 2013: 75-85).

[863] Dillon 2006: 101.
[864] For the battle see Hdts. 7.107; Plut. *Kimon* 7.
[865] Aesch. *Against Ctesiphon* 183, for the inscriptions see 184-185.
[866] See Lyc. *Against Leocrates* 51, who further states that other cities would usually erect statues of athletes in their agoras.
[867] Richter 1965: 1.5.
[868] Pericles: Paus. 1.25.1; Miltiades: Paus. 10.10.1-2, see also **no. 15**; Themistocles: Paus. 1.1.2; according to Pausanias a statue was raised on the Acropolis in honour of Xanthippus, 'who fought against the Persians' (1.25.1). Pausanias places Xanthippus at the battle of Mycale, which falls outside the remit of the Persian Wars as defined within this study, and so this statue is not included as a monument here; see also Richter 1965: 1.5 for further examples; Dillon (2006: 101) also notes that 5th century BC portraits were set up but only in a sanctuary context and usually as privately sponsored votive dedications.

would have been raised shortly after this date.[869] It has been suggested that with the loss of the Peloponnesian War, and the weakening of the Athenian city-state both internally and externally, Athens was increasingly at the mercy of individual initiative, generosity and whim.[870] This dependence would have, in turn, elevated a powerful individual's role, particularly in the areas of generalship and finance. As the state increasingly depended on wealthy individuals, honours bestowed on these statesmen would more likely reflect this relationship; therefore portrait statues increase in frequency.[871] Following the honour bestowed on Conon, in 389 BC Iphikrates received a statue for his defeat of a Spartan hoplite force, in 376 BC Chabrias was voted a bronze statue for his victory at Naxos, and Timotheos (Conon's son) was given a statue for a diplomatic mission to Kerkyra in 375 BC.[872] In addition, there were also others who were honoured in this way who are not mentioned by name.[873]

In addition to honouring living statesmen, it was in the 4th century BC that Athens began regularly honouring historical figures of the city's past with honorific portraits.[874] A statue of Solon is mentioned by Demosthenes and stood in the Athenian agora.[875] Other statues which are thought to have been erected in the 4th century BC include Kallias, who was thought to have negotiated peace with the Persians in *c.* 449 BC.[876] West attributes the statues of Miltiades and Themistocles to these developments in honorific practices. West includes these statues in his data set because he argues they mark an important development in the commemorations of the Persian

---

[869] Dillon 2006: 101, and see n. 20 for further bibliography.
[870] Stewart 1979: 122-124 analyses possible motives behind this development.
[871] Stewart 1979: 123; Smith (1988: 16-18) also interprets the development of honorary portraits as mirroring the political fortunes of the city-state.
[872] Dillon 2006: 102; Iphikrates' statue: Aesch. *Against Ctesiphon* 243, Dem. *Against Aristocrates* 130; Chabrias: Aesch. *Against Ctesiphon* 243, Nep. *Chabrias* 1.2-3; Timotheos: Aesch. *Against Ctesiphon* 243, Nep. *Timotheos*, 2.3, Paus. 1.3.2.
[873] See Aesch. *Against Ctesiphon* 243, who delivered this speech in 330 BC, for this date see Dillon 2006: 102, n. 28.
[874] See Dillon 2006: 104 f.
[875] Dem. *Against Aristogiton 2* 23; a statue of Solon standing in front of the Stoa *Poikile* is also mentioned by Pausanias (1.16.1); Solon was seen by many in the early 4th century BC as the father of Athenian democracy, see Dillon 2006: 104, and n. 53 for further bibliography.
[876] Pausanias (1.8.2) saw the statue of Kallias in the Athenian agora; the 4th century BC date is offered by Dillon 2006: 102.

Wars. These monuments have been argued as contributing to a shift from the religious to the secular in public portraiture in commemorative monuments.[877]

Retrospective portraits were constructed in Athenian public space within the first half of the 4th century BC. Furthermore, Demosthenes specifically mentions Miltiades and Themistocles by name which may indicate specific statues prompted these references. Due to accepting these monuments on the basis of general honorary practices of the 4th century BC, and assuming Demosthenes' specific references were prompted by existing statues, these examples may only be accepted tentatively.

90. Tomb of Aristides

Plutarch is our sole source for the tomb:

Moreover, his tomb is pointed out at Phalerum, and they say the city constructed it for him, since he did not leave even enough to pay for his funeral.[878]

This tomb was paid for by the state and therefore is understood to have acquired the status of a public monument for his service to the city-state.[879] No evidence exists, literary or otherwise, which connects this monument to the Persian Wars. However, probably in the 4th century BC, Athens may have begun honouring the generals who led their forces in the Persian Wars with public honours (such as statues, see **nos. 88** and **89**). This monument is interpreted with some caution due to the late literary source, and the lack of evidence for connecting the tomb with the commemoration of the Persian Wars.

91. Epigram in Thanks to Aphrodite

Plutarch mentions the epigram after describing how Corinthian courtesans prayed to Aphrodite for success against Persia:

---

[877] West 1965: 139.
[878] Plut. *Aristides* 27.1.
[879] As suggested by West 1965: 142-143.

> For it was a thing divulged abroad, concerning which Simonides made an epigram to be inscribed on the brazen image set up in that temple of Venus which is said to have been founded by Medea, when she desired the Goddess, as some affirm, to deliver her from loving her husband Jason, or, as others say, to free him from loving Thetis. The tenor of the epigram follows:
>
> For those who, fighting on their country's side,
> Opposed th' imperial Mede's advancing tide,
> We, votaresses, to Cytherea pray'd;
> Th' indulgent power vouchsafed her timely aid,
> And kept the citadel of Hellas free
> From rude assaults of Persia's archery.[880]

Athenaeus also provides a slightly different version of the epigram:

> Simonides composed this epigram:—
>
> These damsels, in behalf of Greece, and all
> Their gallant countrymen, stood nobly forth,
> Praying to Venus, the all-powerful goddess;
> Nor was the queen of beauty willing ever
> To leave the citadel of Greece to fall
> Beneath the arrows of the unwarlike Persians.[881]

Plutarch attributes the poem to Simonides, which would date it to the 5th century BC, and states that the poem was inscribed. However, no archaeological evidence can support these assertions. Due to the lack of evidence concerning this poem it may only be accepted with caution.

92. Epigram Engraved on a Cenotaph

Pausanias mentions the monument in Megara but does not mention the inscription:

> In the city are tombs of Megarians. They made one for those who died in the Persian invasion, and what is called the Aesymnium (Shrine of Aesymnus) was also a tomb of heroes.[882]

---

[880] Plut. *On the Malice of Herodotus* 39.
[881] Ath. *The Deipnosophists* 13.32.
[882] Paus. 1.43.3.

An inscription was discovered near Megara in the 18th century and is preceded by a short introduction:

> *The epigram for the heroes who died in the Persian Wars and lie buried there, defaced by time, Helladius the high priest inscribed, for the honour of the city. Simonides was the author:*
>
> *While striving to strengthen the day of freedom*
> *For Greece and the Megarians, we received the fate of death,*
> *Some under Euboea and Pelion, where stands*
> *The precinct of the holy archer Artemis,*
> *Some at the mountain of Mykale, some before Salamis,*
> *<>*
> *Others on the Boeotian plain who dared*
> *To come to blows with enemies fighting on horseback.*
> *The citizens granted us together this privilege around the navel*
> *Of the Nisaians in their people-thronged agora.*[883]

According to the excerpt from Pausanias above, tombs were made for the dead of the Persian Wars within Megara. The Megarians provided ships for the Greek navy and took part in the battle of Plataea and, at least at Plataea, the Megarians were afforded burial on the battlefield.[884] In the absence of the bodies, the 'tomb' within the Megarian city, reported by Pausanias, has therefore been interpreted as a cenotaph.[885]

The inscription noted above was discovered in the wall of a church in the village of Palaeochori near Megara in the 18th century by the traveller Michel Fourmont.[886] Fourmont copied the inscription and this version was published by Boeckh in the 19th century.[887] The actual stone was

---

[883] *IG* 7 53; trans. Dillon and Garland 2010: 387; the translation of the introduction is the author's own.
[884] Naval contribution: Hdts. 8.1.1; Plataea: Hdts. 9.69; burial at Plataea: Hdts. 9.85.2.
[885] Frazer 1965: 2.533-534; West 1965: 172; Page (1981: 213) suggests it may be a 'memorial'.
[886] See West 1965: 172-173.
[887] *CIG* 1051.

rediscovered in 1898 by Wilhelm who re-published the inscription.[888] The inscription is thought to be of the 4th century AD at the earliest and is not considered well done.[889] For example, the sixth line of the inscription is omitted (highlighted above by '<>'), a word is missing in the ninth line, the lines are not straight, and the letters are not uniform in size.

According to the introduction before the epigram, the copy was made by 'Helladius the High Priest'. Due to the original epigram being worn with time, the inscription states Helladius had it inscribed rather than 're-inscribed'. Wilhelm suggested that the only the first couplet was copied from the original monument and that the following four couplets were later additions.[890] This suggestion was made on the strength that the final four couplets merely enumerate the battles which the Megarians participated in and add nothing to the poignancy of the first two lines.[891] More recently, two battles have been identified by Dillon and Garland as Artemisium in lines 3-4, and Plataea in lines 7-8.[892]

The original inscription, based on the vocabulary, phrasing, or meter of the preserved copied inscription, has been interpreted as a 5th century epigram.[893] However, the preserved example is an extremely late example, and without further evidence to confirm its accuracy it may only be accepted tentatively.

93. Statues of Skyllis and His Daughter Hydna

Pausanias is our only source for these statues:

> *Beside the Gorgias is a votive offering of the Amphictyons, representing Skyllis of Scione, who, tradition says, dived into the very deepest parts of every sea. He also taught his daughter Hydna to dive. When the fleet of Xerxes was attacked by a violent storm off Mount Pelion, father and*

---

[888] The stone was re-discovered in the church of St. Athanasius in Palaeochori. Wilhelm's publication (originally published in 1899, in *Jahreshefte des Österreichischen Archäologischen Institutes in Wien*, volume 2: 236-244) has been reprinted and is referenced here as Wilhelm 1972.
[889] West (1965: 173) states the spelling is of the 4th century AD; see also Page 1981: XVI, 213.
[890] See Wilhelm 1972: 316-322.
[891] As noted in West 1965: 174.
[892] Dillon and Garland 2010: 387.
[893] Page (1981: 214) states there is 'nothing...incompatible with the early 5th century' about the inscription.

daughter completed its destruction by dragging away under the sea the anchors and any other security the triremes had. In return for this deed the Amphictyons dedicated statues of Skyllis and his daughter.[894]

Pausanias is our sole reference for this monument and no archaeological evidence has been discovered in support.[895] However, Herodotus also mentions the feats of Skyllis, and how he assisted the Greek forces at Artemisium by providing information on the Persian fleet, which indicates he had acquired a reputation by the 5th century BC.[896] Therefore despite Skyllis acquiring some renown in the 5th century BC, without further supporting evidence, this monument may only be accepted tentatively.

94. Altar dedicated to Helios *Eleutherios*

Pausanias is the only source for this monument constructed by the Troezenians:

> They had every reason, it seems to me, for making an altar to Helios Eleutherios, seeing that they escaped being enslaved by Xerxes and the Persians.[897]

Pausanias suggests the monument commemorates the invasion of Xerxes specifically. West proposes that Pausanias bases his suggestion on the epithet '*eleutherios*'.[898] Due to the general association with freedom the monument is counted here among monuments commemorating the Persian Wars in general. However, due to the lack of evidence for this monument, and the uncertainty concerning the date of construction, it may not be accepted with confidence.

95. Statues of Women and Children

Pausanias mentions the monument when describing the market place at Troezen:

---

[894] Paus. 10.19.1-2.
[895] Jacquemin (1999: no. 54) dates the monument to the 5th century BC tentatively.
[896] Hdts, 8.8.
[897] Paus. 2.31.5.
[898] West 1965: 175.

> *Under a portico in the market-place are set up women; both they and their children are of stone. They are the women and children whom the Athenians gave to the Troezenians to be kept safe, when they had resolved to evacuate Athens and not to await the attack of the Persians by land. They are said to have dedicated likenesses, not of all the women—for, as a matter of fact, the statues are not many—but only of those who were of high rank.*[899]

Herodotus also states that Athenians were sheltered at Troezen during the invasion of Xerxes.[900] The monument is therefore understood here to commemorate the contribution Troezen made to the Greek defence, particularly of Attica during Xerxes' invasion.[901] The lack of archaeological, or further literary evidence to support Pausanias' reference, prevents this monument being accepted with confidence. However, on the basis of Herodotus' information concerning Troezen's assistance to the Athenians, which in turn corroborates Pausanias' reasoning behind the monument, it may be accepted tentatively.

96. Trophy with Epigram

Diodorus mentions the trophy at Delphi and recounts the epigram:

> *So the oracle of Delphi, with the aid of some divine Providence, escaped pillage. And the Delphians, desiring to leave to succeeding generations a deathless memorial of the appearance of the gods among men, set up beside the temple of Athena Pronaea a trophy on which they inscribed the following elegiac lines:*
>
> *'To serve as a memorial to war,*
> *The warder-off of men, and as a witness*
> *To victory the Delphians set me up,*
> *Rendering thanks to Zeus and Phoebus who*
> *Thrust back the city-sacking ranks of Medes*
> *And threw their guard about the bronze-crowned shrine.'*[902]

---

[899] Paus. 2.31.7.
[900] Hdts. 8.41.1.
[901] West 1965: 176.
[902] Diod. 11.14.4.

The epigram was copied by the traveller Francis Vernon, who travelled through Greece in 1675 and 1676, and is cited by Meritt.[903] It has been suggested, on a stylistic basis, that the inscribed epigram is not of the early 5th century BC and may have been inscribed about 400 BC or later.[904]

The trophy mentioned by Diodorus may have initially been of the temporary style, a collection of arms and armour from the defeated forces (see chapter section 4.2.2 for definitions).[905] Therefore, the epigram, if it was inscribed at a later date, may have been added to the trophy when it was rebuilt in stone. Due to the uncertainty concerning the date of the epigram, this monument is included here tentatively.

97. Altar of the Winds

Herodotus is the sole reference for this monument which was constructed at Thyia by the Delphians:

> In the meantime, the Delphians, who were afraid for themselves and for Hellas, consulted the god. They were advised to pray to the winds, for these would be potent allies for Hellas. When they had received the oracle, the Delphians first sent word of it to those Greeks who desired to be free; because of their dread of the barbarian, they were forever grateful. Subsequently they erected an altar to the winds at Thyia, the present location of the precinct of Thyia the daughter of Cephisus, and they offered sacrifices to them. This, then, is the reason why the Delphians to this day offer the winds sacrifice of propitiation.[906]

According to Herodotus, the Delphians were advised by the oracle at Delphi to pray to the winds. In doing so an altar was set up in Thyia where continued appeasement of the winds would have taken place.[907] Although Herodotus implies the worshipping of the Winds at Thyia took place after the Persian Wars, the date of the instigation of the worship is not clear. It has been suggested a cult of the Winds was practiced at Thyia before the Persian Wars, and the

---

[903] Meritt 1947: 60; Vernon's copy of the inscription shows that it was inscribed over five lines rather than the four lines recounted by Diodorus, see Meritt 1947: 59-60.
[904] Meritt 1947: 60; Scott 2010: Appendix F, no. 297 dates the inscription to 400 BC.
[905] As suggested by West 1965: 177.
[906] Hdts. 7.178.
[907] Mikalson 2003: 62.

establishment of the altar there by the Delphians has been interpreted as an attempt to give pan-Hellenic significance to the practice.[908] This monument is accepted with confidence on the strength of Herodotus' account.

98. Statue of Apollo

Pausanias mentions the statue constructed by the Epidaurians:

> *The offerings next to Phryne include two images of Apollo, one dedicated from Persian spoils by the Epidaurians of Argolis, the other dedicated by the Megarians to commemorate a victory over the Athenians at Nisaea.*[909]

This statue is thought to have stood east of the temple terrace at Delphi.[910] The supposed location of this monument, and its form as an image of Apollo, has been interpreted as mimicking the pan-Hellenic statue of Apollo which would have stood nearby (**no. 42**).[911] By interpreting the Epidaurian Apollo in conjunction, spatially stylistically, and temporally, with the pan-Hellenic Apollo, the Epidaurian Apollo statue has been suggested to be a monument commemorating the battle of Salamis.[912] However, Epidaurus also contributed ships to the Greek fleet earlier in the invasion, and sent infantry to the Isthmus when the Persians held Attica.[913] Therefore, due to the lack of a specific battle being specified in the surviving evidence, this statue is interpreted here as a monument to the Persian Wars in general.

On the strength of Pausanias' statement, the lack of conflicting sources, and the general likelihood of the Epidaurians participating in the commemorations, this monument is accepted with confidence.

---

[908] Macan 1908: 1.265-266; see also West 1965:178-179.
[909] Paus. 10.15.1.
[910] Scott 2010: 83, Fig. 4.3 no. 106, however, as noted in the image key, the placement is not secure.
[911] Scott 2010: 84.
[912] Epidaurians at Salamis: Hdts. 8.43; see Scott 2010: Appendix C, no. 106; Jacquemin 1999: 171.
[913] Epidaurians contribute ships before Artemisium: Hdts. 8.1; and land forces at the Isthmus: Hdts. 8.72.

99. Bronze Statue of an Ox

Pausanias describes this monument raised at Delphi by the Carystians:

> The Euboeans of Carystus too set up in the sanctuary of Apollo a bronze ox, from spoils taken in the Persian war. The Carystians and the Plataeans dedicated oxen, I believe, because, having repulsed the barbarian, they had won a secure prosperity, and especially a land free to plough.[914]

Pausanias compares the choice of monument form with the ox constructed at Delphi by the Plataeans (**no. 78**).[915] The statue has been suggested to have been located in the area of the east temple terrace.[916] A slab has been discovered near the Bouleterion that may have once stood as part of a plinth on the upper temple terrace.[917] The block has cuttings on the top which suggest it once acted as a statue's plinth, and the bifurcated footprint suggest it was for a figure of an animal. Furthermore, the block is inscribed with two fragmented inscriptions which have been restored as referring to Carystus, the older one of the two being dated to the first third of the 5th century BC based on the letter forms.[918] This block is thought to be part of the top of the plinth which supported the ox, dedicated by Carystus and mentioned by Pausanias.

Pausanias, as our sole literary reference, does not provide a particular battle to which we may attribute this monument. Therefore, the monument is interpreted here as a monument to the Persian Wars in general. Due to Pausanias' reference and the supporting archaeological evidence, this monument is accepted with confidence.

100. Statue Group

This monument once stood in the pan-Hellenic sanctuary at Delphi. The base of this monument is extant and the surviving inscription can be read:

---

[914] Paus. 10.16.6.
[915] See **no. 78** for an outline of differing opinions on what statues of oxen represent.
[916] Scott 201: 83, Fig. 4.3 no. 111.
[917] It has been suggested that it was moved from its intended location by landslide, see *FD* II 311, and for an image of the block 310, Fig. 253.
[918] *FD* II 311, inv. 638.

Persephone
The Hermionaeans dedi[cated to Apollo][919]

The letter forms have been identified as early 5th century BC and it has been suggested that, due to this dating, the monument may be attributed to commemorating the Persian Wars, but there is no firm evidence to support this suggestion.[920] It has also been suggested that another inscribed stone was a part of this statue base, naming other divinities which would have been included in the statue group.[921]

It is quite possible Hermione would commemorate the Persian Wars as they are represented on the inscribed lists of cities on the serpent column at Delphi (**no. 80**) and the statue of Zeus at Olympia (**no. 81**). However, due to relying solely on letter dating to decipher the meaning behind this monument, the attribution is tentative.

101. Gilded Statue of Alexander I

Herodotus is referring to the statue of Apollo holding the beak of a ship commemorating Salamis (**no. 42**) when he mentions the statue of Alexander:

> *After that, they divided the spoils and sent the first-fruits of it to Delphi; of this was made a man's image twelve cubits high, holding in his hand the figurehead of a ship. This stood in the same place as the golden statue of Alexander the Macedonian.*[922]

Pseudo-Demosthenes also mentions the statue:

> *It was my ancestor, Alexander, who first occupied the site, and, as the first-fruits of the Persian captives taken there, set up a golden statue at Delphi.*[923]

---

[919] FD II 235, inv. 2501, author's own trans.; see also Jacquemin 1999: no. 314.
[920] West 1965: 193, and it is further stated that the monument was 'probably intended to suggest the freedom which would allow the people of Hermione to grow their own crops'; the text is described as 'archaic' in *FD* II 235.
[921] *FD* III 4 147; *IG* 4 686; Scott 2010: 81, n. 28.
[922] Hdts. 8.121.2.
[923] [Dem.] *Philip* 21.

Herodotus and pseudo-Demosthenes both state a gold statue was constructed at Delphi by Alexander I of Macedon.[924] Due to Herodotus' positioning of Alexander's statue being near the statue of Apollo holding the beak of a ship **(no. 42)**, the location of Alexander's statue has been identified on the east temple terrace; the proximity of Alexander's statue to the pan-Hellenic statue of Apollo has been interpreted as an effort to represent his own role in the Persian Wars.[925]

We learn from Demosthenes that Macedonians fought and killed Persian forces as they retreated through Macedonian territory from the battle of Plataea.[926] This monument could then be interpreted as directly relating to that battle.[927] However, according to Herodotus, Macedon initially Medised and it was at the battle of Plataea that Alexander reversed his allegiance to assist the Greeks.[928] Therefore this monument is interpreted here as an effort, by Alexander, to present his general realignment of allegiance in the war in general.

Due to general agreement in the literary sources of the existence of a statue dedicated by Alexander at the site of Delphi, which (according to pseudo-Demosthenes) commemorated at least some aspect of the Persian Wars, this monument is accepted with confidence.

102. Bronze Apollo

A limestone block, discovered at Delphi inside the temple of Apollo,[929] bears an inscription which names the dedicator of the monument as the Peparethians:

Diopithes the Athenian made [me].
When the Peparethians captured two ships of the Carians in battle
they erected a tithe to Apollo the Far-Shooter.[930]

---

[924] It is not beyond doubt that the statues mentioned by Herodotus and pseudo-Demosthenes are not the same; however, there is no reason here to assume otherwise.
[925] Scott 2010: 87; see also Jacquemin 1999: 253, and no. 347 who dates the monument 479 BC on the strength of the literary sources.
[926] Dem. *Against Aristocrates* 200; Demosthenes mistakenly states this defeat was inflicted on the Persians by Perdiccas, but Alexander I was ruling Macedonia at the time.
[927] As it is in Scott 2010: Appendix C, no. 114.
[928] Alexander's Medisation: Hdts. 8.142; reversal in allegiance: Hdts. 9.44-45.
[929] *FD* II 283.
[930] *CEG* 325; trans. Bowie 2010: 335.

Judging by the cuttings on the top of the limestone block, the stone would have acted as a base for a bronze statue of a figure approximately 3 m in height.[931] Furthermore, the location of the statue of Apollo has been loosely identified as the area of the east temple terrace.[932] Based on the form of the letters visible on the stone, and the positioning of the cuttings on the stone (from which the statue's position may be deduced), this monument has been dated to the first quarter of the 5th century BC.[933] This statue, then, is thought to have mirrored the pan-Hellenic Apollo statue dedication in its choice of material, the form of its base, its pose and its position on the temple terrace.

Due to the inscription mentioning the Carians, who Herodotus names in the Persian navy,[934] the date proposed based on inscriptional and archaeological evidence this monument is accepted with confidence. However, this statue is attributed to commemorating the Persian Wars in general as it is not clear at which naval battle the Peparethians captured Carian ships.

103. Bronze Apollo

An inscribed limestone block was discovered at Delphi in 1894, near the temple entrance, which bears an inscription identifying the monument as a dedication to Apollo by the Samians.[935] Due to the block's find spot, the statue has been tentatively located slightly to the north on the east temple terrace.[936] Based on the cuttings on the top of the limestone block, the monument is thought to be a bronze statue, probably a figure of Apollo.[937] Based on the lettering form, the dedication of this monument has been dated to later in the first half of the 5th century BC.[938]

---

[931] *FD* II 283.
[932] See Scott 2010: 83, Fig. 4.3; see also *FD* II 284 for the assertion that it is not necessary to look beyond the immediate area of a stone's discovery for its original location.
[933] *FD* II 282-283; Scott 2010: 84; see also Jacquemin 1999: no. 387.
[934] Hdts. 7.93.
[935] *FD* III 4 455, inv. 1790, also pl. 20, A; see also *FD* II 248.
[936] See Scott 2010: 76, Fig. 4.1 no. 94; see also *FD* II 284 for the assertion that it is not necessary to look beyond the immediate area of a stone's discovery for its original location.
[937] *FD* III 4 455; Scott 2010: Appendix C, no. 94.
[938] Scott 2010: 75; *FD* III 4 455; *contra. LSAG* 330, no. 17, where a more specific date of 479 BC is offered, directly following the battle of Mycale; see also Jacquemin 1999: no. 427.

This monument is accepted tentatively due to the lack of evidence concerning Samian involvement in the specific battles that make up the Persian Wars as defined in this study. The monument may commemorate the battle of Mycale and, therefore, fall outside the remit of this study.

104. Bronze Bull

Pausanias mentions this statue, dedicated by the Eretrians, when describing monuments at Olympia:

> *Of the bronze oxen one was dedicated by the Corcyraeans and the other by the Eretrians. Philesius of Eretria was the artist.*[939]

Pausanias is our sole literary source for this monument; however in 1877 the base of a monument bearing an inscription mentioning the Eretrians was uncovered about 30 m east of the northeast corner of the temple of Zeus.[940] The top of the uppermost blocks bear cuttings which appear to have fitted four bifurcated footprints.[941] The upper surface also bears a two line inscription which also supports Pausanias' identification exactly, including the artist's name.[942] The inscription has been dated to the early 5th century BC.[943] The archaeological and inscriptional evidence confirms the description offered by Pausanias. However, the monument is not securely attributed to the Persian Wars.

Before the battle of Marathon, Eretria was sacked by the Persian army which has been considered a considerable blow,[944] and we learn from Herodotus that the Eretrians were enslaved.[945] Despite the removal of Eretrian citizens by the Persians, enough remained to contribute seven ships to the combined Greek navy which fought at Artemisium and

---

[939] Paus. 5.27.9.
[940] Eckstein 1969: 50; this statue has therefore been securely placed to 50 m north of the Bouleterion, see Scott 2010: 166, Fig. 6.7, and 206, Fig. 7.7.
[941] See Eckstein 1969: 51, Textabb 10 for a restoration of the base.
[942] *IvO* 248.
[943] Eckstein 1969: 52.
[944] Francis and Vickers 1983: 52.
[945] Hdts. 6.101 and 6.119.

Salamis,⁹⁴⁶ and alongside the Styrians' made up 600 hoplites at Plataea.⁹⁴⁷ For Eretria's contribution to the Persian Wars, the city-state was included in the Serpent Column inscription at Delphi (see **no. 80**).

Eretria would have undoubtedly suffered financial hardship after being sacked by the Persians and having a number of their citizens enslaved, however the Athenian tribute lists show the city's existence at a respectable level throughout the remainder of the 5th century BC.⁹⁴⁸ Furthermore, the booty from the conflicts of 489-479 BC could have contributed to the cost of constructing of a bronze statue at Olympia.⁹⁴⁹

The fact that the Eretrians constructed this monument at Olympia in the 5th century BC, and that this is the same one mentioned by Pausanias, is accepted with confidence. However due to there being no clear attribution for the monument's purpose, it is accepted here tentatively as a commemoration of the Persian Wars.

105. Inscribed Persian Helmet

The helmet is inscribed:

*The Athenians to Zeus, having taken it from the Medes*⁹⁵⁰

This Persian helmet was discovered at Olympia and bears an inscription that clearly indicates it is a monument from the Persian Wars; therefore it is accepted with confidence.⁹⁵¹ No particular battle is mentioned in the inscription, and so it is treated here as a monument to the Persian Wars in general.

---

⁹⁴⁶ Hdts. 8.1.2.
⁹⁴⁷ Hdts. 9.28.5.
⁹⁴⁸ See Francis and Vickers 1983: 52, and n. 31; Meritt *et al.* 1939: 1.294, and n. 96.
⁹⁴⁹ As suggested by Francis and Vickers 1983: 52.
⁹⁵⁰ *IG* I³ 1472, author's trans.
⁹⁵¹ West 1965: 157; the helmet was first published in Kunze 1961: 129-137, see image on pl. 56; see also Scott 2010: 170, n. 99 for further references.

Bibliography

Albertz, A., 2006. *Exemplarisches Heldentum: Die Rezeptionsgeschichte der Schlacht an den Thermopylen von der Antike bis zur Gegenwart.* Munich: Oldenbourg Wissenschaftsverlag.

Alcock, S. E., 2002. *Archaeologies of the Greek Past: Landscape, Monuments, and Memories.* Cambridge: Cambridge University Press.

Amandry, P., 1946. Le portique des Athéniens à Delphes. *Bulletin de Correspondance Hellenique,* Volume 70: 1-8.

Amandry, P., 1960. Sur les Epigrammes de Marathon, in F. Eckstein, ed. *Theōria: Festschrift für W.-H. Schuchhardt.* Baden-Baden: B. Grimm: 1-8.

Amandry, P., 1998. Notes de topographies et d'architecture delphiques X. Le 'socle marathonien' et le trésor des Athéniens. *Bulletin de Correspondance Hellénique,* Volume 122: 75-90.

Arrington, N., 2010. Topographic Semantics: The Location of the Athenian Public Cemetery and its Significance for the Nascent Democracy. *Hesperia,* 79(4): 499-539.

Arrington, N. T., 2014. *Ashes, Images, and Memories: The Presence of the War Dead in Fifth-Century Athens.* Oxford: Oxford University Press.

Austin, M. M., 2006. *The Hellenistic World from Alexander to the Roman Conquest.* 2nd ed. Cambridge: Cambridge University Press.

Behr, C. A., 1986. *The Complete Works of Aelius Aristides.* Leiden: Brill.

Bengtson, H., 1960. *Griechische Geschichte von den Anfängen bis in die Römische Kaiserzeit.* 2nd ed. Munich: Beck.

Berent, M., 1996. Hobbes and the 'Greek Tongues'. *History of Political Thought,* 17(1): 36-59.

Boardman, J., 1977. The Parthenon Frieze - Another View, in U. Höckmann and A. Krug, eds. *Festschrift für Frank Brommer.* Mainz: von Zabern: 39-49.

Boardman, J., 1984. The Parthenon Frieze, in E. Berger, ed. *Parthenon-Kongress Basel Vols.I-II.* Mainz: von Zabern: 210-215.

Boardman, J., 1999. The Parthenon Frieze, A Closer Look. *Revue Archéologique,* Volume 2: 305-330.

Bommelaer, J. F., 1991. *Guide de Delphes: le site.* Athens: The French School at Athens.

Bowie, E. L., 2010. Epigram as Narration, in M. Baumbach, A. Petrovic and I. Petrovic, eds. *Archaic and Classical Greek Epigram.* Cambridge: Cambridge University Press: 313-384.

Bowra, C. M., 1933. Simonides on the Fallen of Thermopylae. *Classical Philology,* 28(4): 277-281.
Bowra, C. M., 1938. *Early Greek Elegists.* London: Oxford University Press.
Bradeen, D. W., 1964. Athenian Casualty Lists. *Hesperia,* 33(1): 16-62.
Bradeen, D. W., 1969. The Athenian Casualty Lists. *The Classical Quarterly,* 19(1): 145-159.
Brandt, J. R. and Iddeng, J. W., 2012. Introduction: Some Concepts of Ancient Festivals, in J. R. Brandt and J. W. Iddeng, eds. *Greek and Roman Festivals: Content, Meaning, and Practice.* Oxford: Oxford University Press: 1-10.
Brommer, F., 1967. *Die Metopen des Parthenon.* Mainz: von Zabern.
Broneer, O., 1944. The Tent of Xerxes and the Greek Theatre. *University of California Publications in Classical Archaeology,* Volume 1: 305-312.
Buckler, J., 1992. Plutarch and Autopsy. *Aufstieg und Niedergang der römischen Welt,* 33.6(2): 4788-4830.
Camp, J., 1992. *The Athenian Agora: Excavations in the Heart of Classical Athens.* London: Thames and Hudson
Camp, J., 2001. *The Archaeology of Athens.* New Haven: Yale University Press.
Carman, J. and Carman, P., 2006. *Bloody Meadows: Investigating Landscapes of Battle.* Stroud: Sutton Publishing.
Carpenter, R., 1963. Reviews. *The American Journal of Philology,* 84(1): 76-85.
Cartledge, P., 2013. *After Thermopylae: The Oath of Plataea and the End of the Graeco-Persian Wars.* Oxford: Oxford University Press.
Castriota, D., 1992. *Myth, Ethos, and Actuality: Official Art in Fifth-Century B.C. Athens.* Madison, Wis.: University of Wisconsin Press.
Castriota, D., 2005. Feminizing the Barbarian and Barbarizing the Feminine: Amazons, Trojans, and Persians in the Stoa Poikile, in J. M. Barringer and J. M. Hurwit, eds. *Periklean Athens and its Legacy: Problems and Perspectives.* Austin: University of Texas Press: 89-102.
Cawkwell, G., 2005. *The Greek Wars: The Failure of Persia.* Oxford: Oxford University Press.
Chandler, R., 1776. *Travels in Greece.* Oxford: Printed at the Clarendon Press.
Chaniotis, A., 2005. *War in the Hellenistic World: A Social and Cultural History.* Malden, MA: Blackwell Publishing.
Chaniotis, A., 2006. Rituals between Norms and Emotions: Rituals as Shared Experience and Memory, in E. Stravrianopoulou, ed. *Ritual and*

Communication in the Graeco-Roman World. Liège: Centre International d'Etude de la Religion Grecque Antique: 211-238.

Chaniotis, A., 2012. The Ritualised Commemoration of War in the Hellenistic City: Memory, Identity, Meanings, in P. Low, G. Oliver and P. J. Rhodes, eds. *Cultures of Commemoration: War Memorials, Ancient and Modern*. Proceedings of the British Academy 160: Oxford University Press: 13-39.

Clairmont, C. W., 1983. *Patrios Nomos: Public Burial in Athens during the Fifth and Fourth Centuries B.C.: the Archaeological, Epigraphic-Literary and Historical Evidence*. Oxford: B.A.R..

Clarke, E. D., 1818. *Travels in Various Countries of Europe, Asia and Africa*. London: Cadell and Davies.

Connelly, J. B., 1996. Parthenon and Parthenoi: A Mythological Interpretation of the Parthenon Frieze. *American Journal of Archaeology*, 100(1): 58-80.

Cooley, A., 2012. Commemorating the War Dead of the Roman World, in P. Low, G. Oliver and P. J. Rhodes, eds. *Cultures of Commemoration: War Memorials, Ancient and Modern*. Proceedings of the British Academy 160: Oxford University Press: 61-88.

Cooper, F. A., 1990. Reconstruction of the Athenian Treasury at Delphi in the Fourth Century BC. *American Journal of Archaeology*, 94(2): 317-318.

Cullen Davison, C., 2009. *Pheidias: The Sculptures and Ancient Sources Vol. I*. London: Institute of Classical Studies, School of Advanced Study, University of London.

Culley, G. R., 1975. The Restoration of Sanctuaries in Attica: I.G. II2, 1035. *Hesperia*, 44(2): 207-223.

Darling, J. K., 2004. *Architecture of Greece*. Westport, Conn.: Greenwood Press.

Davison, J., 1958. Notes on the Panathenaea. *Journal of Hellenic Studies*, Volume 78: 23-42.

Despines, G., 1971. *Συμβολή στη μελέτη του έργου του Αγορακρίτου*. Athens: Hermēs.

Dillon, M. and Garland, L., 2010. *Ancient Greece: Social and Historical Documents from Archaic Times to the Death of Alexander*. London: Routledge.

Dillon, S., 2006. *Ancient Greek Portrait Sculpture: Contexts, Subjects, and Styles*. Cambridge: Cambridge University Press.

Dimitrova, N. M., 2008. *Theoroi and Initiates in Samothrace: The Epigraphical Evidence*. Princeton, N.J.: American School of Classical Studies at Athens.

Dinsmoor, W. B., 1912. Studies in the Delphian Treasuries. *Bulletin de Correspondance Hellénique*, Volume 36: 439-493.

Dinsmoor, W. B., 1921. Attic Building Accounts. *American Journal of Archaeology*, 25(2): 118-129.

Dinsmoor, W. B., 1934. The Date of the Older Parthenon. *American Journal of Archaeology*, 38(3): 408-448.

Dinsmoor, W. B., 1942. The Correlation of Greek Archaeology with History, in *Studies in the History of Culture: The Disciplines of the Humanities*. Menasha, Wis.: Published for The Conference by the George Banta Pub. Co.: 185-216.

Dinsmoor, W. B., 1950. *The Architecture of Ancient Greece: An Account of its Historic Development*. London: Batsford.

Dinsmoor, W. B., 1951-1953. The Athenian Theater of the Fifth Century, in G. E. Mylonas, ed. *Studies Presented to David Moore Robinson Vols. I-II*. Saint Louis: Washington University: 309-330.

Dittenberger, W. and Purgold, K. eds., 1986. *Die Inschriften von Olympia*. Berlin: A.Asher and Co..

Dodwell, E., 1819. *A Classical and Topographical Tour through Greece: During the Years 1801, 1805 and 1806*. London: Rodwell and Martin.

Eckstein, F., 1969. *Anathemata: Studien zu den Weihgeschenken strengen Stils im Heiligtum von Olympia*. Berlin: Mann.

Edmonds, J. M., 1961. *The Fragments of Attic Comedy III A*. Leiden: E.J. Brill.

Ehrenberg, V., 1969. *The Greek State*. 2nd ed. Oxford: Blackwell.

Emerson, M., 2007. *Greek Sanctuaries: An Introduction*. London: Bristol Classical Press.

Etienne, R. and Pierart, M., 1975. Un decret du koinon des hellenes a Platees en l'honneur de Glaucon, fils d'Eteocles, d'Athenes. *Bulletin de Correspondance Hellénique*, Volume 99: 51-75.

Farnell, L. R., 1896-1809. *The Cults of the Greek States Vols. I-V*. Oxford: Clarendon Press.

Flashar, M., 1995. Die Sieger von Marathon - Zwischen Mythisierung und Vorbildlichkeit, in M. Flashar, H. Gehrke and E. Heinrich, eds. *Retrospektive. Konzepte von Vergangenheit in der griechisch-römischen Antike*. München: Biering und Brinkmann: 63-85.

Flower, M. A., 2000. From Simonides to Isocrates: The Fifth-Century Origins of Fourth-Century Panhellenism. *Classical Antiquity*, 19(1): 65-101.

Forsdyke, E. J., 1919-1920. Some Arrow Heads from the Battlefield of Marathon. *Proceedings of the Society of Antiquaries of London*, Volume 32: 146-157.

Francis, E. D., 1990. *Image and Idea in Fifth-Century Greece*. London: Routledge.

Francis, E. D. and Vickers, M. J., 1983. Signa Priscae Artis: Eretria and Siphnos. *Journal of Hellenic Studies*, Volume 103: 49-67.

Frazer, J. G., 1965. *Pausanias's Description of Greece Vols. I-VI.* New York: Biblo and Tannen.

Funke, P., 2013. Greek Amphiktyonies: An Experiment in Transregional Governance, in H. Beck, ed. *A Companion to Ancient Greek Government.* Chichester: Wiley-Blackwell: 451-465.

Furtwängler, A., 1895. *Masterpieces of Greek Sculpture.* New York: W. Heinemann.

Geagan, D. J., 2011. *Inscriptions: The Dedicatory Monuments.* Princeton, N.J.: American School of Classical Studies at Athens.

Gehrke, H. -J., 2003. Marathon (490 v. Chr.) als Mythos: Von Helden und Barbaren, in G. Krumeich and S. Brandt, eds. *Schlachtenmythen: Ereignis - Erzählung - Erinnerung.* Köln: Böhlau Verlag: 286-313.

Gehrke, H. -J., 2007. Marathon: A European Myth?. *Palmedes*, Volume 2: 93-108.

Gell, W., 1827. *The Itinerary of Greece: Containing One Hundred Routes in Attica, Boeotia, Phocis, Locris, and Thessaly.* London: Rodwell and Martin.

Gray, E. C., 1840. *Tour to the Sepulchres of Etruria in 1839.* London: J. Hatchard and Son.

Grundy, G. B., 1901. *The Great Persian War and its Preliminaries: A Study of the Evidence, Literary and Topographical.* New York: Scribner.

Habicht, C., 1984. Pausanias and the Evidence of Inscriptions. *Classical Antiquity*, 3(1): 40-56.

Habicht, C., 1985. *Pausanias' Guide to Ancient Greece.* Berkeley: University of California Press.

Hall, J. M., 2002. *Hellenicity: Between Ethnicity and Culture.* Chicago: University of Chicago Press.

Hall, J. M., 2013. The Rise of State Action in the Archaic Age, in H. Beck, ed. *A Companion to Ancient Greek Government.* Chichester: Wiley-Blackwell: 9-21.

Hammond, N. G. L., 1956. The Battle of Salamis. *Journal of Hellenic Studies*, Volume 76: 32-54.

Hammond, N. G. L., 1973. *Studies in Greek History.* Oxford: Clarendon Press.

Hansen, M. H., 1997. The Polis as an Urban Centre. The Literary and Epigraphical Evidence, in M. H. Hansen, ed. *The Polis as an Urban Centre and as a Political Community.* Copenhagen: Munksgaard: 9-86.

Hansen, M. H., 2006. *Polis: An Introduction to the Ancient Greek City-State.* Oxford: Oxford University Press.

Hansen, M. H. and Nielsen, T. H., 2004. *An Inventory of Archaic and Classical Poleis.* Oxford: Oxford University Press.

Hansen, O., 1989. Epigraphica Belliaca: On the Dedication of the Athenian Portico at Delphi. *Classica et Mediaevalia,* Volume 40: 133-134.

Harrison, T., 2000. *The Emptiness of Asia: Aeschylus' Persians and the History of the Fifth Century.* London: Duckworth.

Hausoullier, B., 1881. Fouilles à Delphes. *Bulletin de Correspondance Hellénique,* Volume 5: 1-19.

Herter, R., 1935. Nemesis. *Paulys Realencyclopädie der classischen Altertumswissenschaft,* Volume 16: 2338-2380.

Hicks, E. L., 1882. *A Manual of Greek Historical Inscriptions.* Oxford: Clarendon Press.

Hiller von Gaertringen, F. F., 1926. *Historische Griechische Epigramme.* Bonn: Marcus and Weber.

Hiller von Gaertringen, F. F., 1934. Perserepigramme von der Athenischen Agora. *Hermes,* 69(2): 204-206.

Höcker, C. and Schneider, L., 1993. *Phidias.* Reinbek bei Hamburg: Rowohlt.

Hölkeskamp, K.-J., 2001. Marathon-Vom Monument zum Mythos, in D. Papenfuß and V. M. Strocka, eds. *Gab es das Griechische Wunder? Griechenland zwischen dem Ende des 6. und der Mitte des 5. Jahrhunderts v. Chr..* Zabern: Von Zabern : 329-353.

Hölscher, T., 2006. The Transformation of Victory into Power, in S. Dillon and K. E. Welch, eds. *Representations of War in Ancient Rome.* Cambridge: Cambridge University Press: 27-48.

Homolle, T., 1893. Topographie de Delphes. *Bulletin de Correspondance Hellénique,* Volume 17: 611-623.

Hunt, W. I., 1890. Discoveries at Plataia in 1890. IV. Notes on the Battlefield of Plataia. *The American Journal of Archaeology and of the History of the Fine Arts,* 6(4): 463-475.

Hurwit, J. M., 1999. *The Athenian Acropolis: History, Mythology, and Archaeology from the Neolithic Era to the Present.* Cambridge: Cambridge University Press.

Hurwit, J. M., 2004. *The Acropolis in the Age of Pericles.* Cambridge: Cambridge University Press.

Hyde, W. H., 1921. *Olympic Victor Monuments and Greek Athletic Art*. Washington: Carnegie Institution of Washington.

Jacoby, F., 1923-1958. *Die Fragmente der Griechischen Historiker Vols. I-III*. Berlin: Weidmann.

Jacoby, F., 1945. Some Athenian Epigrams of the Persian Wars. *Hesperia*, 14(3): 157-211.

Jacquemin, A., 1999. *Offrandes Monumentales à Delphes*. Paris: de Boccard.

Jacquemin, A. and Laroche, D., 1988. Une base pour l'Apollon de Salamine à Delphes. *Bulletin de Correspondance Hellenique*, Volume 112: 235-246.

Jeffery, L. H., 1990. *The Local Scripts of Archaic Greece: A Study of the Origin of the Greek Alphabet and its Development from the Eighth to the Fifth Centuries B.C.*. Oxford: Oxford University Press.

Jenkins, I., 1994. *The Parthenon Frieze*. London: British Museum Press.

Jung, M., 2006. *Marathon und Plataiai: zwei Perserschlachten als 'lieux de mémoire' im antiken Griechenland*. Göttingen: Vandenhoeck and Ruprecht.

Kagan, D., 1987. *The Fall of the Athenian Empire*. Ithaca, N.Y.: Cornell University Press.

Kardara, C., 1964. Γλαυκῶπις, ο Αρχαϊκός Ναός και το Θέμα της Ζωφόρου του Παρθενώνα'. *Archaiologike Ephemeris*: 62-158.

Keesling, C. M., 2012. The Marathon Casualty List from Eua-Loukou and the Plinthedon Style. *Zeitschrift für Papyrologie und Epigraphik*, Volume 180: 139-148.

Kousser, R., 2009. Destruction and Memory on the Athenian Acropolis. *The Art Bulletin*, 91(3): 263-282.

Kraft, J. C. et al., 1987. The Pass at Thermopylae, Greece. *Journal of Field Archaeology*, 14(2): 181-198.

Krentz, P., 2010. *The Battle of Marathon*. New Haven: Yale University Press.

Kroll, W. and Mittelhaus, K. eds., 1934. *Paulys Realencyclopädie der classischen Altertumswissenschaft V.A2*. Stuttgart: J.B. Metzlersche Verlagsbuchhandlung.

Kunze, E., ed., 1961. *Bericht über die Ausgrabungen in Olympia Vol.VII*. Berlin: Verlag Walter de Gruyter and Co..

Kurtz, D. and Boardman, J., 1971. *Greek Burial Customs*. London: Thames and Hudson.

Lapatin, K. D. S., 1992. A Family Gathering at Rhamnous? Who's Who on the Nemesis Base. *Hesperia*, 61(1): 107-119.

Larsen, J. A., 1940. The Constitution and Original Purpose of the Delian League. *Harvard Studies in Classical Philology,* Volume 51: 175-213.

Leake, W. M., 1829. On the Demi of Attica. *Transactions of the Royal Society of Literature of the United Kingdom Vol.I, Part II:* 114-283.

Leake, W. M., 1835. *Travels in Northern Greece II.* London: Rodwell.

Legrand, P.-E., 1897. Biographie de Louis-Francois-Sebastien Fauvel, Antiquare et Consul (1753-1838). *Revue Archeologique,* 3(30): 41-66.

Lewis, D. M., 1994. *Inscriptiones Graecae Vol. I, Fasc. 2.* 3rd ed. Berlin: W. de Gruyter.

Liddell, G. H., Scott, R. and Jones, H. S. eds., 1996. *A Greek-English Lexicon.* 9th ed. Oxford: Clarendon Press.

Liddel, P., 2008. Scholarship and Morality: Plutarch's Use of Inscriptions, in A. G. Nikolaidis, ed. *The Unity of Plutarch's Work.* New York: De Gruyter: 125-137.

Liddel, P. and Low, P., 2013. Introduction: The Reception of Ancient Inscriptions, in P. Liddel and P. Low, eds. *Inscriptions and Their Uses in Greek and Latin Literature.* Oxford: Oxford University Press: 1-29.

Loraux, N., 2006. *The Invention of Athens: The Funeral Oration in the Classical City.* 2nd rev. ed. Cambridge, Mass.: MIT Press.

Low, P., 2003. Remembering War in Fifth Century Greece: Ideologies, Societies, and Commemoration beyond Democratic Athens. *World Archaeology,* 35(1): 98-111.

Low, P., 2010. Commemoration of the War Dead in Classical Athens: Remembering Defeat and Victory, in D. M. Pritchard, ed. *War, Democracy and Culture in Classical Athens.* Cambridge: Cambridge University Press: 341-358.

Low, P., 2011. The Power of the Dead in Classical Sparta: The Case of Thermopylae, in M. Carroll and J. Rempel, eds. *Living Through the Dead: Burial and Commemoration in the Classical World.* Oxford: Oxbow Books: 1-26.

Low, P., 2012. The Monuments to the War Dead in Classical Athens: Form, Contexts, Meanings, in P. Low, G. Oliver and P. J. Rhodes, eds. *Cultures of Commemoration: War Memorials, Ancient and Modern.* Proceedings of the British Academy 160: Oxford University Press: 13-40.

Low, P. and Oliver, G., 2012. Commemoration in Ancient and Modern Societies, in P. Low, G. Oliver and P. J. Rhodes, eds. *Cultures of Commemoration: War*

Memorials, Ancient and Modern. Proceedings of the British Academy 160: Oxford University Press: 1-12.

Luce, S. B., Fewkes, V. J. and Blegen, E. P., 1939. Archaeological News and Discussions. *American Journal of Archaeology,* 43(4): 672-700.

Macan, R. W., 1908. *Herodotus: The Seventh, Eighth and Ninth Books Vols. I-II.* London: Macmillan.

Madden, T. F., 1992. The Serpent Column of Delphi in Constantinople: Placement, Purposes, and Mutilations. *Byzantine and Modern Greek Studies,* Volume 16: 111-145.

Ma, J., 2013. *Statues and Cities: Honorific Portraits and Civic Identity in the Hellenistic World.* Oxford: Oxford University Press.

Marinatos, S., 1970a. Further News from Marathon. *Archaiologika Analekta ex Athenon,* Volume 3: 152-166.

Marinatos, S., 1970b. Further Discoveries at Marathon. *Archaiologika Analekta ex Athenon,* Volume 3: 349-366.

Matthaiou, A., 1988. Νέος λίθος τοῦ μνημείου μὲ τὰ ἐπιγράμματα γιὰ τούσ Περσικούσ πολέμους. *Horos,* Volume 6: 118-122.

Matthaiou, A., 2000-2003. Εἰς Ag I 4256. *Horos,* Volume 14-16: 143-152.

Matthaiou, A., 2003. Ἀθηναίοισι τεταγμένοισι ἐν τεμένεϊ Ἡρακλέος (Hdt. 6.108.1), in P. Derow and R. Parker, eds. *Herodotus and his World.* Oxford: Oxford University Press: 190-202.

Meiggs, R., 1966. The Dating of Fifth-Century Attic Inscriptions. *The Journal of Hellenic Studies,* Volume 86: 86-98.

Meiggs, R., 1972. *The Athenian Empire.* Oxford: Clarendon Press.

Meiggs, R. and Lewis, D. eds., 1969. *A Selection of Greek Historical Inscritpions to the End of the Fifth Century BC.* Oxford: Clarendon Press.

Meritt, B. D., 1947. The Persians at Delphi. *Hesperia,* 16(2): 58-62.

Meritt, B. D., 1956. Epigrams from the Battle of Marathon, in S. J. Weinberg, ed. *The Aegean and the Near East. Studies Presented to Hetty Goldman.* Locust Valley, New York: J.J.Augustin: 268-280.

Meritt, B. D., 1962. The Marathon Epigrams again. *The American Journal of Philology,* 83(3): 294-298.

Meritt, B. D., Wade-Gery, H. T. and McGregor, M. F., 1939-1953. *The Athenian Tribute Lists Vols. I-III.* Cambridge, Mass.: Harvard University Press.

Mikalson, J. D., 2003. *Herodotus and Religion in the Persian Wars.* Chapel Hill: University of North Carolina Press.

Milchhoefer, A., 1904. Karten von Attika, Erlauternder Text, Heft VII-VIII, in E. Curtius and J. A. Kaupert, eds. *Karten von Attika.* Berlin: D. Reimer: 1-37.

Mitchell, L., 2007. *Panhellenism and the Barbarian in Archaic and Classical Greece.* Swansea: Classical Press of Wales.

Molyneux, J. H., 1992. *Simonides: A Historical Study.* Wauconda, Ill.: Bolchazy-Carducci.

Morgan, C. H., 1952. Pheidias and Olympia. *Hesperia,* 21(4): 295-339.

Neer, R., 2004. The Athenian Treasury at Delphi and the Material of Politics. *Classical Antiquity,* 23(1): 63-93.

Neils, J., 2001. *The Parthenon Frieze.* Cambridge: Cambridge University Press.

Newton, C. T., 1865. *Travels and Discoveries in the Levant Vols. I-II.* London: Day and Son.

Nisbet Ferguson, M. and Nisbet Hamilton Grant, J. P., 1926. *The Letters of Mary Nisbet of Dirleton, Countess of Elgin.* London: Murray.

Olick, J. K., 1999. Collective Memory: The Two Cultures. *Sociological Theory,* 17(3): 333-348.

Oliver, J. H., 1933. Selected Greek Inscriptions. *Hesperia,* 2(4): 480-513.

Oliver, J. H., 1936. The Monument with the Marathon Epigrams. *Hesperia,* 5(2): 225-234.

Oliver, J. H., 1940. Two Monuments Erected after the Victory of Marathon: Addendum. *American Journal of Archaeology,* 44(4): 483-484.

Page, D. L. ed., 1981. *Further Greek Epigrams.* Cambridge: Cambridge University Press.

Parke, H. W., 1939. Delphica. *Hermathena,* 28(53): 59-78.

Parke, H. W., 1948. Consecration to Apollo. Δεκατεύειν τῷ ἐν Δελφοῖς θεῷ. *Hermathena,* Volume 72: 82-114.

Partida, E. C., 2000. *The Treasuries at Delphi: An Architectural Study.* Jonsered: Paul Åströms Förlag.

Pedley, J., 2005. *Sanctuaries and the Sacred in the Ancient Greek World.* Cambridge: Cambridge University Press.

Peek, W., 1934. Zu den neuen Perserepigrammen. *Hermes,* 69(3): 339-343.

Peek, W., 1953. Aus der Werkstatt, in G. E. Mylonas and D. Raymond, eds. *Studies Presented to David Moore Robinson Vol.2.* Saint Louis: Washington University: 305-312.

Peek, W., 1955. *Griechische Vers-Inschriften.* Berlin: Akademie-Verlag.

Petrakos, B., 1996. *Marathon.* Athens: The Archaeological Society at Athens.

Petrovic, A., 2013. The Battle of Marathon in Pre-Herodotean Sources: On Marathon Verse Inscriptions (IG I3 503/504; Seg Lvi 430), in C. Carey and M. Edwards, eds. *Marathon - 2,500 Years.* London: Institute of Classical Studies: 45-62.

Petsalis-Diomidis , A., 2003. Twenty-First Century Perspectives on the Parthenon. *Journal of Hellenic Studies,* Volume 123: 191-196.

Pettersson, M., 1992. *Cults of Apollo at Sparta: The Hyakinthia, the Gymnopaidiai and the Karneia.* Stockholm: P. Aström.

Podlecki, A. J., 1973. Epigraphica Simonidea. *Epigraphica,* Volume 35: 24-39.

Pomtow, H., 1894. *Archäologische Anzeiger ,* Volume 13: 43-45.

Pope, S. A., 2000. Financing and Design: The Development of the Parthenon Program and the Parthenon Building Accounts, in R. R. Holloway, ed. *Miscellanea Mediterranea.* Providence, R.I.: Center for Old World Archaeology and Art, Brown University: 61-69.

Pritchett, W. K., 1957. New Light on Plataia. *American Journal of Archaeology,* 61(1): 9-28.

Pritchett, W. K., 1965-1992. *Studies in Greek Topography Vols. I-VIII.* Berkeley: University of California Press.

Pritchett, W. K., 1971-1991. *The Greek State at War Vols. I-V.* Berkeley: University of California Press.

Proietti, G., 2013. The Marathon Epitaph from Eua-Loukou: Some Notes about its Text and Historical Context. *Zeitschrift für Papyrologie und Epigraphik,* Volume 185: 24-30.

Raaflaub, K., 2004. *The Discovery of Freedom in Ancient Greece.* Chicago: University of Chicago Press.

Rangabē, A. R., 1855. *Antiquités Helléniques ou Répertoire d'Inscriptions et d'autres Antiquités Vol. II.* Athens: Typography et Lithographie Royales.

Raschke, W. J., 1988. Images of Victory: Some New Considerations of Athletic Monuments, in W. J. Raschke, ed. *The Archaeology of the Olympics: The Olympics and Other Festivals in Antiquity.* Madison, Wis.: University of Wisconsin Press: 38-54.

Raubitschek, A. E., 1940. Two Monuments Erected after the Victory of Marathon. *American Journal of Archaeology,* 44(1): 53-59.

Raubitschek, A. E. and Stevens, G. P., 1946. The Pedestal of the Athena Promachos. *Hesperia,* Volume 15: 107-114.

Rhodes, P. J. and Osborne, R. eds., 2003. *Greek Historical Inscriptions 404-323 BC.* Oxford: Oxford University Press.

Richter, G. M. A., 1950. *The Sculpture and Sculptors of the Greeks.* New rev. ed. New Haven: Yale University Press.

Richter, G. M. A., 1965. *The Portraits of the Greeks Vols.I-III.* London: Phaidon Press.

Robert, L., 1938. *Études épigraphiques et philologiques.* Paris: Champion.

Robertson, M., 1939. Archaeology in Greece 1938-39. *Journal of Hellenic Studies,* Volume 59: 189-209.

Rouse, W. H., 1902. *Greek Votive Offerings: An Essay in the History of Greek Religion.* Cambridge: Cambridge University Press.

Roux, G., 1980. Les quatres grand sanctuaires panhelléniques. *Les Dossiers d'Archéologie,* Volume 45: 20-38.

Samuel, R., 1994. *Theatres of Memory.* London: Verso.

Schachter, A., 1994. *Cults of Boiotia. Vol. III.* London: Institute of Classical Studies.

Schliemann, H., 1884a. Das Sogenannte Grab der 192 Athener in Marathon. *Zeitschrift für Ethnologie:* 85-88.

Schliemann, H., 1884b. Exploration of the Tumulus at Marathon. *The Academy,* Volume 25: 138-139.

Scott, M., 2010. *Delphi and Olympia: The Spatial Politics of Panhellenism in the Archaic and Classical Periods.* Cambridge: Cambridge University Press.

Shear, T. L. J., 1984. The Athenian Agora: Excavations of 1980-1982. *Hesperia,* 53(1): 1-57.

Simon, E., 1983. *Festivals of Attica: An Archaeological Commentary.* Madison, Wis.: University of Wisconsin Press.

Skia, A., 1917. Ἐπιγραφαι ἐκ Πλαταιῶν. *Ephemeris Archaiologike:* 157-167.

Smith, A. H., 1892-1904. *Catalogue of Sculptures in the British Museum Vols. I-III.* London: Printed by order of the Trustees.

Smith, R. R. R., 1988. *Hellenistic Royal Portraits.* Oxford: Clarendon Press.

Spence, I. G., 1993. *The Cavalry of Classical Greece.* Oxford: Clarendon Press.

Staes, V., 1890. Ανασκαφαί τύμβων εν Αττική. Ο τύμβος των Μαραθωνομάχων. *Deltion Archaiologikon:* 65-71 and 123-132.

Stansbury-O'Donnell, M. D., 2005. The Painting Program in the Stoa Poikile, in J. M. Barringer and J. M. Hurwit, eds. *Periklean Athens and its Legacy: Problems and Perspectives.* Austin: University of Texas Press: 73-87.

Steinbock, B., 2013. *Social Memory in Athenian Public Discourse: Uses and Meanings of the Past*. Ann Arbor: University of Michigan Press.

Steinhauer, G., 2004-2009. Στήλη πεσόντων της Ερεχθηίδος. *Horos*, Issue 17-21: 679-692.

Steskal, M., 2004. *Der Zerstörungsbefund 480/79 der Athener Akropolis: Eine Fallstudie zum etablierten Chronologiegerüst*. Hamburg: Kovač.

Stevens, G. P., 1936. The Periclean Entrance Court of the Acropolis. *Hesperia*, 5(4): 443-520.

Stewart, A., 1979. *Attika: Studies in Athenian Sculpture of the Hellenistic Age*. London: Society for the Promotion of Hellenic Studies.

Strauss, B., 2013. The Classical Greek Polis and Its Government, in H. Beck, ed. *A Companion to Ancient Greek Government*. Chichester: Wiley-Blackwell: 22-37.

Stuart, J. and Revett, N., 1762. *The Antiquities of Athens*. London: s.n.

Svoronos, J. N., 1909-1937. *Das Athener Nationalmuseum Vols. I-III*. Athens: Beck and Barth.

Thompson, D. B., 1956. The Persian Spoils in Athens, in S. Weinberg, ed. *The Aegean and the Near East: Studies Presented to Hetty Goldman*. Locust Valley, N.Y.: J. J. Augustin: 281-291.

Tod, M. N., 1946. *A Selection of Greek Historical Inscriptions Vols. I-II*. 2nd ed. Oxford: Clarendon Press.

Vanderpool, E., 1942. An Inscribed Stele from Marathon. *Hesperia*, 11(4): 329-337.

Vanderpool, E., 1966. A Monument to the Battle of Marathon. *Hesperia*, 35(2): 93-106.

Vidal-Naquet, P., 1986. *The Black Hunter: Forms of Thought and Forms of Society in the Greek World*. Baltimore: Johns Hopkins University Press.

Wade-Gery, H. T., 1933. Classical Epigrams and Epitaphs: A Study of the Kimonian Age. *The Journal of Hellenic Studies*, Volume 53: 71-104.

Wallace, P. W., 1969. Psyttaleia and the Trophies of the Battle of Salamis. *American Journal of Archaeology*, 73(3): 293-304.

Walsh, J., 1986. The Date of the Athenian Stoa at Delphi. *American Journal of Archaeology*, 90(3): 319-336.

Way, A. S., 1939. *Greek Anthology, Books V-VII*. London: Macmillan and Co..

Waywell, G., 1999. Sparta and Its Topography. *Bulletin of the Institute of Classical Studies*, 43(1): 1-26.

Weber, L., 1929. Zum athenischen Staatsfriedhof. *Philologus*, 84(1): 35-50.
Westcoat, B. D., 2005. Buildings for Votive Ships on Delos and Samothrace, in M. Yeroulanou and M. Stamatopoulou, eds. *Architecture and Archaeology in the Cyclades: Papers in Honour of J.J. Coulton.* Oxford: Archeopress: 153-172.
West, S., 1985. Herodotus' Epigraphical Interests. *Classical Quarterly*, 35(2): 278-305.
West, W. C., 1965. *'Greek Public Monuments of the Persian Wars'*. PhD Thesis: University of North Carolina.
West, W. C., 1969. The Trophies of the Persian Wars. *Classical Philology*, 64(1): 7-19.
Whittaker, H., 1991. Pausanias and his Use of Inscriptions. *Symbolae Osloenses*, Volume 66: 171-186.
Wiesner, J., 1939. Zeus der Platäer. *Real-Encyclopädie der klassischen Altertumswissenschaft*, 18(1): 151-152.
Wilhelm, A., 1898. Altattische Schriftdenkmaeler. *Mitteilungen des Deutschen Archäologischen Instituts, Athenischer Abteilung*, Volume 23: 466-492.
Wilhelm, A., 1934. Drei auf Schlacht von Marathon bezügliche Gedichte. *Anzeiger der Oesterreichische Akademie in Wien*, Volume 71: 89-117.
Wilhelm, A., 1972. Simonideische Gedichte, in G. Pfohl, ed. *Die Griechische Elegie.* Darmstadt: Wissenschaftliche Buchgesellschaft: 290-322.
Woodford, S., 1971. Cults of Heracles in Attica, in D. G. Mitten, J. G. Pedley and J. A. Scott, eds. *Studies Presented to George M.A. Hanfmann.* Mainz: Verlag P. von Zabern: 211-225.
Yates, D., 2011. *'Remembering the Persian War Differently'*. PhD Thesis: Brown University.
Zimmer, G., 1990. *Griechische Bronzegusswerkstätten: zur Technologieentwicklung eines antiken Kunsthandwerkes.* Mainz am Rhein: P. von Zabern.